THE 100 MOST INFLUENTIAL
SCIENTISTS
OF ALL TIME

The Britannica Guide to the World's Most Influential People

The 100 Most Influential
SCIENTISTS
of All Time

Edited by Kara Rogers, Senior Editor, Biomedical Sciences

Britannica®
Educational Publishing

IN ASSOCIATION WITH

ROSEN
EDUCATIONAL SERVICES

Published in 2010 by Britannica Educational Publishing
(a trademark of Encyclopædia Britannica, Inc.)
in association with Rosen Educational Services, LLC
29 East 21st Street, New York, NY 10010.

Distributed exclusively by Rosen Educational Services.
For a listing of additional Britannica Educational Publishing titles, call toll free (800) 237-9932.

First Edition

Britannica Educational Publishing
Michael I. Levy: Executive Editor
Marilyn L. Barton: Senior Coordinator, Production Control
Steven Bosco: Director, Editorial Technologies
Lisa S. Braucher: Senior Producer and Data Editor
Yvette Charboneau: Senior Copy Editor
Kathy Nakamura: Manager, Media Acquisition
Kara Rogers: Senior Editor, Biomedical Sciences

Rosen Educational Services
Jeanne Nagle: Senior Editor
Nelson Sá: Art Director
Introduction by Kristi Lew

Library of Congress Cataloging-in-Publication Data

The 100 most influential scientists of all time / edited by Kara Rogers.—1st ed.
    p. cm.—(The Britannica guide to the world's most influential people)
"In association with Britannica Educational Publishing, Rosen Educational Services."
Includes index.
ISBN 978-1-61530-002-0 (library binding: alk. paper)
1. Science—Popular works. 2. Science—History—Popular works. 3. Scientists—
Biography—Popular works. I. Rogers, Kara. II. Title: One hundred influential scientists
of all time.
Q162.A15 2010
509.2'2—dc22

                                                                    2009026069

Manufactured in the United States of America

On the cover: Discoveries such as Einstein's theory of relativity—shown in original
manuscript form—are hallmarks of the genius exhibited by the world's most influential
scientists. *Jon Levy/AFP/Getty Images*

CONTENTS

186

247

INTRODUCTION

In science the credit goes to the man who convinces the world,
not to the man to whom the idea first occurs.
—Francis Darwin (1848–1925)

From the very first moment humans appeared on the planet, we have attempted to understand and explain the world around us. The most insatiably curious among us often have become scientists.

The scientists discussed in this book have shaped humankind's knowledge and laid the foundation for virtually every scientific discipline, from basic biology to black holes. Some of these individuals were inclined to ponder questions about what was contained within the human body, while others were intrigued by celestial bodies. Their collective vision has been concentrated enough to examine microscopic particles and broad enough to unlock tremendous universal marvels such as gravity, relativity— even the nature of life itself. Acknowledgement of their importance comes from a variety of knowledgeable and well-respected sources; luminaries such as Isaac Asimov and noted biochemist Marcel Florkin have written biographies contained herein.

The influence wielded by the profiled men and women within the realm of scientific discovery becomes readily apparent as the reader delves deeper into each individual's life and contributions to his or her chosen field. Oftentimes, more than one field has been the beneficiary of these brilliant minds. Many early scientists studied several different branches of science during their lifetimes. Indeed, as the founder of formal logic and the study of chemistry, biology, physics, zoology, botany, psychology, history, and literary theory in the Middle Ages, Aristotle is considered one of the greatest thinkers in history.

Breakthroughs in the medical sciences have been numerous and extremely valuable. Study in this discipline begins with a contemporary of Aristotle's named Hippocrates, who is commonly regarded as the "father of medicine." Perhaps Hippocrates' most enduring legacy to the field is the Hippocratic Oath, the ethical code that doctors still abide by today. By taking the Hippocratic Oath, doctors pledge to Asclepius, the Greco-Roman god of medicine, that to the best of their knowledge and abilities, they will prescribe the best course of medical care for their patients. They also promise to, above all, cause no harm to any patient.

The Greeks were not the only ones studying medicine. The Muslim scholar Avicenna also advanced the discipline by writing one of the most influential medical texts in history, *The Canon of Medicine*. Avicenna also produced an encyclopedic volume describing Aristotle's philosophic and scientific thoughts about logic, biology, psychology, geometry, astronomy, music, and metaphysics. This hefty tome was called the *Kitāb al-shifā* ("Book of Healing"). About 450 years later, a German-Swiss physician named Philippus Aureolus Theophrastus Bombastus Von Hohenheim, or Paracelsus, once again advanced medical science by integrating medicine with chemistry and linking specific diseases to medications that could treat them.

The Renaissance period brought to light the scientific genius of painter and sculptor Leonardo da Vinci. His drawings of presciently detailed flying machines preceded the advent of human flight by more than 300 years. What's more, da Vinci's drawings of the human anatomy structure not only illuminated many of the body's features and functions, they also laid the foundation for modern scientific illustration.

Anatomical drawings were also the purview of Flemish physician Andreas Vesalius. Unlike da Vinci's illustrations, which were mainly for his own artistic education, Vesalius incorporated his sketches and the explanations of them into the first anatomy textbook. His observations of human anatomy also helped to advance physiology, the study of the way the body functions.

Other physicians took their investigation of anatomy off the page and onto the operating table. Ancient Greek physician Galen of Pergamum greatly influenced the study of medicine by performing countless autopsies on monkeys, pigs, sheep, and goats. His observations allowed him to ascertain the functions of the nervous system and note the difference between arteries and veins. Galen was also able to dispel the notion that arteries carry air, an idea that had persisted for 400 years.

Centuries later, in the 1600s, Englishman William Harvey built on Galen's theories and observations, and helped lay the foundation for modern physiology with his numerous animal dissections. As a result of his work, Harvey was the first person to describe the function of the circulatory system, providing evidence that veins and arteries had separate and distinct functions. Before his realization that the heart acts as a pump that keeps blood flowing throughout the body, people thought that constrictions of the blood vessels caused the blood to move.

Other groundbreaking scientists have relied on observations outside the body. A gifted Dutch scientist and lens grinder named Antonie van Leeuwenhoek refined the main tool of his trade, the microscope, which allowed him to become the first person to observe tiny microbes. Leeuwenhoek's observations helped build the framework for bacteriology and protozoology.

As several of the stories in this book confirm, science is a competitive yet oddly cooperative field, with researchers frequently either refuting or capitalizing on one another's findings. Some ideas survive the test of time and remain intact while others are discarded or changed to fit more recent data. As an example of the former, Sir Isaac Newton developed three laws of motion that are still the basic tenets of mechanics to this day. Newton also proved instrumental to the advancement of science when he invented calculus, a branch of mathematics used by physicists and many others.

Then there are the numerous advances made in the name of science that began with the development of vaccines. Smallpox was a leading cause of death in 18th-century England. Yet Edward Jenner, an English surgeon, noticed something interesting occurring in his small village. People who were exposed to cowpox, a disease contracted from infected cattle that had relatively minor symptoms, did not get smallpox when they were exposed to the disease. Concluding that cowpox could protect people from smallpox, Jenner purposely infected a young boy who lived in the village first with cowpox, then with smallpox. Thankfully, Jenner's hypothesis proved to be correct. He had successfully administered the world's first vaccine and eradicated the disease.

More than fifty years later, another scientist by the name of Louis Pasteur would expand Jenner's ideas by explaining that the microbes, first discovered by Leeuwenhoek, caused diseases like smallpox. Today this idea is called the germ theory. Pasteur would go on to discover the vaccines for anthrax, rabies, and other diseases. He also came to understand the role microbes played in the contamination and spoilage of food. The process he invented to prevent these problems, known as pasteurization, is still in use today.

Other scientists, including Joseph Lister, Robert Koch, Sir Alexander Fleming, Selman Waksman, and

Jonas Salk, would build on Pasteur's germ theory, leading to subsequent discoveries of medical import. Anyone who ever needs to have an operation has Lister, the founder of antiseptic medicine, to thank for today's sterile surgical techniques. Koch, with his numerous experiments and meticulous record keeping, was instrumental in advancing the idea that particular microbes caused particular illnesses, greatly improving diagnostic medicine. Fleming was responsible for discovering the first antibiotic, penicillin, in 1928. Fleming's work was continued by Waksman, who systematically searched for other antibiotics. This led to the discovery of one of the most widely used antibiotics of modern times, streptomycin, in 1943. Less than 10 years later, Salk would develop a vaccine that could protect children from the debilitating and deadly disease poliomyelitis. Since that time, scientists have almost succeeded in eliminating polio worldwide.

Medical scientists are certainly not the only ones to build on one another's work. Discoveries of one scientist, no matter what field he or she works in, are almost always examined, recreated, and expanded on by others. Luigi Galvani, an Italian physicist and physician, for example, discovered that animal tissue (specifically frog legs) could conduct an electric current. Building on Galvani's observations, his friend, Italian scientist Alessandro Volta, constructed the first battery in 1800.

Expanding on Volta's work and that of Danish physicist Hans Christiaan Ørsted, who discovered that electricity running through a wire could deflect a magnetic compass needle, French physicist André-Marie Ampère founded a new scientific field called electromagnetism. The English physicist Michael Faraday would pick up the work from there, using a magnetic field to produce an electric current. In turn, this enabled him to invent and build the first electric motor.

Reviewing Faraday's experiments and theoretical work allowed James Clerk Maxwell to unify the ideas of electricity and magnetism into an electromagnetic theory and to mathematically describe the electromagnetic force. Another physicist, Albert Michelson, determined that the speed of light was a never-changing constant. Using Maxwell's mathematical theories and Michelson's experimental data, Albert Einstein was able to develop his special theory of relativity, which resulted in what is arguably the most famous equation in the world: $E=mc^2$. This elegantly simple but extremely powerful equation states that mass and energy are two different forms of the same thing. In other words, they are interchangeable. This idea has been indescribably important to the development of modern physics and astronomy.

Einstein suggested that his idea could be tested using radium, a radioactive element discovered shortly before he announced his special theory of relativity. Discovered by Marie Curie, a Polish-born French chemist, and her husband, Pierre, radium continuously converts some of its mass into energy, a process Madame Curie named radioactivity. Her studies would eventually result in her becoming the first woman to ever be awarded a Nobel Prize. She was awarded a second Nobel Prize in 1911 for the discovery of polonium and radium.

Building on the work of Curie and Einstein, future scientists would be successful—for better or worse—in harnessing nuclear energy. These concepts would be used to build fission reactors in nuclear power plants, producing electricity for towns and cities. However, the same concepts would also be used by a group of scientists, including Enrico Fermi, J. Robert Oppenheimer, Luis Alvarez, and many others, to develop nuclear weapons.

In 1675, Isaac Newton wrote a letter to Robert Hooke in which he said, "If I have seen further it is by standing on the shoulders of giants." Thanks to the pioneering efforts of the scientists mentioned in this introduction, along with the other chemists, biologists, astronomers, ecologists, and geneticists in the remainder of this book, today's scientists have a solid foundation upon which to make astounding leaps of logic. Without the work of these men and women, we would not have computers, electricity, or many other modern conveniences. We would not have the vaccines and medications that help keep us healthy. And, in general, we would know a lot less about the way the human body functions and the way the world works.

Today's scientists owe a huge debt of gratitude to the scientists of days past. By standing on the shoulders of these giants, who knows how far they may be able to see.

ASCLEPIUS

In the *Iliad*, the writer Homer mentions Asclepius only as a skillful physician and the father of two Greek doctors at Troy, Machaon and Podalirius. In later times, however, he was honoured as a hero, and eventually worshiped as a god. Asclepius (Greek: Asklepios, Latin: Aesculapius), the son of Apollo (god of healing, truth, and prophecy) and the mortal princess Coronis, became the Greco-Roman god of medicine. Legend has it that the Centaur Chiron, who was famous for his wisdom and knowledge of medicine, taught Asclepius the art of healing. At length Zeus, the king of the gods, afraid that Asclepius might render all men immortal, slew him with a thunderbolt. Apollo slew the Cyclopes who had made the thunderbolt and was then forced by Zeus to serve Admetus.

Asclepius's cult began in Thessaly but spread to many parts of Greece. Because it was supposed that Asclepius effected cures of the sick in dreams, the practice of sleeping in his temples in Epidaurus in South Greece became common. This practice is often described as Asclepian incubation. In 293 BCE his cult spread to Rome, where he was worshiped as Aesculapius.

Asclepius was frequently represented standing, dressed in a long cloak, with bare breast; his usual attribute was a staff with a serpent coiled around it. This staff is the only true symbol of medicine. A similar but unrelated emblem, the caduceus, with its winged staff and intertwined serpents, is frequently used as a medical emblem but is without medical relevance since it represents the magic wand of Hermes, or Mercury, the messenger of the gods and the patron of trade. However, its similarity to the staff of Asclepius resulted in modern times in the adoption of the caduceus as a symbol of the physician and as the emblem of the U.S. Army Medical Corp.

The plant genus *Asclepias*, which contains various species of milkweed, was named for Asclepius. Many of these plants possess some degree of medicinal value.

HIPPOCRATES

(b. *c.* 460 BCE, island of Cos, Greece—d. *c.* 375 BCE, Larissa, Thessaly)

Hippocrates was an ancient Greek physician who lived during Greece's Classical period and is traditionally regarded as the father of medicine. It is difficult to isolate the facts of Hippocrates' life from the later tales told about him or to assess his medicine accurately in the face of centuries of reverence for him as the ideal physician. About 60 medical writings have survived that bear his name, most of which were not written by him. He has been revered for his ethical standards in medical practice, mainly for the Hippocratic Oath, which, it is suspected, he did not write.

LIFE AND WORKS

What is known is that while Hippocrates was alive, he was admired as a physician and teacher. In the *Protagoras* Plato called Hippocrates "the Asclepiad of Cos," who taught students for fees. Further, he implied that Hippocrates was as well known as a physician as Polyclitus and Phidias were as sculptors. Plato also referenced Hippocrates in the *Phaedrus*, in which Hippocrates is referred to as a famous Asclepiad who had a philosophical approach to medicine.

Meno, a pupil of Aristotle, specifically stated in his history of medicine the views of Hippocrates on the causation of diseases, namely, that undigested residues were produced by unsuitable diet and that these residues excreted vapours, which passed into the body generally and produced diseases. Aristotle said that Hippocrates was called "the Great Physician" but that he was small in stature.

Hippocrates appears to have traveled widely in Greece and Asia Minor practicing his art and teaching his pupils. He presumably taught at the medical school at Cos quite frequently. His reputation, and myths about his life and his family, began to grow in the Hellenistic period, about a century after his death. During this period, the Museum of Alexandria in Egypt collected for its library literary material from preceding periods in celebration of the past greatness of Greece. So far as it can be inferred, the medical works that remained from the Classical period (among the earliest prose writings in Greek) were assembled as a group and called the works of Hippocrates (*Corpus Hippocraticum*).

The virtues of the Hippocratic writings are many, and, although they are of varying lengths and literary quality, they are all simple and direct, earnest in their desire to help, and lacking in technical jargon and elaborate argument. The works show such different views and styles that they cannot be by one person, and some were clearly written in later periods. Yet all the works of the *Corpus* share basic assumptions about how the body works and what disease is, providing a sense of the substance and appeal of ancient Greek medicine as practiced by Hippocrates and other physicians of his era. Prominent among these attractive works are the *Epidemics*, which give annual records of weather and associated diseases, along with individual case histories and records of treatment, collected from cities in northern Greece. Diagnosis and prognosis are frequent subjects.

Other treatises explain how to set fractures and treat wounds, feed and comfort patients, and take care of the body to avoid illness. Treatises called *Diseases* deal with serious illnesses, proceeding from the head to the feet, giving symptoms, prognoses, and treatments. There are works on diseases of women, childbirth, and pediatrics. Prescribed medications, other than foods and local salves, are generally purgatives to rid the body of the noxious substances thought to cause disease. Some works argue that medicine is indeed a science, with firm principles and methods, although explicit medical theory is very rare. The medicine depends on a mythology of how the body works and how its inner organs are connected. The myth is laboriously constructed from experience, but it must be remembered that there was neither systematic research nor dissection of human beings in Hippocrates' time. Hence, while much of the writing seems wise and correct, there are large areas where much is unknown.

Over the next four centuries, imaginative writings, some obviously fiction, were added to the original collection of Hippocratic works and enhanced Hippocrates' reputation, providing the basis for the traditional picture of Hippocrates as the father of medicine. Still other works were added to the Hippocratic *Corpus* between its first collection and its first scholarly edition around the beginning of the 2nd century CE. Among them were the Hippocratic Oath and other ethical writings that prescribe principles of behaviour for the physician.

Hippocratic Oath

The Hippocratic Oath dictates the obligations of the physician to students of medicine and the duties of pupil to teacher. In the oath, the physician pledges to prescribe only beneficial treatments, according to his abilities and judgment; to refrain from causing harm or hurt; and to live an exemplary personal and professional life. The text of the Hippocratic Oath (*c.* 400 BCE) provided below is a translation from Greek by Francis Adams (1849). It is considered a classical version and differs from contemporary versions, which are reviewed and revised frequently to fit with changes in modern medical practice.

I swear by Apollo the physician, and Aesculapius, and Health, and All-heal, and all the gods and goddesses, that, according to my ability and judgment, I will keep this Oath and this stipulation—to reckon him who taught me this Art equally dear to me as my parents, to share my substance with him, and relieve his necessities if required; to look upon his offspring in the same footing as my own brothers, and to teach them this Art, if they shall wish to learn it, without fee or stipulation; and that by precept, lecture, and every other mode of instruction, I will impart a knowledge of the Art to my own sons, and those of my teachers, and to disciples bound by a stipulation and oath according to the law of medicine, but to none others. I will follow that system of regimen which, according to my ability and judgment, I consider for the benefit of my patients, and abstain from whatever is deleterious and mischievous. I will give no deadly medicine to any one if asked, nor suggest any such counsel; and in like manner I will not give to a woman a pessary to produce abortion. With purity and with holiness I will pass my life and practice my Art. I will not cut persons laboring under the stone, but will leave this to be done by men who are practitioners of this work. Into whatever houses I enter, I will go into them for the benefit of the sick, and will abstain from every voluntary act of mischief and corruption; and, further from the seduction of females or males, of freemen and slaves. Whatever, in connection with my professional practice or not, in connection with it, I see or hear, in the life of men, which ought not to be spoken of abroad, I will not divulge, as reckoning that all such should be kept secret. While I continue to keep this Oath unviolated, may it be granted to me to enjoy life and the practice of the art, respected by all men, in all times! But should I trespass and violate this Oath, may the reverse be my lot!

INFLUENCE

Technical medical science developed in the Hellenistic period and after. Surgery, pharmacy, and anatomy advanced; physiology became the subject of serious speculation; and philosophic criticism improved the logic of medical theories. Competing schools in medicine (first Empiricism and later Rationalism) claimed Hippocrates as the origin and inspiration of their doctrines. For later physicians, Hippocrates stood as the inspirational source, and today Hippocrates still continues to represent the humane, ethical aspects of the medical profession.

ARISTOTLE

(b. 384 BCE, Stagira, Chalcidice, Greece—d. 322 BCE, Chalcis, Euboea)

Aristotle (Greek: Aristoteles) was an ancient Greek philosopher and scientist, and one of the greatest intellectual figures of Western history. He was the author of a philosophical and scientific system that became the framework and vehicle for both Christian Scholasticism and medieval Islamic philosophy. Aristotle's intellectual range was vast, covering most of the sciences and many of the arts, including biology, botany, chemistry, ethics, history, logic, metaphysics, rhetoric, philosophy of mind, philosophy of science, physics, poetics, political theory, psychology, and zoology. He was the founder of formal logic, devising for it a finished system that for centuries was regarded as the sum of the discipline. Aristotle also pioneered the study of zoology, both observational and theoretical, in which some of his work remained unsurpassed until the 19th century. His writings in metaphysics

This statue of Aristotle, the Greek philosopher who taught Alexander the Great, stands in the Palazzo Spada in Rome. Popperfoto/Getty Images and the philosophy of science continue to be studied, and his work remains a powerful current in contemporary philosophical debate.

PHYSICS AND METAPHYSICS

Aristotle divided the theoretical sciences into three groups: physics, mathematics, and theology. Physics as he understood it was equivalent to what would now be called "natural philosophy," or the study of nature; in this sense it encompasses not only the modern field of physics but also biology, chemistry, geology, psychology, and even meteorology. Metaphysics, however, is notably absent from Aristotle's classification; indeed, he never uses the word, which first appears in the posthumous catalog of his writings as a name for the works listed after the *Physics*. He does, however, recognize the branch of philosophy now called metaphysics. He calls it "first philosophy" and defines it as the discipline that studies "being as being."

Aristotle's contributions to the physical sciences are less impressive than his researches in the life sciences. In works such as *On Generation and Corruption* and *On the Heavens*, he presented a world-picture that included many features inherited from his pre-Socratic predecessors. From Empedocles (*c.* 490–430 BCE) he adopted the view that the universe is ultimately composed of different combinations of the four fundamental elements of earth, water, air, and fire. Each element is characterized by the possession of a unique pair of the four elementary qualities of heat, cold, wetness, and dryness: earth is cold and dry, water is cold and wet, air is hot and wet, and fire is hot and dry. Each element also has a natural place in an ordered cosmos, and each has an innate tendency to move toward this natural place. Thus, earthy solids naturally fall, while fire, unless prevented, rises ever higher. Other motions of the elements are possible but are considered "violent." (A relic of Aristotle's distinction is preserved in the modern-day contrast between natural and violent death.)

Aristotle's vision of the cosmos also owes much to Plato's dialogue *Timaeus*. As in that work, the Earth is at the centre of the universe, and around it the Moon, the Sun, and the other planets revolve in a succession of concentric crystalline spheres. The heavenly bodies are not compounds of the four terrestrial elements but are made up of a superior fifth element, or "quintessence." In addition, the heavenly bodies have souls, or supernatural intellects, which guide them in their travels through the cosmos.

Even the best of Aristotle's scientific work has now only a historical interest. The abiding value of treatises such as the *Physics* lies not in their particular scientific assertions but in their philosophical analyses of some of the concepts that pervade the physics of different eras — concepts such as place, time, causation, and determinism.

PHILOSOPHY OF SCIENCE

In his *Posterior Analytics*, Aristotle applies the theory of the syllogism (a form of deductive reasoning) to scientific and epistemological ends (epistemology is the philosophy of the nature of knowledge). Scientific knowledge, he urges, must be built up out of demonstrations. A demonstration is a particular kind of syllogism, one whose premises can be traced back to principles that are true, necessary, universal, and immediately intuited. These first, self-evident principles are related to the conclusions of science as axioms are related to theorems: the axioms both necessitate and explain the truths that constitute a science. The most important axioms, Aristotle thought, would be those that define the proper subject matter of a science. Thus, among the axioms of geometry would be the definition of a triangle. For this reason much of the second book of the *Posterior Analytics* is devoted to definition.

The account of science in the *Posterior Analytics* is impressive, but it bears no resemblance to any of Aristotle's own scientific works. Generations of scholars have tried in vain to find in his writings a single instance of a demonstrative syllogism. Moreover, the whole history of scientific endeavour contains no perfect instance of a demonstrative science.

PLINY THE ELDER

(b. 23 CE, Novum Comum, Transpadane Gaul [now in Italy]—d. Aug. 24, 79, Stabiae, near Mt. Vesuvius)

Pliny the Elder (Latin: Gaius Plinius Secundus) was a Roman savant and author of the celebrated *Natural History*, an encyclopaedic work of uneven accuracy that was an authority on scientific matters up to the Middle Ages. Seven writings are ascribed to Pliny, of which only the *Natural History* is extant. There survive, however, a few fragments of his earlier writings on grammar, a biography of Pomponius Secundus, a history of Rome, a study of the Roman campaigns in Germany, and a book on hurling the lance. These writings probably were lost in antiquity and have played no role in perpetuating Pliny's fame, which rests solely on the *Natural History*.

The *Natural History*, divided into 37 *libri*, or "books," was completed, except for finishing touches, in 77 CE. In the preface, dedicated to Titus (who became emperor shortly before Pliny's death), Pliny justified the title and explained his purpose on utilitarian grounds as the study of "the nature of things, that is, life." Heretofore, he continued, no one had attempted to bring together the older, scattered material that belonged to "encyclic culture" (*enkyklios paideia*, the origin of the word encyclopaedia). Disdaining high literary style and political mythology, Pliny adopted a plain style—but one with an unusually rich vocabulary—as best suited to his purpose. A novel feature of the *Natural History* is the care taken by Pliny in naming his sources, more than 100 of which are mentioned. Book I, in fact, is a summary of the remaining 36 books, listing the authors and sometimes the titles of the books (many of which are now lost) from which Pliny derived his material.

The *Natural History* properly begins with Book II, which is devoted to cosmology and astronomy. Here, as elsewhere, Pliny demonstrated the extent of his reading, especially of Greek texts. By the same token, however, he was sometimes careless in translating details, with the result that he distorted the meaning of many technical and mathematical passages. In Books III through VI, on the physical and historical geography of the ancient world, he gave much attention to major cities, some of which no longer exist.

Books VII through XI treat zoology, beginning with humans, then mammals and reptiles, fishes and other marine animals, birds, and insects. Pliny derived most of the biological data from Aristotle, while his own contributions were concerned with legendary animals and unsupported folklore.

In Books XII through XIX, on botany, Pliny came closest to making a genuine contribution to science. Although he drew heavily upon Theophrastus, he reported some independent observations, particularly those made during his travels in Germany. Pliny is one of the chief sources of modern knowledge of Roman gardens, early botanical writings, and the introduction into Italy of new horticultural and agricultural species. Book XVIII, on agriculture, is especially important for agricultural techniques such as crop rotation, farm management, and the names of legumes and other crop plants. His description of an ox-driven grain harvester in Gaul, long regarded by scholars as imaginary, was confirmed by the discovery in southern Belgium in 1958 of a 2nd-century stone relief depicting such an implement. Moreover, by recording the Latin synonyms of Greek plant names, he made most of the plants mentioned in earlier Greek writings identifiable.

Books XX through XXXII focus on medicine and drugs. Like many Romans, Pliny criticized luxury on moral and medical grounds. His random comments on diet and on the commercial sources and prices of the ingredients of costly drugs provide valuable evidence relevant to contemporary Roman life. The subjects of Books XXXIII through XXXVII include minerals, precious stones, and metals, especially those used by Roman craftsmen. In describing their uses, he referred to famous artists and their creations and to Roman architectural styles and technology.

INFLUENCE

Perhaps the most important of the pseudoscientific methods advocated by Pliny was the doctrine of signatures: a resemblance between the external appearance of a plant, animal, or mineral and the outward symptoms of a disease was thought to indicate the therapeutic usefulness of the plant. With the decline of the ancient world and the loss of the Greek texts on which Pliny had so heavily depended, the *Natural History* became a substitute for a general education. In the European Middle Ages many of the larger monastic libraries possessed copies of the work. These and many abridged versions ensured Pliny's place in European literature. His authority was unchallenged, partly because of a lack of more reliable information and partly because his assertions were not and, in many cases, could not be tested.

However, Pliny's influence diminished starting in the late 15th century, when writers began to question his statements. By the end of the 17th century, the *Natural History* had been rejected by the leading scientists. Up to that time, however, Pliny's influence, especially on nonscientific writers, was undiminished. He was, for example, almost certainly known to William Shakespeare and John Milton. Although Pliny's work was never again accepted as an authority in science, 19th-century Latin scholars conclusively demonstrated the historical importance of the *Natural History* as one of the greatest literary monuments of classical antiquity.

PTOLEMY

(b. *c.* 100 CE – d. *c.* 170)

Ptolemy (Latin: Claudius Ptolemaeus) was an Egyptian astronomer, mathematician, and geographer of Greek descent who flourished in Alexandria during the 2nd century CE. In several fields his writings represent the culminating achievement of Greco-Roman science, particularly his geocentric (Earth-centred) model of the universe now known as the Ptolemaic system.

Virtually nothing is known about Ptolemy's life except what can be inferred from his writings. His first major astronomical work, the *Almagest*, was completed about 150 CE and contains reports of astronomical observations that Ptolemy had made over the preceding quarter of a century. The size and content of his subsequent literary production suggests that he lived until about 170 CE.

The book that is now generally known as the *Almagest* (from a hybrid of Arabic and Greek, "the greatest") was called by Ptolemy *Hē mathēmatikē syntaxis* (*The Mathematical Collection*) because he believed that its subject, the motions of the heavenly bodies, could be explained in mathematical terms. The opening chapters present empirical arguments for the basic cosmological framework within which Ptolemy worked. Earth, he argued, is a stationary sphere at the centre of a vastly larger celestial sphere that revolves at a perfectly uniform rate around Earth, carrying with it the stars, planets, Sun, and Moon—thereby causing their daily risings and settings. Through the course of a year the Sun slowly traces out a great circle, known as the ecliptic, against the rotation of the celestial sphere. The Moon and planets similarly travel backward against the

In this drawing, part of the Studio Raffaele collection in Venice, from around 130 CE, the Greek astronomer Ptolemy studies a sphere. Hulton Archive/Getty Images

"fixed stars" found in the ecliptic. Hence, the planets were also known as "wandering stars." The fundamental assumption of the *Almagest* is that the apparently irregular movements of the heavenly bodies are in reality combinations of regular, uniform, circular motions.

How much of the *Almagest* is original is difficult to determine because almost all of the preceding technical astronomical literature is now lost. Ptolemy credited Hipparchus (mid-2nd century BCE) with essential elements of his solar theory, as well as parts of his lunar theory, while denying that Hipparchus constructed planetary models. Ptolemy made only a few vague and disparaging remarks regarding theoretical work over the intervening three centuries; yet the study of the planets undoubtedly made great strides during that interval. Moreover, Ptolemy's veracity, especially as an observer, has been controversial since the time of the astronomer Tycho Brahe (1546–1601). Brahe pointed out that solar observations Ptolemy claimed to have made in 141 BCE are definitely not genuine, and there are strong arguments for doubting that Ptolemy independently observed the more than 1,000 stars listed in his star catalog. What is not disputed, however, is the mastery of mathematical analysis that Ptolemy exhibited.

Ptolemy was preeminently responsible for the geocentric cosmology that prevailed in the Islamic world and in medieval Europe. This was not due to the *Almagest* so much as a later treatise, *Hypotheseis tōn planōmenōn* (*Planetary Hypotheses*). In this work he proposed what is now called the Ptolemaic system, a unified system in which each heavenly body is attached to its own sphere and the set of spheres nested so that it extends without gaps from the Earth to the celestial sphere. The numerical tables in the *Almagest* (which enabled planetary positions and other celestial phenomena to be calculated for arbitrary dates) had a profound influence on medieval astronomy, in part through a separate, revised version of the tables that Ptolemy published as *Procheiroi kanones* (*Handy Tables*). Ptolemy taught later astronomers how to use dated, quantitative observations to revise cosmological models.

Ptolemy also attempted to place astrology on a sound basis in *Apotelesmatika* (*Astrological Influences*), later known as the *Tetrabiblos* for its four volumes. He believed that astrology is a legitimate, though inexact, science that describes the physical effects of the heavens on terrestrial life. Ptolemy accepted the basic validity of the traditional astrological doctrines, but he revised the details to reconcile the practice with an Aristotelian conception of nature, matter, and change. Of Ptolemy's writings, the *Tetrabiblos* is the most foreign to modern readers, who do not accept astral prognostication and a cosmology driven by the interplay of basic qualities such as hot, cold, wet, and dry.

GALEN OF PERGAMUM

(b. 129 CE, Pergamum, Mysia, Anatolia [now Bergama, Tur.]—d. *c.* 216)

Galen of Pergamum (Latin: Galenus) was a Greek physician, writer, and philosopher who exercised a dominant influence on medical theory and practice in Europe from the Middle Ages until the mid-17th century. His authority in the Byzantine world and the Muslim Middle East was similarly long-lived.

ANATOMICAL AND MEDICAL STUDIES

Galen regarded anatomy as the foundation of medical knowledge, and he frequently dissected and experimented on such lower animals as the Barbary ape (or African monkey), pigs, sheep, and goats. Galen's advocacy of dissection, both to improve surgical skills and for research purposes, formed part of his self-promotion, but there is no doubt that he was an accurate observer. He distinguished seven pairs of cranial nerves, described the valves of the heart, and observed the structural differences between arteries and veins. One of his most important demonstrations was that the arteries carry blood, not air, as had been taught for 400 years. Notable also were his vivisection experiments, such as tying off the recurrent laryngeal nerve to show that the brain controls the voice, performing a series of transections of the spinal cord to establish the functions of the spinal nerves, and tying off the ureters to demonstrate kidney and bladder functions. Galen was seriously hampered by the prevailing social taboo against dissecting human corpses, however, and the inferences he made about human anatomy based on his dissections of animals often led him into errors. His anatomy of the uterus, for example, is largely that of the dog's.

Galen's physiology was a mixture of ideas taken from the philosophers Plato and Aristotle as well as from the physician Hippocrates, whom Galen revered as the fount of all medical learning. Galen viewed the body as consisting of three connected systems: the brain and nerves, which are responsible for sensation and thought; the heart and arteries, responsible for life-giving energy; and the liver and veins, responsible for nutrition and growth. According to Galen, blood is formed in the liver and is then carried by the veins to all parts of the body, where it is used up as nutriment or is transformed into flesh and other substances. A small amount of blood seeps through the lungs between the pulmonary artery and pulmonary veins, thereby becoming mixed with air, and then seeps from the right to the left ventricle of the heart through minute pores in the wall separating the two chambers. A small proportion of this blood is further refined in a network of nerves at the base of the skull (in reality found only in ungulates) and the brain to make psychic pneuma, a subtle material that is the vehicle of sensation. Galen's physiological theory proved extremely seductive, and few possessed the skills needed to challenge it in succeeding centuries.

Building on earlier Hippocratic conceptions, Galen believed that human health requires an equilibrium between the four main bodily fluids, or humours—blood, yellow bile, black bile, and phlegm. Each of the humours is built up from the four elements and displays two of the four primary qualities: hot, cold, wet, and dry. Unlike Hippocrates, Galen argued that humoral imbalances can be located in specific organs, as well as in the body as a whole. This modification of the theory allowed doctors to make more precise diagnoses and to prescribe specific remedies to restore the body's balance. As a continuation of earlier Hippocratic conceptions, Galenic physiology became a powerful influence in medicine for the next 1,400 years.

Galen was both a universal genius and a prolific writer. About 300 titles of works by him are known, of which about 150 survive wholly or in part. He was perpetually inquisitive, even in areas remote from medicine, such as linguistics, and he was an important logician who wrote major studies of scientific method. Galen was also a skilled polemicist and an incorrigible publicist of his own genius, and these traits, combined with the enormous range of his writings, help to explain his subsequent fame and influence.

INFLUENCE

Galen's writings achieved wide circulation during his lifetime, and copies of some of his works survive that were written within a generation of his death. By 500 CE his works were being taught and summarized at Alexandria, and his theories were already crowding out those of others in the medical handbooks of the Byzantine world. Greek manuscripts began to be collected and translated by enlightened Arabs in the 9th century, and in about 850 Ḥunayn ibn Isḥāq, an Arab physician at the court of Baghdad, prepared an annotated list of 129 works of Galen that he and his followers had translated from Greek into Arabic or Syriac. Learned medicine in the Arabic world thus became heavily based upon the commentary, exposition, and understanding of Galen.

Galen's influence was initially almost negligible in western Europe except for drug recipes, but from the late 11th century Ḥunayn's translations, commentaries on them by Arab physicians, and sometimes the original Greek writings themselves were translated into Latin. These Latin versions came to form the basis of medical education in the new medieval universities. From about 1490, Italian humanists felt the need to prepare new Latin versions of Galen directly from Greek manuscripts in order to free his texts from medieval preconceptions and misunderstandings. Galen's works were first printed in Greek in their entirety in 1525, and printings in Latin swiftly followed. These texts offered a different picture from that of the Middle Ages, one that emphasized Galen as a clinician, a diagnostician, and above all, an anatomist. His new followers stressed his methodical techniques of identifying and curing illness, his independent judgment, and his cautious empiricism. Galen's injunctions to investigate the body were eagerly followed, since physicians wished to repeat the experiments and observations that he had recorded. Paradoxically, this soon led to the overthrow of Galen's authority as an anatomist. In 1543 the Flemish physician Andreas Vesalius showed that Galen's anatomy of the body was more animal than human in some of its aspects, and it became clear that Galen and his medieval followers had made many errors. Galen's notions of physiology, by contrast, lasted for a further century, until the English physician William Harvey correctly explained the circulation of the blood. The renewal and then the overthrow of the Galenic tradition in the Renaissance had been an important element in the rise of modern science.

AVICENNA

(b. 980, Bukhara, Iran—d. 1037, Hamadan)

Avicenna (Arabic: Ibn Sīnā) was an Iranian physician and the most famous and influential of the philosopher-scientists of Islam. He was particularly noted for his contributions in the fields of Aristotelian philosophy and medicine. He composed the *Kitāb al-shifā'* (*Book of Healing*), a vast philosophical and scientific encyclopaedia, and *Al-Qānūn fī al-tibb* (*The Canon of Medicine*), which is among the most famous books in the history of medicine.

Avicenna's *Book of Healing* is probably the largest work of its kind ever written by one man. It discusses logic, the natural sciences, including psychology, the *quadrivium* (geometry, astronomy, arithmetic, and music), and metaphysics, but there is no real exposition of ethics or of politics. His thought in this work owes a great deal to Aristotle but also to other Greek influences and to Neoplatonism.

The Canon of Medicine is the most famous single book in the history of medicine in both East and West. It is a systematic encyclopaedia based for the most part on the achievements of Greek physicians of the Roman imperial age and on other Arabic works and, to a lesser extent, on his own experience (his own clinical notes were lost during his journeys). Occupied during the day with his duties at court as both physician and administrator, Avicenna spent almost every night with his students composing these and other works and carrying out general philosophical and scientific discussions related to them.

Avicenna's *Book of Healing* was translated partially into Latin in the 12th century, and the complete *Canon* appeared in the same century. These translations and others spread the thought of Avicenna far and wide in the West. His thought, blended with that of St. Augustine, the Christian philosopher and theologian, was a basic ingredient in the thought of many of the medieval Scholastics, especially in the Franciscan schools. In medicine, the *Canon* became *the* medical authority for several centuries, and Avicenna enjoyed an undisputed place of honour equaled only by the early Greek physicians Hippocrates and Galen. In the East his dominating influence in medicine, philosophy, and theology has lasted over the ages and is still alive within the circles of Islamic thought.

ROGER BACON

(b. *c.* 1220, Ilchester, Somerset, or Bisley, Gloucester?, Eng.—d. 1292, Oxford?)

Roger Bacon, who was also known as Doctor Mirabilis (Latin for "Wonderful Teacher"), was an English Franciscan philosopher and educational reformer, as well as a major medieval proponent of experimental science. Bacon studied mathematics, astronomy, optics, alchemy, and languages. He was the first European to describe in detail the process of making gunpowder, and he proposed flying machines and motorized ships and carriages. Bacon (as he himself complacently remarked) displayed a prodigious energy and zeal in the pursuit of experimental science; indeed, his studies were talked about everywhere and eventually won him a place in popular literature as a kind of wonder worker. Bacon therefore represents a historically precocious expression of the empirical spirit of experimental science, even though his actual practice of it seems to have been exaggerated.

UNIVERSITY AND SCIENTIFIC CAREER

In the earlier part of his career, Bacon lectured in the faculty of arts at the University of Paris on Aristotelian and pseudo-Aristotelian treatises, displaying no indication of his later preoccupation with science. However, beginning in about 1247, Bacon expended much time and energy and huge sums of money in experimental research, in acquiring "secret" books, in the construction of instruments and of tables, in the training of assistants, and in seeking the friendship of savants—activities that marked a definite departure from the usual routine of the faculty of arts. From 1247 to 1257, he devoted himself wholeheartedly to the cultivation of new branches of learning, including languages, optics, and alchemy, and to further studies in astronomy and mathematics. Bacon extolled experimentation so ardently that he has often been viewed as a harbinger of modern science more than 300 years before it came to bloom. However, Bacon's originality lay not so much in any positive contribution to the sum of knowledge but rather in his insistence on fruitful lines of research and methods of experimental study.

Bacon's studies on the nature of light and on the rainbow are especially noteworthy, and he seems to have planned and interpreted these experiments carefully. But his many other "experiments" seem never to have been actually performed; they were merely described. He suggested, for example, that a balloon of thin copper sheet be made and filled with "liquid fire"; he felt that it would float in the air as many light objects do in water. He seriously studied the problem of flying in a machine with flapping wings. Bacon also elucidated the principles of reflection, refraction, and spherical aberration and proposed mechanically propelled ships and carriages. He used a camera obscura, which projects an image through a pinhole, to observe eclipses of the Sun.

THE ORDER OF FRIARS MINOR

By 1257, Bacon had entered into the Order of Friars Minor, a branch of the Franciscan Christian religious order. However, he soon fell ill and felt (as he wrote) forgotten by everyone and all but buried. Furthermore, his feverish activity, his amazing credulity, his superstition, and his vocal contempt for those not sharing his interests displeased his superiors in the order and brought him under severe discipline. He appealed to Pope Clement IV, arguing that a more accurate experimental knowledge of nature would be of great value in confirming the Christian faith. Bacon felt that his proposals would be of great importance for the welfare of the church and of the universities.

The pope desired to become more fully informed of these projects. In obedience to the pope's command, Bacon set to work and in a remarkably short time had dispatched the *Opus majus* ("Great Work"), the *Opus minus* ("Lesser Work"), and the *Opus tertium* ("Third Work"). He had to do this secretly, and even when the irregularity of his conduct attracted the attention of his superiors and the terrible weapons of spiritual coercion were brought to bear upon him, he was deterred from explaining his position by the papal command of secrecy. Under the circumstances, his achievement was truly astounding. The *Opus majus* was an effort to persuade the pope of the urgent necessity and broad utility of the reforms that he proposed. But the death of Clement in 1268 extinguished Bacon's dreams of gaining for the sciences their rightful place in the curriculum of university studies.

Sometime between 1277 and 1279, Bacon was condemned to prison by his fellow Franciscans because of certain "suspected novelties" in his teaching. The condemnation was probably issued in part because of his excessive credulity in alchemy and astrology. How long he was imprisoned is unknown.

LEONARDO DA VINCI

(b. April 15, 1452, Anchiano, near Vinci, Republic of Florence [now in Italy]—d. May 2, 1519, Cloux [now Clos-Lucé], France)

Leonardo da Vinci was an Italian painter, draftsman, sculptor, architect, and engineer. His genius, perhaps more than that of any other figure, epitomized the Renaissance humanist ideal. His *Last Supper* (1495–98) and *Mona Lisa* (c. 1503–06) are among the most widely popular and influential paintings of the Renaissance. His notebooks reveal a spirit of scientific inquiry and a mechanical inventiveness that were centuries ahead of their time.

The unique fame that Leonardo enjoyed in his lifetime and that, filtered by historical criticism, has remained undimmed to the present day rests largely on his unlimited desire for knowledge, which guided all his thinking and behaviour. An artist by disposition and endowment, he considered his eyes to be his main avenue to knowledge; to Leonardo, sight was man's highest sense because it alone conveyed the facts of experience immediately, correctly, and with certainty. Hence, every phenomenon perceived became an object of knowledge. *Saper vedere* ("knowing how to see") became the great theme of his studies. He applied his creativity to every realm in which graphic representation is used: He was a painter, sculptor, architect, and engineer. But he went even beyond that. He used his superb intellect, unusual powers of observation, and mastery of the art of drawing to study nature itself, a line of inquiry that allowed his dual pursuits of art and science to flourish.

ANATOMICAL STUDIES AND DRAWINGS

Leonardo's fascination with anatomical studies reveals a prevailing artistic interest of the time. In his own 1435 treatise *Della pittura* ("On Painting"), theorist Leon Battista Alberti urged painters to construct the human figure as it exists in nature, supported by the skeleton and musculature, and only then clothed in skin. The date of Leonardo's initial involvement with anatomical study is not known nor can it be determined exactly when Leonardo began to perform dissections, but it might have been several years after he first moved to Milan, at the time a centre of medical investigation. His study of anatomy, originally pursued for his training as an artist, had grown by the 1490s into an independent area of research. As his sharp eye uncovered the structure of the human body, Leonardo became fascinated by the *figura istrumentale dell'omo* ("man's instrumental figure"), and he sought to comprehend its physical working as a creation of nature. Over the following two decades, he did practical work in anatomy on the dissection table in Milan, then at hospitals in Florence and Rome, and in Pavia, where he collaborated with the physician-anatomist Marcantonio della Torre. By his own count Leonardo dissected 30 corpses in his lifetime.

Leonardo's early anatomical studies dealt chiefly with the skeleton and muscles. Yet even at the outset, he combined anatomical with physiological research. From observing the static structure of the body, Leonardo proceeded to study the role of individual parts of the body in mechanical activity. This led him finally to the study of the internal organs; among them he probed most deeply into the brain, heart, and lungs as the "motors" of the senses and of life. His findings from these studies were recorded in the famous anatomical drawings, which are among the most significant achievements of Renaissance science. The drawings are based on a connection between natural and abstract representation. He represented parts of the body in transparent layers that afford an "insight" into the organ by using sections in perspective, reproducing muscles as "strings," indicating hidden parts by dotted lines, and devising a hatching system. The genuine value of these *dimostrazione* lay in their ability to synthesize a multiplicity of individual experiences at the dissecting table and make the data immediately and accurately visible. As Leonardo proudly emphasized, these drawings were superior to descriptive words. The wealth of Leonardo's anatomical studies that have survived forged the basic principles of modern scientific illustration. It is worth noting, however, that during his lifetime, Leonardo's medical investigations remained private. He did not consider himself a professional in the field of anatomy, and he neither taught nor published his findings.

Although he kept his anatomical studies to himself, Leonardo did publish some of his observations on human proportion. Working with the mathematician Luca Pacioli, he considered the proportional theories of Vitruvius, the 1st-century BCE Roman architect, as presented in his treatise *De architectura* (*On Architecture*). Imposing the principles of geometry on the configuration of the human body, Leonardo demonstrated that the ideal proportion of the human figure corresponds with the forms of the circle and the square. In his illustration of this theory, the so-called Vitruvian Man, Leonardo demonstrated that when a man places his feet firmly on the ground and stretches out his arms, he can be contained within the four lines of a square, but when in a spread-eagle position, he can be inscribed in a circle.

Leonardo da Vinci's world-renowned drawing the Vitruvian Man was created in the late 1400s and is accompanied by his notes based on the works of Vitruvius. Stuart Gregory/Photographer's Choice RF/Getty Images

Leonardo envisaged the great picture chart of the human body he had produced through his anatomical drawings and Vitruvian Man as a *cosmografia del minor mondo* ("cosmography of the microcosm"). He believed the workings of the human body to be an analogy, in microcosm, for the workings of the universe. Leonardo wrote: "Man has been called by the ancients a lesser world, and indeed the name is well applied; because, as man is composed of earth, water, air, and fire ... this body of the earth is similar." He compared the human skeleton to rocks ("supports of the earth") and the expansion of the lungs in breathing to the ebb and flow of the oceans.

MECHANICS AND COSMOLOGY

According to Leonardo's observations, the study of mechanics, with which he became quite familiar as an architect and engineer, also reflected the workings of nature. Throughout his life Leonardo was an inventive builder. He thoroughly understood the principles of mechanics of his time and contributed in many ways to advancing them. His two Madrid notebooks deal extensively with his theory of mechanics; the first was written in the 1490s, and the second was written between 1503 and 1505. Their importance lay less in their description of specific machines or work tools than in their use of demonstration models to explain the basic mechanical principles and functions employed in building machinery. As in his anatomical drawings, Leonardo developed definite principles of graphic representation— stylization, patterns, and diagrams—that offer a precise demonstration of the object in question.

Leonardo was especially intrigued by problems of friction and resistance, and with each of the mechanical elements he presented—such as screw threads, gears, hydraulic jacks, swiveling devices, and transmission gears—drawings took precedence over the written word. Throughout his career he also was intrigued by the mechanical potential of motion. This led him to design a machine with a differential transmission, a moving fortress that resembles a modern tank, and a flying machine. His "helical airscrew" (c. 1487) almost seems a prototype for the modern helicopter, but, like the other vehicles Leonardo designed, it presented a singular problem: it lacked an adequate source of power to provide propulsion and lift.

Wherever Leonardo probed the phenomena of nature, he recognized the existence of primal mechanical forces that govern the shape and function of the universe. This is seen in his studies of the flight of birds, in which his youthful idea of the feasibility of a flying apparatus took shape and that led to exhaustive research into the element of air; in his studies of water, the *vetturale della natura* ("conveyor of nature"), in which he was as much concerned with the physical properties of water as with its laws of motion and currents; in his research on the laws of growth of plants and trees, as well as the geologic structure of earth and hill formations; and finally in his observation of air currents, which evoked the image of the flame of a candle or the picture of a wisp of cloud and smoke. In his drawings based on the numerous experiments he undertook, Leonardo found a stylized form of representation that was uniquely his own, especially in his studies of whirlpools. He managed to break down a phenomenon into its component parts—the traces of water or eddies of the whirlpool—yet at the same time preserve the total picture, creating both an analytic and a synthetic vision.

Leonardo as Artist Scientist

In an era that often compared the process of divine creation to the activity of an artist, Leonardo reversed the analogy, using art as his own means to approximate the mysteries of creation, asserting that, through the science of painting, "the mind of the painter is transformed into a copy of the divine mind, since it operates freely in creating many kinds of animals, plants, fruits, landscapes, countrysides, ruins, and awe-inspiring places." With this sense of the artist's high calling, Leonardo approached the vast realm of nature to probe its secrets. His utopian idea of transmitting in ency-clopaedic form the knowledge thus won was still bound up with medieval Scholastic conceptions; however, the results of his research were among the first great achievements of the forthcoming age's thinking because they were based to an unprecedented degree on the principle of experience.

NICOLAUS COPERNICUS

(b. Feb. 19, 1473, Toruń, Pol.—d. May 24, 1543, Frauenburg, East Prussia [now Frombork, Pol.])

Polish astronomerNicolaus Copernicus (Polish: Mikołaj Kopernik) proposed that the planets have the Sun as the fixed point to which their motions are to be referred; that the Earth is a planet which, besides orbiting the Sun annually, also turns once daily on its own axis; and that very slow, long-term changes in the direction of this axis account for the precession of the equinoxes. This representation of the heavens is usually called the heliocentric, or "Sun-centred," system—derived from the Greek *helios*, meaning "Sun."

Copernicus's theory had important consequences for later thinkers of the scientific revolution, including such major figures as Galileo, Kepler, Descartes, and Newton. Copernicus probably hit upon his main idea sometime between 1508 and 1514, and during those years he wrote a manuscript usually called the *Commentariolus* ("Little Commentary"). However, the book that contains the final version of his theory, *De revolutionibus orbium coelestium libri vi* ("Six Books Concerning the Revolutions of the Heavenly Orbs"), did not appear in print until 1543, the year of his death.

SCIENCE OF THE STARS

In Copernicus's period, astrology and astronomy were considered subdivisions of a common subject called the "science of the stars," whose main aim was to provide a description of the arrangement of the heavens as well as the theoretical tools and tables of motions that would permit accurate construction of horoscopes and annual prognostications. At this time the terms *astrologer*, *astronomer*, and *mathematician* were virtually interchangeable; they generally denoted anyone who studied the heavens using mathematical techniques. Furthermore, practitioners of astrology were in disagreement about everything, from the divisions of the zodiac to the minutest observations to the order of the planets; there was also a long-standing disagreement concerning the status of the planetary models.

From antiquity, astronomical modeling was governed by the premise that the planets move with uniform angular motion on fixed radii at a constant distance from their centres of motion. Two types of models derived from this premise. The first, represented by that of Aristotle, held that the planets are carried around the centre of the universe embedded in unchangeable, material, invisible spheres at fixed distances. Since all planets have the same centre of motion, the universe is made of nested, concentric spheres with no gaps between them. As a predictive model, this account was of limited value. Among other things, it had the distinct disadvantage that it could not account for variations in the apparent brightness of the planets since the distances from the centre were always the same.

A second tradition, deriving from Claudius Ptolemy, solved this problem by postulating three mechanisms: uniformly revolving, off-centre circles called eccentrics; epicycles, little circles whose centres moved uniformly on the circumference of circles of larger radius (deferents); and equants. The equant, however, broke with the main assumption of ancient astronomy because it separated the condition of uniform motion from that of constant distance from the centre. A planet viewed from a specific point at the centre of its orbit would appear to move sometimes faster, sometimes slower. As seen from the Earth and removed a certain distance from the specific centre point, the planet would also appear to move nonuniformly. Only from the equant, an imaginary point at a calculated distance from the Earth, would the planet appear to move uniformly. A planet-bearing sphere revolving around an equant point will wobble; situate one sphere within another, and the two will collide, disrupting the heavenly order. In the 13th century a group of Persian astronomers at Marāgheh discovered that, by combining two uniformly revolving epicycles to generate an oscillating point that would account for variations in distance, they could devise a model that produced the equalized motion without referring to an equant point. This insight was the starting point for Copernicus's attempt to resolve the conflict raised by wobbling physical spheres.

An Orderly Universe

In the *Commentariolus*, Copernicus postulated that, if the Sun is assumed to be at rest and if the Earth is assumed to be in motion, then the remaining planets fall into an orderly relationship whereby their sidereal periods increase from the Sun as follows: Mercury (88 days), Venus (225 days), Earth (1 year), Mars (1.9 years), Jupiter (12 years), and Saturn (30 years). This theory did resolve the disagreement about the ordering of the planets but, in turn, raised new problems. To accept the theory's premises, one had to abandon much of Aristotelian natural philosophy and develop a new explanation for why heavy bodies fall to a moving Earth. It was also necessary to explain how a transient body like the Earth, filled with meteorological phenomena, pestilence, and wars, could be part of a perfect and imperishable heaven. In addition, Copernicus was working with many observations that he had inherited from antiquity and whose trustworthiness he could not verify. In constructing a theory for the precession of the equinoxes, for example, he was trying to build a model based upon very small, long-term effects. Also, his theory for Mercury was left with serious incoherencies.

Any of these considerations alone could account for Copernicus's delay in publishing his work. (He remarked in the preface to *De revolutionibus* that he had chosen to withhold publication not for merely the nine years recommended by the Roman poet Horace but for 36 years, four times that period.) When a description of the main elements of the heliocentric hypothesis was first published in 1540 and 1541 in the *Narratio Prima* ("First Narration"), it was not under Copernicus's own name but under that of the 25-year-old Georg Rheticus, a Lutheran from the University of Wittenberg, Germany, who stayed with Copernicus at Frauenburg for about two and a half years, between 1539 and 1542. The *Narratio prima* was, in effect, a joint production of Copernicus and Rheticus, something of a "trial balloon" for the main work. It provided a summary of the theoretical principles contained in the manuscript of *De revolutionibus*, emphasized their value for computing new planetary tables, and presented Copernicus as following admiringly in the footsteps of Ptolemy even as he broke fundamentally with his ancient predecessor. It also provided what was missing from the

Commentariolus: a basis for accepting the claims of the new theory.

Both Rheticus and Copernicus knew that they could not definitively rule out all possible alternatives to the heliocentric theory. But they could underline what Copernicus's theory provided that others could not: a singular method for ordering the planets and for calculating the relative distances of the planets from the Sun. Rheticus compared this new universe to a well-tuned musical instrument and to the interlocking wheel-mechanisms of a clock. In the preface to *De revolutionibus*, Copernicus used an image from Horace's *Ars poetica* ("Art of Poetry"). The theories of his predecessors, he wrote, were like a human figure in which the arms, legs, and head were put together in the form of a disorderly monster. His own representation of the universe, in contrast, was an orderly whole in which a displacement of any part would result in a disruption of the whole. In effect, a new criterion of scientific adequacy was advanced together with the new theory of the universe.

PARACELSUS

(b. Nov. 11 or Dec. 17, 1493, Einsiedeln, Switz.—d. Sept. 24, 1541, Salzburg, Archbishopric of Salzburg [now in Austria])

Philippus Aureolus Theophrastus Bombastus Von Hohenheim, better known as Paracelsus, was a German-Swiss physician and alchemist. He established the role of chemistry in medicine. He published *Der grossen Wundartzney* ("Great Surgery Book") in 1536 and a clinical description of syphilis in 1530.

EDUCATION

Paracelsus is said to have graduated from the University of Vienna with a baccalaureate in medicine in 1510. It is

This painting by Flemish artist Peter Paul Rubens depicts the alchemist and physician known as Paracelsus. Hulton Archive/Getty Images

believed that he received his doctoral degree in 1516 from the University of Ferrara in Italy, where he was free to express his rejection of the prevailing view that the stars and planets controlled all the parts of the human body. He is thought to have begun using the name "para-Celsus" (above or beyond Celsus) at about that time because he regarded himself as even greater than Celsus, a renowned 1st-century Roman physician.

Soon after taking his degree, he set out upon many years of wandering through Europe and took part in the "Netherlandish wars" as an army surgeon. Later Paracelsus went to Russia, was held captive by the Tatars, escaped into Lithuania, went south into Hungary, and again served as an army surgeon in Italy in 1521. Ultimately his wanderings brought him to Egypt, Arabia, the Holy Land, and, finally, Constantinople. Everywhere he sought out the most learned exponents of practical alchemy, not only to discover the most effective means of medical treatment but also—and even more important—to discover "the latent forces of Nature," and how to use them.

CAREER AT BASEL

In 1524 Paracelsus returned to his home at Villach in southern Austria to find that his fame for many miraculous cures had preceded him. He was subsequently appointed town physician and lecturer in medicine at the University of Basel in Switzerland, and students from all parts of Europe came to the city to hear his lectures. Pinning a program of his forthcoming lectures to the notice board of the university on June 5, 1527, he invited not only students but anyone and everyone.

Three weeks later, on June 24, 1527, Paracelsus reportedly burned the books of Avicenna, the Arab "Prince of Physicians," and those of Galen, in front of the university.

This incident is said to have recalled in many people's minds Martin Luther, who on Dec. 10, 1520, at the Elster Gate of Wittenberg had burned a papal bull, or edict, that threatened excommunication. While Paracelsus seemingly remained a Catholic to his death, it is suspected that his books were placed on the *Index Expurgatorius*, a catalogue of books from which passages of text considered immoral or against the Catholic religion are removed.

Paracelsus reached the peak of his career at Basel. In his lectures he stressed the healing power of nature and discouraged the use of methods of treating wounds, such as padding with moss or dried dung, that prevented natural draining. He also attacked many other medical malpractices of his time, including the use of worthless salves, fumigants, and drenches. However, by the spring of 1528 Paracelsus fell into disrepute with local doctors, apothecaries, and magistrates. He left Basel, heading first to Colmar in Upper Alsace, about 50 miles north of the university. He continued to travel for the next eight years. During this time, he revised old manuscripts and wrote new treatises. With the publication of *Der grossen Wundartzney* in 1536 he restored, and even extended, the revered reputation he had earned at Basel.

CONTRIBUTIONS TO MEDICINE

In 1530 Paracelsus wrote a clinical description of syphilis, in which he maintained that the disease could be successfully treated by carefully measured doses of mercury compounds taken internally. He stated that the "miners' disease" (silicosis) resulted from inhaling metal vapours and was not a punishment for sin administered by mountain spirits. He was the first to declare that, if given in small doses, "what makes a man ill also cures him," an anticipation of the modern practice of homeopathy. Paracelsus is said to have cured many people in the plague-stricken town of Stertzing in the summer of 1534 by administering orally a pill made of bread containing a minute amount of the patient's excreta he had removed on a needle point.

Paracelsus was the first to connect goitre with minerals, especially lead, in drinking water. He prepared and used new chemical remedies, including those containing mercury, sulfur, iron, and copper sulfate—thus uniting medicine with chemistry, as the first *London Pharmacopoeia*, in 1618, indicates. Paracelsus, in fact, contributed substantially to the rise of modern medicine, including psychiatric treatment.

ANDREAS VESALIUS

(b. Dec. 1514, Brussels [now in Belgium]—d. June 1564, island of Zacynthus, Republic of Venice [now in Greece])

Andreas Vesalius (Flemish: Andries Van Wesel) was a Renaissance Flemish physician who revolutionized the study of biology and the practice of medicine by his careful description of the anatomy of the human body. Basing his observations on dissections he made himself, he wrote and illustrated the first comprehensive textbook of anatomy.

LIFE

Vesalius was from a family of physicians and pharmacists. He attended the Catholic University of Leuven (Louvain) from 1529 to 1533. From 1533 to 1536, he studied at the medical school of the University of Paris, where he learned to dissect animals. He also had the opportunity to dissect human cadavers, and he devoted much of his time to a study of human bones, at that time easily available in the Paris cemeteries.

In 1536 Vesalius returned to his native Brabant to spend another year at the Catholic University of Leuven, where the influence of Arab medicine was still dominant.

Following the prevailing custom, he prepared, in 1537, a paraphrase of the work of the 10th-century Arab physician, Rhazes, probably in fulfillment of the requirements for the bachelor of medicine degree. He then went to the University of Padua, a progressive university with a strong tradition of anatomical dissection. On receiving the M.D. degree the same year, he was appointed a lecturer in surgery with the responsibility of giving anatomical demonstrations. Since he knew that a thorough knowledge of human anatomy was essential to surgery, he devoted much of his time to dissections of cadavers and insisted on doing them himself, instead of relying on untrained assistants.

At first, Vesalius had no reason to question the theories of Galen, the Greek physician who had served the emperor Marcus Aurelius in Rome and whose books on anatomy were still considered as authoritative in medical education in Vesalius's time. In January 1540, breaking with this tradition of relying on Galen, Vesalius openly demonstrated his own method—doing dissections himself, learning anatomy from cadavers, and critically evaluating ancient texts. He did so while visiting the University of Bologna. Such methods soon convinced him that Galenic anatomy had not been based on the dissection of the human body, which had been strictly forbidden by the Roman religion. Galenic anatomy, he maintained, was an application to the human form of conclusions drawn from the dissections of animals, mostly dogs, monkeys, or pigs.

It was this conclusion that he had the audacity to declare in his teaching as he hurriedly prepared his complete textbook of human anatomy for publication. Early in 1542 he traveled to Venice to supervise the preparation of drawings to illustrate his text, probably in the studio of the great Renaissance artist Titian. The drawings of his dissections were engraved on wood blocks, which he took, together with his manuscript, to Basel, Switzerland, where his major work, *De humani corporis fabrica libri septem* ("The Seven Books on the Structure of the Human Body"), commonly known as the *Fabrica*, was printed in 1543. In this epochal work, Vesalius deployed all his scientific, humanistic, and aesthetic gifts. The *Fabrica* was a more extensive and accurate description of the human body than any put forward by his predecessors. It gave anatomy a new language, and, in the elegance of its printing and organization, an unparalleled perfection.

Early in 1543, Vesalius left for Mainz, to present his book to the Holy Roman emperor Charles V, who engaged him as regular physician to the household. Thus, when not yet 28 years old, Vesalius had attained his goal. After relinquishing his post in Padua, and returning in the spring of 1544 to his native land to marry Anne van Hamme, he took up new duties in the service of the Emperor on his travels in Europe. From 1553 to 1556 Vesalius spent most of his time in Brussels, where he built an imposing house in keeping with his growing affluence and attended to his flourishing medical practice. His prestige was further enhanced when Charles V, on abdication from the Spanish throne in 1556, provided him with a lifetime pension and made him a count.

Vesalius went to Spain in 1559 with his wife and daughter to take up an appointment, made by Philip II, son of Charles V, as one of the physicians in the Madrid court. In 1564 Vesalius obtained permission to leave Spain to go on pilgrimage to the Holy Sepulchre. He traveled to Jerusalem, with stops at Venice and Cyprus, his wife and daughter having returned to Brussels.

ASSESSMENT

Vesalius's work represented the culmination of the humanistic revival of ancient learning, the introduction of human dissections into medical curricula, and the growth of a European anatomical literature. Vesalius performed his dissections with a thoroughness hitherto unknown. After Vesalius, anatomy became a scientific discipline, with far-reaching implications not only for physiology but for all of biology. During his own lifetime, however, Vesalius found it easier to correct points of Galenic anatomy than to challenge his physiological framework.

Conflicting reports obscure the final days of Vesalius's life. Apparently he became ill aboard ship while returning to Europe from his pilgrimage. He was put ashore on the Greek island of Zacynthus, where he died.

TYCHO BRAHE

(b. Dec. 14, 1546, Knudstrup, Scania, Denmark—d. Oct. 24, 1601, Prague)

Tycho Brahe was a Danish astronomer whose work in developing astronomical instruments and in measuring and fixing the positions of stars paved the way for future discoveries. His observations—the most accurate possible before the invention of the telescope—included a comprehensive study of the solar system and accurate positions of more than 777 fixed stars.

The new star in the constellation Cassiopeia caused Tycho to dedicate himself to astronomy; one immediate decision was to establish a large observatory for regular observations of celestial events. His plan to establish this observatory in Germany prompted King Frederick II to keep him in Denmark by granting him title in 1576 to the island of Ven (formerly Hven), in the middle of The Sound and about halfway between Copenhagen and Helsingør, together with financial support for the observatory and laboratory buildings. Tycho called the observatory Uraniborg, after Urania, the Muse of astronomy. Surrounded by scholars and visited by learned travelers from all over Europe, Tycho and his assistants collected observations and substantially corrected nearly every known astronomical record.

Tycho was an artist as well as a scientist and craftsman, and everything he undertook or surrounded himself with had to be innovative and beautiful. He established a printing shop to produce and bind his manuscripts in his own way, he imported Augsburg craftsmen to construct the finest astronomical instruments, he induced Italian and Dutch artists and architects to design and decorate his observatory, and he invented a pressure system to provide the then uncommon convenience of sanitary lavatory facilities. Uraniborg fulfilled the hopes of Tycho's king and friend, Frederick II, that it would become the centre of astronomical study and discovery in northern Europe. But Frederick died in 1588, and under his son, Christian IV, Tycho's influence dwindled; most of his income was stopped, partly because of the increasing needs of the state for money. Spoiled by Frederick, however, Tycho had become both unreasonably demanding of more money and less inclined to carry out the civic duties required by his income from state lands.

At odds with the three great powers—king, church, and nobility—Tycho left Ven in 1597, and, after short stays at Rostock and at Wandsbek, near Hamburg, he settled in Prague in 1599 under the patronage of Emperor Rudolf II, who also in later years supported the astronomer Johannes Kepler.

The major portion of Tycho's lifework—making and recording accurate astronomical observations—had already been done at Uraniborg. To his earlier observations, particularly his proof that the nova of 1572 was a star, he added a comprehensive study of the solar system and his proof that the orbit of the comet of 1577 lay beyond the Moon.

He proposed a modified Copernican system in which the planets revolved around the Sun, which in turn moved around the stationary Earth. What Tycho accomplished, using only his simple instruments and practical talents, remains an outstanding accomplishment of the Renaissance.

Tycho attempted to continue his observations at Prague with the few instruments he had salvaged from Uraniborg, but the spirit was not there, and he died in 1601, leaving all his observational data to Kepler, his pupil and assistant in the final years. With these data Kepler laid the groundwork for the work of Sir Isaac Newton.

GIORDANO BRUNO

(b. 1548, Nola, near Naples—d. Feb. 17, 1600, Rome)

Giordano Bruno was an Italian philosopher, astronomer, mathematician, and occultist whose theories anticipated modern science. The most notable of these were his theories of the infinite universe and the multiplicity of worlds, in which he rejected the traditional geocentric astronomy and intuitively went beyond the Copernican heliocentric theory, which still maintained a finite universe with a sphere of fixed stars. Bruno is, perhaps, chiefly remembered for the tragic death he suffered at the stake because of the tenacity with which he maintained his unorthodox ideas at a time when both the Roman Catholic and the Reformed churches were reaffirming rigid Aristotelian and Scholastic principles in their struggle for the evangelization of Europe.

WORKS

In the spring of 1583 Bruno moved from Paris to London and was soon attracted to Oxford, where, during the summer, he started a series of lectures in which he expounded the Copernican theory maintaining the reality of the movement of the Earth. In February 1584 he was invited to discuss his theory of the movement of the Earth with some doctors from the University of Oxford. However, the discussion degenerated into a quarrel, and a few days later he started writing his Italian dialogues, which constitute the first systematic exposition of his philosophy. There are six dialogues, three of which are cosmological— on the theory of the universe.

In the *Cena de le Ceneri* (1584; "The Ash Wednesday Supper"), he not only reaffirmed the reality of the heliocentric theory but also suggested that the universe is infinite, constituted of innumerable worlds substantially similar to those of the solar system. In the same dialogue he anticipated his fellow Italian astronomer Galileo Galilei by maintaining that the Bible should be followed for its moral teaching but not for its astronomical implications. He also strongly criticized the manners of English society and the pedantry of the Oxford doctors.

In the *De la causa, principio e uno* (1584; *Concerning the Cause, Principle, and One*) he elaborated the physical theory on which his conception of the universe was based: "form" and "matter" are intimately united and constitute the "one." Thus, the traditional dualism of the Aristotelian physics was reduced by him to a monistic conception of the world, implying the basic unity of all substances and the coincidence of opposites in the infinite unity of Being.

In the *De l'infinito universo e mondi* (1584; *On the Infinite Universe and Worlds*), he developed his cosmological theory by systematically criticizing Aristotelian physics; he also formulated his Averroistic view of the relation between philosophy and religion, according to which religion is considered as a means to instruct and govern ignorant people, philosophy as the discipline of the elect who are able to behave themselves and govern others.

In October 1585 Bruno returned to Paris, but found himself at odds with the political climate there. As a result, he went to Germany, where he wandered from one university city to another, lecturing and publishing a variety of minor works, including the *Articuli centum et sexaginta* (1588; "160 Articles") against contemporary mathematicians and philosophers, in which he expounded his conception of religion—a theory of the peaceful coexistence of all religions based upon mutual understanding and the freedom of reciprocal discussion. At Helmstedt, however, in January 1589 he was excommunicated by the local Lutheran Church. He remained in Helmstedt until the spring, completing works on natural and mathematical magic (posthumously published) and working on three Latin poems—*De triplici minimo et mensura* ("On the Threefold Minimum and Measure"), *De monade, numero et figura* ("On the Monad, Number, and Figure"), and *De immenso, innumerabilibus et infigurabilibus* ("On the Immeasurable and Innumerable")—which reelaborated the theories expounded in the Italian dialogues and developed Bruno's concept of an atomic basis of matter and being.

To publish these, he went in 1590 to Frankfurt am Main, where the senate rejected his application to stay. Nevertheless, he took up residence in the Carmelite convent, lecturing to Protestant doctors and acquiring a reputation of being a "universal man" who, the Prior thought, "did not possess a trace of religion" and who "was chiefly occupied in writing and in the vain and chimerical imagining of novelties."

FINAL YEARS

In August 1591, at the invitation of the Venetian patrician Giovanni Mocenigo, Bruno made the fatal move of returning to Italy. During the late summer of 1591, he composed the *Praelectiones geometricae* ("Lectures on Geometry") and *Ars deformationum* ("Art of Deformation"). In Venice, as the guest of Mocenigo, Bruno took part in the discussions of progressive Venetian aristocrats who, like Bruno, favoured philosophical investigation irrespective of its theological implications. Bruno's liberty came to an end when Mocenigo—disappointed by his private lessons from Bruno on the art of memory and resentful of Bruno's intention to go back to Frankfurt to have a new work published—denounced him to the Venetian Inquisition in May 1592 for his heretical theories. Bruno was arrested and tried. He defended himself by admitting minor theological errors, emphasizing, however, the philosophical rather than the theological character of his basic tenets. The Roman Inquisition demanded his extradition, and on Jan. 27, 1593, Bruno entered the jail of the Roman palace of the Sant'Uffizio (Holy Office).

During the seven-year Roman period of the trial, Bruno at first developed his previous defensive line, disclaiming any particular interest in theological matters and reaffirming the philosophical character of his speculation. This distinction did not satisfy the inquisitors, who demanded an unconditional retraction of his theories. Bruno then made a desperate attempt to demonstrate that his views were not incompatible with the Christian conception of God and creation. The inquisitors rejected his arguments and pressed him for a formal retraction. Bruno finally declared that he had nothing to retract and that he did not even know what he was expected to retract. At that point, Pope Clement VIII ordered that he be sentenced as an impenitent and pertinacious heretic. On Feb. 8, 1600, when the death sentence was formally read to him, he addressed his judges, saying, "Perhaps your fear in passing judgment on me is greater than mine in receiving it." Not long after, he was brought to the Campo de' Fiori, his tongue in a gag, and burned alive.

INFLUENCE

Bruno's theories influenced 17th-century scientific and philosophical thought and, since the 18th century, have been absorbed by many modern philosophers. As a symbol of the freedom of thought, he inspired the European liberal movements of the 19th century, particularly the Italian Risorgimento (the movement for national political unity). Because of the variety of his interests, modern scholars are divided as to the chief significance of his work. Bruno's cosmological vision certainly anticipates some fundamental aspects of the modern conception of the universe. His ethical ideas, in contrast with religious ascetical ethics, appeal to modern humanistic activism, and his ideal of religious and philosophical tolerance has influenced liberal thinkers. On the other hand, his emphasis on the magical and the occult has been the source of criticism as has his impetuous personality. Bruno stands, however, as one of the important figures in the history of Western thought, a precursor of modern civilization.

GALILEO

(b. Feb. 15, 1564, Pisa [Italy]—d. Jan. 8, 1642, Arcetri, near Florence)

Galileo Galilei was an Italian natural philosopher, astronomer, and mathematician who made fundamental contributions to the sciences of motion, astronomy, and strength of materials and to the development of the scientific method. His formulation of (circular) inertia, the law of falling bodies, and parabolic trajectories marked the beginning of a fundamental change in the study of motion. His insistence that the book of nature was written in the language of mathematics changed natural philosophy from a verbal, qualitative account to a mathematical one in which experimentation became a recognized method for discovering the facts of nature. Finally, his discoveries with the telescope revolutionized astronomy and paved the way for the acceptance of the Copernican heliocentric system, but his advocacy of that system eventually resulted in an Inquisition process against him.

TELESCOPIC DISCOVERIES

In the spring of 1609 Galileo heard that in the Netherlands an instrument had been invented that showed distant things as though they were nearby. By trial and error, he quickly figured out the secret of the invention and made his own three-powered spyglass from lenses for sale in spectacle makers' shops. Others had done the same; what set Galileo apart was that he quickly figured out how to improve the instrument, taught himself the art of lens grinding, and produced increasingly powerful telescopes.

In the fall of 1609 Galileo began observing the heavens with instruments that magnified up to 20 times. In December he drew the Moon's phases as seen through the telescope, showing that the Moon's surface is not smooth, as had been thought, but is rough and uneven. In January 1610 he discovered four moons revolving around Jupiter. He also found that the telescope showed many more stars than are visible with the naked eye. These discoveries were earthshaking, and Galileo quickly produced a little book, *Sidereus Nuncius* (*The Sidereal Messenger*), in which he described them. He dedicated the book to Cosimo II de Medici (1590–1621), the grand duke of his native Tuscany, whom he had tutored in mathematics for several summers, and he named the moons of Jupiter after the Medici family: the Sidera Medicea, or "Medicean Stars."

Italian astronomer, mathematician, and philosopher Galileo Galilei (1564–1642) pores over a book while holding a compass. Hulton Archive/ Getty Images

Galileo also had discovered the puzzling appearance of Saturn, later to be shown as caused by a ring surrounding it, and he discovered that Venus goes through phases just as the Moon does. Although these discoveries did not prove that the Earth is a planet orbiting the Sun, they undermined Aristotelian cosmology: the absolute difference between the corrupt earthly region and the perfect and unchanging heavens was proved wrong by the mountainous surface of the Moon, the moons of Jupiter showed that there had to be more than one centre of motion in the universe, and the phases of Venus showed that it (and, by implication, Mercury) revolves around the Sun. As a result, Galileo was confirmed in his belief, which he had

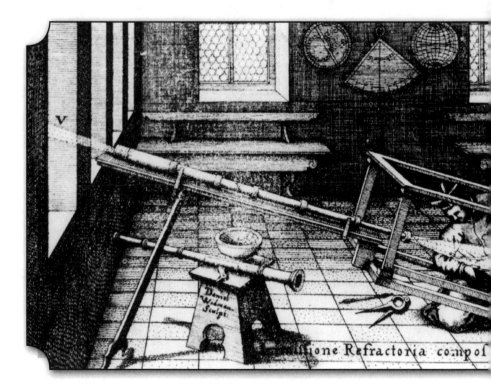

Christoph Scheiner, observing sunspots, c. 1620. © Photos.com/Jupiterimages

probably held for decades but which had not been central to his studies, that the Sun is the centre of the universe and that the Earth is a planet, as Copernicus had argued. Galileo's conversion to Copernicanism would be a key turning point in the scientific revolution.

After a brief controversy about floating bodies, Galileo again turned his attention to the heavens and entered a debate with Christoph Scheiner (1573–1650), a German Jesuit and professor of mathematics at Ingolstadt, about the nature of sunspots (of which Galileo was an independent discoverer). This controversy resulted in Galileo's *Istoria e dimostrazioni intorno alle macchie solari e loro accidenti* ("History and Demonstrations Concerning Sunspots and Their Properties," or "Letters on Sunspots"), which appeared in 1613. Against Scheiner, who, in an effort to save the perfection of the Sun, argued that sunspots are satellites of the Sun, Galileo argued that the spots are on or near the Sun's surface, and he bolstered his argument with a series of detailed engravings of his observations.

GALILEO'S COPERNICANISM

Following the appearance of three comets in 1618, Galileo entered a controversy about the nature of comets, which led to the publication of *Il saggiatore* (*The Assayer*) in 1623. This work was a brilliant polemic on physical reality and an exposition of the new scientific method. In 1624 Galileo went to Rome and met with Pope Urban VIII. Galileo told the pope about his theory of the tides (developed earlier), which he put forward as proof of the annual and diurnal motions of the Earth. The pope gave Galileo permission to write a book about theories of the universe but warned him to treat the Copernican theory only hypothetically.

The book, *Dialogo sopra i due massimi sistemi del mondo, tolemaico e copernicano* (*Dialogue Concerning the Two Chief World Systems, Ptolemaic & Copernican*), was finished in 1630, and Galileo sent it to the Roman censor. Because of an outbreak of the plague, communications between Florence and Rome were interrupted, and Galileo asked for the censoring to be done instead in Florence. The Roman censor had a number of serious criticisms of the book and forwarded these to his colleagues in Florence. After writing a preface in which he professed that what followed was written hypothetically, Galileo had little trouble getting the book through the Florentine censors, and it appeared in Florence in 1632.

In the *Dialogue* Galileo gathered together all the arguments (mostly based on his own telescopic discoveries) for the Copernican theory and against the traditional geocentric cosmology. As opposed to Aristotle's, Galileo's approach to cosmology is fundamentally spatial and geometric: the Earth's axis retains its orientation in space as the Earth circles the Sun, and bodies not under a force retain their velocity (although this inertia is ultimately circular). But in the work, Galileo ridiculed the notion that God could have made the universe any way he wanted to and still made it appear to us the way it does. The reaction against the book was swift. The pope convened a special commission to examine the book and make recommendations; the commission found that Galileo had not really treated the Copernican theory hypothetically and recommended that a case be brought against him by the Inquisition.

He was pronounced to be vehemently suspect of heresy and was condemned to life imprisonment. However, Galileo was never in a dungeon or tortured; during the Inquisition process he stayed mostly at the house of the Tuscan ambassador to the Vatican and for a short time in a comfortable apartment in the Inquisition building. After the process he spent six months at the palace of Ascanio Piccolomini (*c.* 1590–1671), the archbishop of Siena and a friend and patron, and then moved into a villa near Arcetri, in the hills above Florence. He spent the rest of his life there.

Galileo was then 70 years old. Yet he kept working. In Siena he had begun a new book on the sciences of motion and strength of materials. The book was published in Leiden, Netherlands, in 1638 under the title *Discorsi e dimostrazioni matematiche intorno a due nuove scienze attenenti alla meccanica* (*Dialogues Concerning Two New Sciences*). Galileo here treated for the first time the bending and breaking of beams and summarized his mathematical and experimental investigations of motion, including the law of falling bodies and the parabolic path of projectiles as a result of the mixing of two motions, constant speed and uniform acceleration. By then Galileo had become blind, and he spent his time working with a young student, Vincenzo Viviani, who was with him when he died on Jan. 8, 1642.

JOHANNES KEPLER

(b. Dec. 27, 1571, Weil der Stadt, Württemberg [Ger.]—d. Nov. 15, 1630, Regensburg)

German astronomer Johannes Kepler discovered three major laws of planetary motion, conventionally designated as follows: (1) the planets move in elliptical orbits with the Sun at one focus; (2) the time necessary to traverse any arc of a planetary orbit is proportional to the area of the sector between the central body and that arc (the "area law"); and (3) there is an exact relationship between the squares of the planets' periodic times and the cubes of the radii of their orbits (the "harmonic law").

Kepler himself did not call these discoveries "laws," as would become customary after Isaac Newton derived them from a new and quite different set of general physical principles. He regarded them as celestial harmonies that reflected God's design for the universe. Kepler's discoveries turned Nicolaus Copernicus's Sun-centred system into a dynamic universe, with the Sun actively pushing the planets around in noncircular orbits. And it was Kepler's notion of a physical astronomy that fixed a new problematic for other important 17th-century world-system builders, the most famous of whom was Newton.

Among Kepler's many other achievements, he provided a new and correct account of how vision occurs; he developed a novel explanation for the behaviour of light in the newly invented telescope; he discovered several new, semiregular polyhedrons; and he offered a new theoretical foundation for astrology while at the same time restricting the domain in which its predictions could be considered reliable. A list of his discoveries, however, fails to convey the fact that they constituted for Kepler part of a common edifice of knowledge. The matrix of theological, astrological, and physical ideas from which Kepler's scientific achievements emerged is unusual and fascinating in its own right.

Although Kepler's scientific work was centred first and foremost on astronomy, that subject as then understood—the study of the motions of the heavenly bodies—was classified as part of a wider subject of investigation called "the science of the stars." The science of the stars was regarded as a mixed science consisting of a mathematical and a physical component and bearing a kinship to other like disciplines, such as music (the study of ratios of tones) and optics (the study of light). It also was subdivided into theoretical and practical categories. Besides the theory of heavenly motions, one had the practical construction of planetary tables and instruments; similarly, the theoretical principles of astrology had a corresponding practical part that dealt with the making of annual astrological forecasts about individuals, cities, the human body, and the weather. Within this framework, Kepler made astronomy an integral part of natural philosophy, but he did so in an unprecedented way—in the process, making unique contributions to astronomy as well as to all its auxiliary disciplines.

The ideas that Kepler would pursue for the rest of his life were already present in his first work, *Mysterium cosmographicum* (1596; "Cosmographic Mystery"). In 1595 Kepler realized that the spacing among the six Copernican planets might be explained by circumscribing and inscribing each orbit with one of the five regular polyhedrons. If the ratios of the mean orbital distances agreed with the ratios obtained from circumscribing and inscribing the polyhedrons, then, Kepler felt confidently, he would have discovered the architecture of the universe. Remarkably, Kepler did find agreement within 5 percent, with the exception of Jupiter.

In place of the tradition that individual incorporeal souls push the planets and instead of Copernicus's passive, resting Sun, Kepler hypothesized that a single force from the Sun accounts for the increasingly long periods of motion as the planetary distances increase. Kepler did not yet have an exact mathematical description for this relation, but he intuited a connection. A few years later he acquired William Gilbert's groundbreaking book *De Magnete, Magneticisque Corporibus, et de Magno Magnete*

Tellure (1600; "On the Magnet, Magnetic Bodies, and the Great Magnet, the Earth"), and he immediately adopted Gilbert's theory that the Earth is a magnet. From this Kepler generalized to the view that the universe is a system of magnetic bodies in which, with corresponding like poles repelling and unlike poles attracting, the rotating Sun sweeps the planets around.

In 1601 Kepler published *De Fundamentis Astrologiae Certioribus* (*Concerning the More Certain Fundamentals of Astrology*). This work proposed to make astrology "more certain" by basing it on new physical and harmonic principles. In 1605 Kepler discovered his "first law"—that Mars moves in an elliptical orbit. During the creative burst when Kepler won his "war on Mars" (he did not publish his discoveries until 1609 in the *Astronomia Nova* [*New Astronomy*]), he also wrote important treatises on the nature of light and on the sudden appearance of a new star (1606; *De Stella Nova*, "On the New Star"). Kepler first noticed the star—now known to have been a supernova-—in October 1604, not long after a conjunction of Jupiter and Saturn in 1603. The astrological importance of the long-anticipated conjunction (such configurations take place every 20 years) was heightened by the unexpected appearance of the supernova. Kepler used the occasion both to render practical predictions (e.g., the collapse of Islam and the return of Christ) and to speculate theoretically about the universe—for example, that the star was not the result of chance combinations of atoms and that stars are not suns.

Kepler's interest in light was directly related to his astronomical concerns. Kepler wrote about his ideas on light in *Ad Vitellionem Paralipomena, Quibus Astronomiae Pars Optica Traditur* (1604; "Supplement to Witelo, in Which Is Expounded the Optical Part of Astronomy"). Kepler wrote that every point on a luminous body in the field of vision emits rays of light in all directions but that the only rays that can enter the eye are those that impinge on the pupil. He also stated that the rays emanating from a single luminous point form a cone the circular base of which is in the pupil. All the rays are then refracted within the normal eye to meet again at a single point on the retina. For more than three centuries eyeglasses had helped people see better. But nobody before Kepler was able to offer a good theory for why these little pieces of curved glass had worked.

After Galileo built a telescope in 1609 and announced hitherto-unknown objects in the heavens (e.g., moons revolving around Jupiter) and imperfections of the lunar surface, he sent Kepler his account in *Siderius Nuncius*

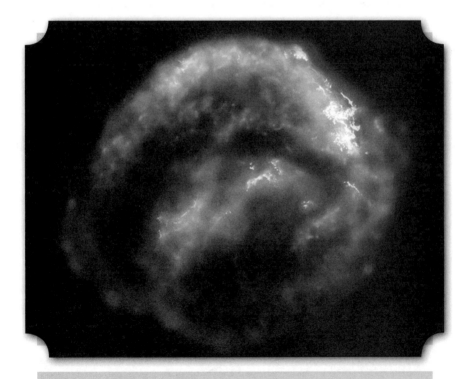

Composite image of Kepler's Nova, or Kepler's Supernova, taken by the Chandra X-ray Observatory. NASA, ESA, R. Sankrit and W. Blair, Johns Hopkins University

(1610; *The Sidereal Messenger*). Kepler responded with three important treatises. The first was his *Dissertatio cum Nuncio Sidereo* (1610; "Conversation with the Sidereal Messenger"), in which, among other things, he speculated that the distances of the newly discovered Jovian moons might agree with the ratios of the rhombic dodecahedron, triaconta-hedron, and cube. The second was a theoretical work on the optics of the telescope, *Dioptrice* (1611; "Dioptrics"), including a description of a new type of telescope using two convex lenses. The third was based upon his own observations of Jupiter, made between August 30 and September 9, 1610, and published as *Narratio de Jovis Satellitibus* (1611; "Narration Concerning the Jovian Satellites"). These works provided strong support for Galileo's discoveries.

Kepler also published the first textbook of Copernican astronomy, *Epitome Astronomiae Copernicanae* (1618–21; *Epitome of Copernican Astronomy*), which proved to be the most important theoretical resource for the Copernicans in the 17th century. Galileo and French mathematician and philosopher René Descartes were probably influenced by it.

WILLIAM HARVEY

(b. April 1, 1578, Folkestone, Kent, Eng. – d. June 3, 1657, London)

English physician William Harvey was the first to rec-ognize the full circulation of the blood in the human body and to provide experiments and arguments to sup-port this idea.

DISCOVERY OF CIRCULATION

Harvey's key work was *Exercitatio Anatomica de Motu Cordis et Sanguinis in Animalibus* (*Anatomical Exercise on the*

Motion of the Heart and Blood in Animals), published in 1628. Harvey's greatest achievement was to recognize that the blood flows rapidly around the human body, being pumped through a single system of arteries and veins, and to support this hypothesis with experiments and arguments.

Prior to Harvey, it was believed there were two separate blood systems in the body. One carried purple, "nutritive" blood and used the veins to distribute nutrition from the liver to the rest of the body. The other carried scarlet, "vivyfying" (or "vital") blood and used the arteries to distribute a life-giving principle from the lungs. Today these blood systems are understood as deoxygenated blood and oxygenated blood. However, at the time, the influence of oxygen on blood was not understood. Furthermore, blood was not thought to circulate around the body—it was believed to be consumed by the body at the same rate that it was produced. The capillaries, small vessels linking the arteries and veins, were unknown at the time, and their existence was not confirmed until later in the 17th century, after Harvey, when the microscope had been invented.

Harvey claimed he was led to his discovery of the circulation by consideration of the venous valves. It was known that there were small flaps inside the veins that allowed free passage of blood in one direction but strongly inhibited the flow of blood in the opposite direction. It was thought that these flaps prevented pooling of the blood under the influence of gravity, but Harvey was able to show that all these flaps are cardiocentrically oriented. For example, he showed that in the jugular vein of the neck they face downward, inhibiting blood flow away from the heart, instead of upward, inhibiting pooling due to gravity.

Harvey's main experiment concerned the amount of blood flowing through the heart. He made estimates of the volume of the ventricles, how efficient they were in expelling blood, and the number of beats per minute made by the heart. He was able to show, even with conservative estimates, that more blood passed through the heart than could possibly be accounted for based on the then current understanding of blood flow. Harvey's values indicated the heart pumped 0.5–1 litre of blood per minute (modern values are about 4 litres per minute at rest and 25 litres per minute during exercise). The human body contains about 5 litres of blood. The body simply could not produce or consume that amount of blood so rapidly; therefore, the blood had to circulate.

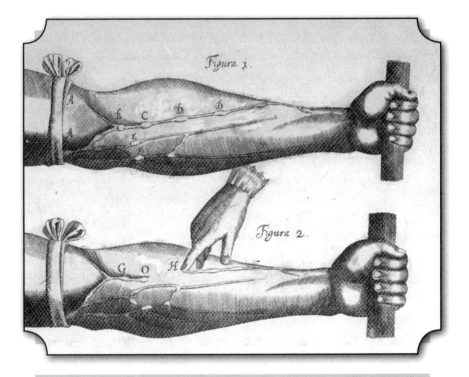

This engraving from a groundbreaking work by the physician and human anatomy expert William Harvey demonstrates how blood flows through the veins of the arm. Time & Life Pictures/Getty Images

It is also important that Harvey investigated the nature of the heartbeat. Prior to Harvey, it was thought that the active phase of the heartbeat, when the muscles contract, was when the heart increased its internal volume. So the active motion of the heart was to draw blood into itself. Harvey observed the heart beating in many animals—particularly in cold-blooded animals and in animals near death, because their heartbeats were slow. He concluded that the active phase of the heartbeat, when the muscles contract, is when the heart decreases its internal volume and that blood is expelled with considerable force from the heart. Although Harvey did quantify blood flow, his quantification is very approximate, and he deliberately used underestimates to further his case. This is very different from the precise quantification leading to the mathematical laws of someone like Galileo.

Harvey's theory of circulation was opposed by conservative physicians, but it was well established by the time of his death. It is likely that Harvey actually made his discovery of the circulation about 1618–19. Such a major shift in thinking about the body needed to be very well supported by experiment and argument to avoid immediate ridicule and dismissal; hence the delay before the publication of his central work. In 1649 Harvey published *Exercitationes Duae Anatomicae de Circulatione Sanguinis, ad Joannem Riolanem, Filium, Parisiensem* (*Two Anatomical Exercises on the Circulation of the Blood*) in response to criticism of the circulation theory by French anatomist Jean Riolan.

RENAISSANCE INFLUENCES

Harvey was very much influenced by the ideas of Greek philosopher Aristotle and the natural magic tradition of the Renaissance. His key analogy for the circulation of the blood was a macrocosm/microcosm analogy with the weather system. A macrocosm/microcosm analogy sees similarities between a small system and a large system. Thus, one might say that the solar system is a macrocosm and the atom is a microcosm. The Renaissance natural magic tradition was very keen on the idea of the human body as a microcosm. The macrocosm for Harvey was the Earth's weather cycle. Water was changed into vapour by the action of the Sun, and the vapour rose, was cooled, and fell again as rain. The microcosm was the human body, where the action of the heart was supposed to heat and change the blood, which was cooled again in the extremities of the body. It also should be noted that much of his terminology for change was drawn from the alchemy of his time. Harvey was very much a man of the later Renaissance—not a man of the scientific revolution and its mechanical nature.

STUDIES OF REPRODUCTION

Harvey spent much of the latter part of his career working on the nature of reproduction in animals. He worked on chickens as an example of oviparous reproduction, in which embryonic development occurs within eggs hatched outside the mother's body, and on deer as an example of viviparous reproduction, in which embryonic development occurs within the mother's body, resulting in the birth of live young. Harvey's work in this area generated a wealth of observational detail. At the time, reproduction was poorly understood, and Harvey investigated issues of the role of sperm and menstrual blood in the formation of the embryo. His observations were excellent, but such matters could not be resolved properly without the use of the microscope.

ROBERT BOYLE

(b. Jan. 25, 1627, Lismore Castle, County Waterford, Ire.—d. Dec. 31, 1691, London, Eng.)

British natural philosopher and theological writer Robert Boyle was a preeminent figure of 17th-century intellectual culture. He was best known as a natural philosopher, particularly in the field of chemistry, but his scientific work covered many areas including hydrostatics, physics, medicine, earth sciences, natural history, and alchemy. His prolific output also included Christian devotional and ethical essays and theological tracts on biblical language, the limits of reason, and the role of the natural philosopher as a Christian. He sponsored many religious missions as well as the translation of the Scriptures into several languages. In 1660 he helped found the Royal Society of London.

Boyle spent much of 1652–54 in Ireland overseeing his hereditary lands, and he also performed some anatomic dissections. In 1654 he was invited to Oxford, and he took up residence at the university from c. 1656 until 1668. In Oxford he was exposed to the latest developments in natural philosophy and became associated with a group of notable natural philosophers and physicians, including John Wilkins, Christopher Wren, and John Locke. These individuals, together with a few others, formed the "Experimental Philosophy Club," which at times convened in Boyle's lodgings. Much of Boyle's best-known work dates from this period.

In 1659 Boyle and Robert Hooke, the clever inventor and subsequent curator of experiments for the Royal Society, completed the construction of their famous air pump and used it to study pneumatics. Their resultant discoveries regarding air pressure and the vacuum appeared in Boyle's first scientific publication, *New Experiments Physico-Mechanicall, Touching the Spring of the Air and its Effects* (1660).

Boyle and Hooke discovered several physical characteristics of air, including its role in combustion, respiration, and the transmission of sound. One of their findings, published in 1662, later became known as "Boyle's law." This law expresses the inverse relationship that exists between the pressure and volume of a gas, and it was determined by measuring the volume occupied by a constant quantity of air when compressed by differing weights of mercury. Other natural philosophers, including Henry Power and Richard Towneley, concurrently reported similar findings about air.

Boyle's scientific work is characterized by its reliance on experiment and observation and its reluctance to formulate generalized theories. He advocated a "mechanical philosophy" that saw the universe as a huge machine or clock in which all natural phenomena were accountable purely by mechanical, clockwork motion. His contributions to chemistry were based on a mechanical "corpuscularian hypothesis"—a brand of atomism which claimed that everything was composed of minute (but not indivisible) particles of a single universal matter and that these particles were only differentiable by their shape and motion. Among his most influential writings were *The Sceptical Chymist* (1661), which assailed the then-current Aristotelian and especially Paracelsian notions about the composition of matter and methods of chemical analysis, and the *Origine of Formes and Qualities* (1666), which used chemical phenomena to support the corpuscularian hypothesis.

Boyle also maintained a lifelong pursuit of transmutational alchemy, endeavouring to discover the secret of transmuting base metals into gold and to contact individuals believed to possess alchemical secrets. Overall, Boyle argued so strongly for the need of applying the principles and methods of chemistry to the study of the natural world and to medicine that he later gained the appellation of the "father of chemistry."

ANTONIE VAN LEEUWENHOEK

(b. Oct. 24, 1632, Delft, Neth.—d. Aug. 26, 1723, Delft)

Dutch microscopist Antonie van Leeuwenhoek was the first to observe bacteria and protozoa. His researches on lower animals refuted the doctrine of spontaneous generation, and his observations helped lay the foundations for the sciences of bacteriology and protozoology. The dramatic nature of his discoveries made him world famous, and he was visited by many notables—including Peter I the Great of Russia, James II of England, and Frederick II the Great of Prussia.

Little is known of Leeuwenhoek's early life. When his stepfather died in 1648, he was sent to Amsterdam to become an apprentice to a linendraper. Returning to Delft when he was 20, he established himself as a draper and haberdasher. In 1660 he obtained a position as chamberlain to the sheriffs of Delft. His income was thus secure and sufficient enough to enable him to devote much of his time to his all-absorbing hobby, that of grinding lenses and using them to study tiny objects.

Leeuwenhoek made microscopes consisting of a single, high-quality lens of very short focal length; at the time, such simple microscopes were preferable to the compound microscope, which increased the problem of chromatic aberration. Although Leeuwenhoek's studies lacked the organization of formal scientific research, his powers of careful observation enabled him to make discoveries of fundamental importance. In 1674 he began to observe bacteria and protozoa, his "very little animalcules," which he was able to isolate from different sources, such as rainwater, pond and well water, and the human mouth and intestine, and he calculated their sizes.

In 1677 he described for the first time the spermatozoa from insects, dogs, and man, though Stephen Hamm probably was a codiscoverer. Leeuwenhoek studied the structure of the optic lens, striations in muscles, the mouthparts of insects, and the fine structure of plants and discovered parthenogenesis in aphids. In 1680 he noticed that yeasts consist of minute globular particles. He extended Marcello Malpighi's demonstration in 1660 of the blood capillaries by giving (in 1684) the first accurate description of red blood cells. In his observations on rotifers in 1702, Leeuwenhoek remarked that "in all falling rain, carried from gutters into water-butts, animalcules are to be found; and that in all kinds of water, standing in the open air, animalcules can turn up. For these animalcules can be carried over by the wind, along with the bits of dust floating in the air."

A friend of Leeuwenhoek put him in touch with the Royal Society of England, to which, from 1673 until 1723, he communicated by means of informal letters most of his discoveries and to which he was elected a fellow in 1680. His discoveries were for the most part made public in the society's *Philosophical Transactions*. The first representation of bacteria is to be found in a drawing by Leeuwenhoek in that publication in 1683.

His researches on the life histories of various low forms of animal life were in opposition to the doctrine that they could be produced spontaneously or bred from corruption. Thus, he showed that the weevils of granaries (in his time commonly supposed to be bred from wheat as well as in it) are really grubs hatched from eggs deposited by winged insects. His letter on the flea, in which he not only described its structure but traced out the whole history of its metamorphosis, is of great interest, not so much for the exactness of his observations as for an illustration of his opposition to the spontaneous generation of many lower organisms, such as "this minute and despised creature." Some theorists asserted that the flea was produced from sand, others from dust or the like, but Leeuwenhoek proved that it bred in the regular way of winged insects.

Leeuwenhoek also carefully studied the history of the ant and was the first to show that what had been commonly reputed to be ants' eggs were really their pupae, containing the perfect insect nearly ready for emergence, and that the true eggs were much smaller and gave origin to maggots, or larvae. He argued that the sea mussel and other shellfish were not generated out of sand found at the seashore or mud in the beds of rivers at low water but from spawn, by the regular course of generation. He maintained the same to be true of the freshwater mussel, whose embryos he examined so carefully that he was able to observe how they were consumed by "animalcules," many of which, according to his description, must have included ciliates in conjugation, flagellates, and the *Vorticella*. Similarly, he investigated the generation of eels, which were at that time supposed to be produced from dew without the ordinary process of generation.

Leeuwenhoek's methods of microscopy, which he kept secret, remain something of a mystery. During his lifetime he ground more than 400 lenses, most of which were very small—some no larger than a pinhead—and usually mounted them between two thin brass plates, riveted together. A large sample of these lenses, bequeathed to the Royal Society, were found to have magnifying powers of between 50 and, at the most, 300 times. In order to observe phenomena as small as bacteria, Leeuwenhoek must have employed some form of oblique illumination, or other technique, for enhancing the effectiveness of the lens, but this method he would not reveal. Leeuwenhoek continued his work almost to the end of his long life of 90 years.

Leeuwenhoek's contributions to the *Philosophical Transactions* amounted to 375 and those to the *Memoirs of the Paris Academy of Sciences* to 27. Two collections of his works appeared during his life, one in Dutch (1685–1718) and the other in Latin (1715–22); a selection was translated by S. Hoole, *The Select Works of A. van Leeuwenhoek* (1798–1807).

ROBERT HOOKE

(b. July 18, 1635, Freshwater, Isle of Wight, Eng.—d. March 3, 1703, London)

English physicist Robert Hooke discovered the law of elasticity, known as Hooke's law. He also conducted research in a remarkable variety of fields.

In 1655 Hooke was employed by Robert Boyle to construct the Boylean air pump. Five years later, Hooke discovered his law of elasticity, which states that the stretching of a solid body (e.g., metal, wood) is proportional to the force applied to it. The law laid the basis for studies of stress and strain and for understanding of elastic materials. He applied these studies in his designs for the balance springs of watches. In 1662 he was appointed curator of experiments to the Royal Society of London and was elected a fellow the following year.

One of the first men to build a Gregorian reflecting telescope, Hooke discovered the fifth star in the Trapezium, an asterism in the constellation Orion, in 1664 and first suggested that Jupiter rotates on its axis. His detailed sketches of Mars were used in the 19th century to determine that planet's rate of rotation. In 1665 he was appointed professor of geometry in Gresham College. In *Micrographia* (1665; "Small Drawings") he included his studies and illustrations of the crystal structure of snowflakes, discussed the possibility of manufacturing artificial fibres by a process similar to the spinning of the silkworm, and first used the word cell to name the microscopic honeycomb cavities in cork. His studies of microscopic fossils led him to become one of the first proponents of a theory of evolution.

Hooke suggested that the force of gravity could be measured by utilizing the motion of a pendulum (1666) and attempted to show that the Earth and Moon follow an elliptical path around the Sun. In 1672 he discovered the phenomenon of diffraction (the bending of light rays around corners); to explain it, he offered the wave theory of light. He stated the inverse square law to describe planetary motions in 1678, a law that Newton later used in modified form. Hooke complained that he was not given sufficient credit for the law and became involved in bitter controversy with Newton. Hooke was the first man to state in general that all matter expands when heated and that air is made up of particles separated from each other by relatively large distances.

JOHN RAY

(b. Nov. 29, 1627, Black Notley, Essex, Eng.—d. Jan. 17, 1705, Black Notley)

John Ray (spelled Wray until 1670) was a leading 17th-century English naturalist and botanist who contributed significantly to progress in taxonomy. His enduring legacy to botany was the establishment of species as the ultimate unit of taxonomy.

EDUCATION AND EXPEDITIONS

Ray was the son of the village blacksmith in Black Notley and attended the grammar school in nearby Braintree. In 1644, with the aid of a fund that had been left in trust to support needy scholars at the University of Cambridge, he enrolled at one of the colleges there, St. Catherine's Hall, and moved to Trinity College in 1646. Ray had come to

Cambridge at the right time for one with his talents, for he found a circle of friends with whom he pursued anatomical and chemical studies. He also progressed well in the curriculum, taking his bachelor's degree in 1648 and being elected to a fellowship at Trinity the following year; during the next 13 years he lived quietly in his collegiate cloister.

Ray's string of fortunate circumstances ended with the Restoration. Although he was never an excited partisan, he was thoroughly Puritan in spirit and refused to take the oath that was prescribed by the Act of Uniformity. In 1662 he lost his fellowship. Prosperous friends supported him during the subsequent 43 years while he pursued his career as a naturalist, which began with the publication of his first work in 1660, a catalog of plants growing around Cambridge. After he had exhausted the Cambridge area as a subject for his studies, Ray began to explore the rest of Britain. An expedition in 1662 to Wales and Cornwall with the naturalist Francis Willughby was a turning point in his life. Willughby and Ray agreed to undertake a study of the complete natural history of living things, with Ray responsible for the plant kingdom and Willughby the animal.

The first fruit of the agreement, a tour of the European continent lasting from 1663 to 1666, greatly extended Ray's first-hand knowledge of flora and fauna. Back in England, the two friends set to work on their appointed task. In 1670 Ray produced a *Catalogus Plantarum Angliae* ("Catalog of English Plants"). Then in 1672 Willughby suddenly died, and Ray took up the completion of Willughby's portion of their project. In 1676 Ray published *F. Willughbeii . . . Ornithologia* (*The Ornithology of F. Willughby . . .*) under Willughby's name, even though Ray had contributed at least as much as Willughby. Ray also completed *F. Willughbeii . . . de Historia Piscium* (1685; "History of Fish"), with the Royal Society, of which Ray was a fellow, financing its publication.

IMPORTANT PUBLICATIONS

Ray had never interrupted his research in botany. In 1682 he had published a *Methodus Plantarum Nova* (revised in 1703 as the *Methodus Plantarum Emendata . . .*), his contribution to classification, which insisted on the taxonomic importance of the distinction between monocotyledons and dicotyledons, plants whose seeds germinate with one leaf and those with two, respectively. Ray's enduring legacy to botany was the establishment of species as the ultimate unit of taxonomy. On the basis of the *Methodus*, he constructed his masterwork, the *Historia Plantarum*, three huge volumes that appeared between 1686 and 1704. After the first two volumes, he was urged to compose a complete system of nature. To this end he compiled brief synopses of British and European plants, a *Synopsis Methodica Avium et Piscium* (published posthumously, 1713; "Synopsis of Birds and Fish"), and a *Synopsis Methodica Animalium Quadrupedum et Serpentini Generis* (1693; "Synopsis of Quadrupeds"). Much of his final decade was spent on a pioneering investigation of insects, published posthumously as *Historia Insectorum*.

In all this work, Ray contributed to the ordering of taxonomy. Instead of a single feature, he attempted to base his systems of classification on all the structural characteristics, including internal anatomy. By insisting on the importance of lungs and cardiac structure, he effectively established the class of mammals, and he divided insects according to the presence or absence of metamorphoses. Although a truly natural system of taxonomy could not be realized before the age of Darwin, Ray's system approached that goal more than the frankly artificial systems of his contemporaries. He was one of the great predecessors who made possible Carolus Linnaeus's contributions in the following century.

Nor was this the sum of his work. In the 1690s Ray also published three volumes on religion. *The Wisdom of God Manifested in the Works of the Creation* (1691), an essay in natural religion that called on the full range of his biological learning, was his most popular and influential book. It argued that the correlation of form and function in organic nature demonstrates the necessity of an omniscient creator. This argument from design, common to most of the leading scientists of the 17th century, implied a static view of nature that was distinctly different from the evolutionary ideas of the early and mid-19th century. Still working on his *Historia Insectorum*, John Ray died at the age of 77.

SIR ISAAC NEWTON

(b. Dec. 25, 1642 [Jan. 4, 1643, New Style], Woolsthorpe,
Lincolnshire, Eng.—d. March 20 [March 31], 1727, London)

English physicist and mathematician Sir Isaac Newton was the culminating figure of the scientific revolution of the 17th century. In optics, his discovery of the composition of white light integrated the phenomena of colours into the science of light and laid the foundation for modern physical optics. In mechanics, his three laws of motion, the basic principles of modern physics, resulted in the formulation of the law of universal gravitation. In mathematics, he was the original discoverer of the infinitesimal calculus. Newton's *Philosophiae Naturalis Principia Mathematica* (*Mathematical Principles of Natural Philosophy*), 1687, was one of the most important single works in the history of modern science.

THE *OPTICKS*

Newton was elected to a fellowship in Trinity College in 1667, and from 1670 to 1672 he delivered a series of lectures and developed them into the essay "Of Colours," which was later revised to become Book One of his *Opticks*. Newton held that light consists of material corpuscles in motion. The corpuscular conception of light was always a speculative theory on the periphery of his optics, however. The core of Newton's contribution had to do with colours. He realized that light is not simple and homogeneous—it is instead complex and heterogeneous and the phenomena of colours arise from the analysis of the heterogeneous mixture into its simple components.

The ultimate source of Newton's conviction that light is corpuscular was his recognition that individual rays of light have immutable properties. He held that individual rays (that is, particles of given size) excite sensations of individual colours when they strike the retina of the eye. He also concluded that rays refract at distinct angles—hence, the prismatic spectrum, a beam of heterogeneous rays, i.e., alike incident on one face of a prism, separated or analyzed by the refraction into its component parts—and that phenomena such as the rainbow are produced by refractive analysis. Because he believed that chromatic aberration could never be eliminated from lenses, Newton turned to reflecting telescopes; he constructed the first ever built. The heterogeneity of light has been the foundation of physical optics since his time.

In 1675 Newton brought forth a second paper, an examination of the colour phenomena in thin films, which was identical to most of Book Two as it later appeared in the *Opticks*. The purpose of the paper was to explain the colours of solid bodies by showing how light can be analyzed into its components by reflection as well as refraction. The paper was significant in demonstrating for the first time the existence of periodic optical phenomena. He discovered the concentric coloured rings in the thin film of air between a lens and a flat sheet of glass; the distance

The English scientist and mathematician Isaac Newton is seen here creating a shaft of light. Hulton Archive/Getty Images

between these concentric rings (Newton's rings) depends on the increasing thickness of the film of air.

A second piece which Newton had sent with the paper of 1675 provoked new controversy. Entitled "An Hypothesis Explaining the Properties of Light," it was in fact a general system of nature. Robert Hooke, who had earlier established himself as an opponent of Newton's ideas, apparently claimed that Newton had stolen its content from him. The issue was quickly controlled, however, by an exchange of formal, excessively polite letters that fail to conceal the complete lack of warmth between the men.

Newton was also engaged in another exchange on his theory of colours with a circle of English Jesuits in Liège, perhaps the most revealing exchange of all. Although their objections were shallow, their contention that his experiments were mistaken lashed him into a fury. The correspondence dragged on until 1678, when a final shriek of rage from Newton, apparently accompanied by a complete nervous breakdown, was followed by silence. For six years he withdrew from intellectual commerce except when others initiated a correspondence, which he always broke off as quickly as possible.

During his time of isolation, Newton, who was always somewhat interested in alchemy, now immersed himself in it. His conception of nature underwent a decisive change. Newton's "Hypothesis of Light" of 1675, with its universal ether, was a standard mechanical system of nature. However, about 1679, Newton abandoned the ether and its invisible mechanisms and began to ascribe the puzzling phenomena—chemical affinities, the generation of heat in chemical reactions, surface tension in fluids, capillary action, the cohesion of bodies, and the like—to attractions and repulsions between particles of matter.

More than 35 years later, in the second English edition of the *Opticks*, Newton accepted an ether again, although it was an ether that embodied the concept of action at a distance by positing a repulsion between its particles. As he conceived of them, attractions were quantitatively defined, and they offered a bridge to unite the two basic themes of 17th-century science — the mechanical tradition, which had dealt primarily with verbal mechanical imagery, and the Pythagorean tradition, which insisted on the mathematical nature of reality. Newton's reconciliation through the concept of force was his ultimate contribution to science.

THE *PRINCIPIA*

In 1684 Newton was at work on the problem of orbital dynamics, and two and a half years later, a short tract he had written, entitled *De Motu* ("On Motion"), had grown into *Philosophiae Naturalis Principia Mathematica*. This work is not only Newton's masterpiece but also the fundamental work for the whole of modern science. Significantly, *De Motu* did not state the law of universal gravitation. For that matter, even though it was a treatise on planetary dynamics, it did not contain any of the three Newtonian laws of motion. Only when revising *De Motu* did Newton embrace the principle of inertia (the first law) and arrive at the second law of motion.

The mechanics of the *Principia* was an exact quantitative description of the motions of visible bodies. It rested on Newton's three laws of motion: (1) that a body remains in its state of rest unless it is compelled to change that state by a force impressed on it; (2) that the change of motion (the change of velocity times the mass of the body) is proportional to the force impressed; (3) that to every action there is an equal and opposite reaction. Using these laws, Newton found that the centripetal force holding the planets in their given orbits about the Sun must decrease with the square of the planets' distances from the Sun.

Newton also compared the distance by which the Moon, in its orbit of known size, is diverted from a tangential path in one second with the distance that a body at the surface of the Earth falls from rest in one second. When the latter distance proved to be 3,600 (60 × 60) times as great as the former, he concluded that one and the same force, governed by a single quantitative law, is operative in all three cases, and from the correlation of the Moon's orbit with the measured acceleration of gravity on the surface of the Earth, he applied the ancient Latin word *gravitas* (literally, "heaviness" or "weight") to it. The law of universal gravitation, which he also confirmed from such further phenomena as the tides and the orbits of comets, states that every particle of matter in the universe attracts every other particle with a force that is proportional to the product of their masses and inversely proportional to the square of the distance between their centres. The *Principia* immediately raised Newton to international prominence.

CAROLUS LINNAEUS

(b. May 23, 1707, Råshult, Småland, Swed.—d. Jan. 10, 1778, Uppsala)

Swedish naturalist and explorer Carolus Linnaeus was the first to frame principles for defining natural genera and species of organisms and to create a uniform system for naming them (binomial nomenclature).

THE "SEXUAL SYSTEM" OF CLASSIFICATION

In 1735 Linnaeus published *Systema Naturae* ("The System of Nature"), a folio volume of only 11 pages, which presented a hierarchical classification, or taxonomy, of the three kingdoms of nature: stones, plants, and animals. Each kingdom was subdivided into classes, orders, genera, species, and varieties. This hierarchy of taxonomic ranks replaced traditional systems of biological classification that were based on mutually exclusive divisions, or dichotomies.

In particular, it was the botanical section of *Systema Naturae* that built Linnaeus's scientific reputation. After reading essays on sexual reproduction in plants by Vaillant and by German botanist Rudolph Jacob Camerarius, Linnaeus had become convinced of the idea that all organisms reproduce sexually. As a result, he expected each plant to possess male and female sexual organs (stamens and pistils), or "husbands and wives," as he also put it. On this basis, he designed a simple system of distinctive characteristics to classify each plant. The number and position of the stamens, or husbands, determined the class to which it belonged, whereas the number and position of pistils, or wives, determined the order. This "sexual system," as Linnaeus called it, became extremely popular.

CLASSIFICATION BY "NATURAL CHARACTERS"

In 1736 Linnaeus, then in the Netherlands, published a booklet, the *Fundamenta Botanica* ("The Foundations of Botany"), that framed the principles and rules to be followed in the classification and naming of plants. The year before, Linnaeus was introduced to George Clifford, a local English merchant and banker who had close connections to the Dutch East India Company. Impressed by Linnaeus's knowledge, Clifford offered Linnaeus a position as curator of his botanical garden. Linnaeus accepted the position and used this opportunity to expand certain chapters of the *Fundamenta Botanica* in separate publications: the *Bibliotheca Botanica* (1736; "The Library of Botany"); *Critica Botanica* (1737; "A Critique of Botany"), on botanical nomenclature; and *Classes Plantarum* (1738; "Classes of Plants"). He applied the theoretical framework laid down in these books in two further publications: *Hortus Cliffortianus* (1737), a catalogue of the species contained in Clifford's collection; and the *Genera Plantarum* (1737; "Genera of Plants"), which modified and updated definitions of plant genera first offered by Joseph Pitton de Tournefort.

Genera Plantarum was considered by Linnaeus to be his crowning taxonomic achievement. In contrast to earlier attempts by other botanists at generic definition, which proceeded by a set of arbitrary divisions, *Genera Plantarum* presented a system based on what Linnaeus called the "natural characters" of genera—morphological descriptions of all the parts of flower and fruit. In contrast to systems based on arbitrary divisions (including his own sexual system), a system based on natural characters could accommodate the growing number of new species—often possessing different morphological features—pouring into Europe from its oversea trading posts and colonies.

Linnaeus's distinction between artificial and natural classifications of organisms, however, raised the question of the mechanism that allowed organisms to fall into natural hierarchies. He could only answer this question with regard to species: species, according to Linnaeus, were similar in form because they derived from the same parental pair created by God at the beginning of the world. Linnaeus tried to explain the existence of natural genera, orders, or classes within the context of hybridization; however, the question of natural hierarchies would not receive a satisfying answer until English naturalist Charles Darwin explained similarity by common descent in his *Origin of Species* (1859).

BINOMIAL NOMENCLATURE

In 1738 Linnaeus began a medical practice in Stockholm, Swed., which he maintained until 1742, when he received the chair in medicine and botany at Uppsala University. Linnaeus built his further career upon the foundations he laid in the Netherlands. Linnaeus used the international contacts to create a network of correspondents that provided him with seeds and specimens from all over the world. He then incorporated this material into the botanical garden at Uppsala, and these acquisitions helped him develop and refine the empirical basis for revised and enlarged editions of his major taxonomic works. During his lifetime he completed 12 editions of the *Systema Naturae*, six editions of the *Genera Plantarum*, two editions of the *Species Plantarum* ("Species of Plants," which succeeded the *Hortus Cliffortianus* in 1753), and a revised edition of the *Fundamenta Botanica* (which was later renamed the *Philosophia Botanica* [1751; "Philosophy of Botany"]).

Linnaeus's most lasting achievement was the creation of binomial nomenclature, the system of formally classifying and naming organisms according to their genus and species. In contrast to earlier names that were made up of diagnostic phrases, binomial names (or "trivial" names as Linnaeus himself called them) conferred no prejudicial information about the plant species named. Rather, they served as labels by which a species could be universally addressed. This naming system was also implicitly hierarchical, as each species is classified within a genus. The first use of binomial nomenclature by Linnaeus occurred within the context of a small project in which students were asked to identify the plants consumed by different kinds of cattle. In this project, binomial names served as a type of shorthand for field observations. Despite the advantages of this naming system, binomial names were used consistently in print by Linnaeus only after the publication of the *Species Plantarum* (1753).

The rules of nomenclature that Linnaeus put forward in his *Philosophia Botanica* rested on a recognition of the "law of priority," the rule stating that the first properly published name of a species or genus takes precedence over all other proposed names. These rules became firmly established in the field of natural history and also formed the backbone of international codes of nomenclature—such as the Strickland Code (1842)—created for the fields of botany and zoology in the mid-19th century. The first edition of the *Species Plantarum* (1753) and the 10th edition of the *Systema Naturae* (1758) are the agreed starting points for botanical and zoological nomenclature, respectively.

OTHER CONTRIBUTIONS

Toward the end of his life, Linnaeus became interested in other aspects of the life sciences. Of greatest influence were his physico-theological writings, *Oeconomia Naturae* (1749; "The Economy of Nature") and *Politiae Naturae* (1760; "The Politics of Nature"). Both works were of great importance to Charles Darwin. His studies of plant hybridization influenced the experimental tradition that led directly to the pea plant experiments of Austrian botanist Gregor Mendel.

HENRY CAVENDISH

(b. Oct. 10, 1731, Nice, France—d. Feb. 24, 1810, London, Eng.)

H enry Cavendish was a natural philosopher and is considered to be the greatest experimental and theoretical English chemist and physicist of his age. Cavendish was distinguished for great accuracy and precision in researches into the composition of atmospheric air, the properties of different gases, the synthesis of water, the law governing electrical attraction and repulsion, a mechanical theory of heat, and calculations of the density (and hence the weight) of the Earth. His experiment to weigh the Earth has come to be known as the Cavendish experiment.

RESEARCH IN CHEMISTRY

Cavendish was a shy man who was uncomfortable in society and avoided it when he could. About the time of his father's death, Cavendish began to work closely with Charles Blagden, an association that helped Blagden enter fully into London's scientific society. In return, Blagden helped to keep the world at a distance from Cavendish. Cavendish published no books and few papers, but he achieved much. Several areas of research, including mechanics, optics, and magnetism, feature extensively in his manuscripts, but they scarcely feature in his published work.

His first publication (1766) was a combination of three short chemistry papers on "factitious airs," or gases produced in the laboratory. He produced "inflammable air" (hydrogen) by dissolving metals in acids and "fixed air" (carbon dioxide) by dissolving alkalis in acids, and he collected these and other gases in bottles inverted over water or mercury. He then measured their solubility in water and their specific gravity and noted their combustibility. Cavendish was awarded the Royal Society's Copley Medal for this paper. Gas chemistry was of increasing importance in the latter half of the 18th century and became crucial for Frenchman Antoine-Laurent Lavoisier's reform of chemistry, generally known as the chemical revolution.

In 1783 Cavendish published a paper on eudiometry (the measurement of the goodness of gases for breathing). He described a new eudiometer of his own invention, with which he achieved the best results to date, using what in other hands had been the inexact method of measuring gases by weighing them. He next published a paper on the production of water by burning inflammable air (that is, hydrogen) in dephlogisticated air (now known to be oxygen), the latter a constituent of atmospheric air. Cavendish concluded that dephlogisticated air was dephlogisticated water and that hydrogen was either pure phlogiston or phlogisticated water. He reported these findings to Joseph Priestley, an English clergyman and scientist, no later than March 1783, but did not publish them until the following year.

The Scottish inventor James Watt published a paper on the composition of water in 1783; Cavendish had performed the experiments first but published second. Controversy about priority ensued. In 1785 Cavendish carried out an investigation of the composition of common (i.e., atmospheric) air, obtaining, as usual, impressively accurate results. He observed that, when he had determined the amounts of phlogisticated air (nitrogen) and dephlogisticated air (oxygen), there remained a volume of gas amounting to 1/120 of the original volume of common air.

In the 1890s, two British physicists, William Ramsay and Lord Rayleigh, realized that their newly discovered inert gas, argon, was responsible for Cavendish's problematic residue; he had not made an error. What he had done was perform rigorous quantitative experiments, using standardized instruments and methods, aimed at reproducible results; taken the mean of the result of several experiments; and identified and allowed for sources of error.

Cavendish, as noted before, used the language of the old phlogiston theory in chemistry. In 1787 he became one of the earliest outside France to convert to the new antiphlogistic theory of Lavoisier, though he remained skeptical about the nomenclature of the new theory. He also objected to Lavoisier's identification of heat as having a material or elementary basis. Working within the framework of Newtonian mechanism, Cavendish had tackled the problem of the nature of heat in the 1760s, explaining heat as the result of the motion of matter. In 1783 he published a paper on the temperature at which mercury freezes and in that paper made use of the idea of latent heat, although he did not use the term because he believed that it implied acceptance of a material theory of heat. He made his objections explicit in his 1784 paper on air. He went on to develop a general theory of heat, and the manuscript of that theory has been persuasively dated to the late 1780s. His theory was at once mathematical and mechanical; it contained the principle of the conservation of heat (later understood as an instance of conservation of energy) and even contained the concept (although not the label) of the mechanical equivalent of heat.

EXPERIMENTS WITH ELECTRICITY

Cavendish also worked out a comprehensive theory of electricity. Like his theory of heat, this theory was mathematical in form and was based on precise quantitative experiments. In 1771 he published an early version of his theory, based on an expansive electrical fluid that exerted pressure. He demonstrated that if the intensity of electric force was inversely proportional to distance, then the electric fluid in excess of that needed for electrical neutrality would lie on the outer surface of an electrified sphere; and he confirmed this experimentally. Cavendish continued to work on electricity after this initial paper, but he published no more on the subject.

Beginning in the mid-1780s Cavendish carried out most of his experiments at his house in London. The most famous of those experiments, published in 1798, was to determine the density of the Earth. His apparatus for weighing the world was a modification of the Englishman John Michell's torsion balance. The balance had two small lead balls suspended from the arm of a torsion balance and two much larger stationary lead balls. Cavendish calculated the attraction between the balls from the period of oscillation of the torsion balance, and then he used this value to calculate the density of the Earth. What was extraordinary about Cavendish's experiment was its elimination of every source of error and every factor that could disturb the experiment and its precision in measuring an astonishingly small attraction, a mere 1/50,000,000 of the weight of the lead balls. The result that Cavendish obtained for the density of the Earth is within 1 percent of the currently accepted figure.

The combination of painstaking care, precise experimentation, thoughtfully modified apparatus, and fundamental theory carries Cavendish's unmistakable signature. It is fitting that the University of Cambridge's great physics laboratory is named the Cavendish Laboratory.

JOSEPH PRIESTLEY

(b. March 13, 1733, Birstall Fieldhead, near Leeds, Yorkshire [now West Yorkshire], Eng.—d. Feb. 6, 1804, Northumberland, Pa., U.S.)

English clergyman, political theorist, and physical scientist Joseph Priestley contributed to advances in liberal political and religious thought and in experimental chemistry. He is best remembered for his contribution to the chemistry of gases.

WORK IN ELECTRICITY

In 1765 Priestley met the American scientist and statesman Benjamin Franklin, who encouraged him to publish *The History and Present State of Electricity, with Original Experiments* (1767). In this work, Priestley used history to show that scientific progress depended more on the accumulation of "new facts" that anyone could discover than on the theoretical insights of a few men of genius. This view shaped Priestley's electrical experiments, in which he anticipated the inverse square law of electrical attraction, discovered that charcoal conducts electricity, and noted the relationship between electricity and chemical change.

THE CHEMISTRY OF GASES

In 1767 Priestley began intensive experimental investigations into chemistry. Between 1772 and 1790, he published six volumes of *Experiments and Observations on Different Kinds of Air* and more than a dozen articles in the Royal Society's *Philosophical Transactions* describing his experiments on gases, or "airs," as they were then called. British pneumatic chemists had previously identified three types of gases: air, carbon dioxide (fixed air), and hydrogen (inflammable air). Priestley incorporated an explanation of the chemistry of these gases into the phlogiston theory, according to which combustible substances released phlogiston (an immaterial "principle of inflammability") during burning.

Priestley discovered 10 new gases: nitric oxide (nitrous air), nitrogen dioxide (red nitrous vapour), nitrous oxide (inflammable nitrous air, later called "laughing gas"), hydrogen chloride (marine acid air), ammonia (alkaline air), sulfur dioxide (vitriolic acid air), silicon tetrafluoride (fluor acid air), nitrogen (phlogisticated air), oxygen (dephlogisticated air, independently codiscovered by Carl Wilhelm Scheele), and a gas later identified as carbon monoxide. Priestley's experimental success resulted predominantly from his ability to design ingenious apparatuses and his skill in their manipulation. He gained particular renown for an improved pneumatic trough in which, by collecting gases over mercury instead of in water, he was able to isolate and examine gases that were soluble in water. For his work on gases, Priestley was awarded the Royal Society's prestigious Copley Medal in 1773.

Upon contemplating the processes of vegetation and the "agitation" of seas and lakes, Priestley envisioned the means by which a benevolent nature restored the "common air" that had been "vitiated and diminished" by such "noxious" processes as combustion and respiration. Apart from strengthening his own spiritual views, these observations informed the photosynthesis experiments performed by his contemporaries, the Dutch physician Jan Ingenhousz and the Swiss clergyman and naturalist Jean Senebier.

When confronted by the multitude of diseases that plagued the growing populations in towns and military installations, Priestley designed an apparatus that produced carbonated water, a mixture that he thought would provide medicinal benefit to sufferers of scurvy and various fevers. Although it ultimately proved ineffective in treating these disorders, the "gasogene" that employed this technique later made possible the soda-water industry. Priestley also designed the "eudiometer," which was used in the general movement for sanitary reform and urban design to measure the "purity" (oxygen content) of atmospheric air.

THE DISCOVERY OF OXYGEN AND THE CHEMICAL REVOLUTION

Priestley's lasting reputation in science is founded upon the discovery he made on Aug. 1, 1774, when he obtained a colourless gas by heating red mercuric oxide. Finding that a candle would burn and that a mouse would thrive in this gas, he called it "dephlogisticated air," based upon the belief that ordinary air became saturated with phlogiston once it could no longer support combustion and life. Priestley was not yet sure, however, that he had discovered a "new species of air." The following October, while in Paris on a journey through Europe, he informed the

French chemist Antoine-Laurent Lavoisier how he obtained the new "air." This meeting between the two scientists was highly significant for the future of chemistry. Lavoisier immediately repeated Priestley's experiments and, between 1775 and 1780, conducted intensive investigations from which he derived the elementary nature of oxygen, recognized it as the "active" principle in the atmosphere, interpreted its role in combustion and respiration, and gave it its name. Lavoisier's pronouncements of the activity of oxygen revolutionized chemistry.

In 1800 Priestley published a slim pamphlet, *Doctrine of Phlogiston Established, and That of the Composition of Water Refuted*, which he expanded to book length in 1803. The *Doctrine of Phlogiston* provided a detailed account of what he envisioned to be the empirical, theoretical, and methodological shortcomings of the oxygen theory. Priestley called for a patient, humble, experimental approach to God's infinite creation. Chemistry could support piety and liberty only if it avoided speculative theorizing and encouraged the observation of God's benevolent creation. The phlogiston theory was superseded by Lavoisier's oxidation theory of combustion and respiration.

TURMOIL AND EXILE

The English press and government decreed that Priestley's support, together with that of his friend, the moral philosopher Richard Price, of the American and French Revolutions was "seditious." On July 14, 1791, the "Church-and-King mob" destroyed Priestley's house and laboratory. Priestley and his family retreated to the security of Price's congregation at Hackney, near London. Priestley later began teaching at New College, Oxford, and defended his anti-British government views in *Letters to the Right Honourable Edmund Burke* (1791).

In 1794 Priestley fled to the United States, where he discovered a form of government that was "relatively tolerable." His best-known writing in the United States, *Letters to the Inhabitants of Northumberland* (1799), became part of the Republican response to the Federalists. Priestley died at Northumberland, Pennsylvania, mourned and revered by Thomas Jefferson, the third president of the United States.

LUIGI GALVANI

(b. Sept. 9, 1737, Bologna, Papal States [Italy]—d. Dec. 4, 1798, Bologna, Cisalpine Republic)

Luigi Galvani was an Italian physician and physicist who investigated the nature and effects of what he conceived to be electricity in animal tissue. His discoveries led to the invention of the voltaic pile, a kind of battery that makes possible a constant source of current electricity.

EARLY YEARS

Galvani followed his father's preference for medicine by attending the University of Bologna, graduating in 1759. On obtaining the doctor of medicine degree, with a thesis (1762) *De ossibus* on the formation and development of bones, he was appointed lecturer in anatomy at the University of Bologna and professor of obstetrics at the separate Institute of Arts and Sciences. Beginning with his doctoral thesis, his early research was in comparative anatomy—such as the structure of renal tubules, nasal mucosa, and the middle ear—with a tendency toward physiology, a direction appropriate to the later work for which he is noted.

Galvani's developing interest was indicated by his lectures on the anatomy of the frog in 1773 and in electrophysiology in the late 1770s, when, following the acquisition of an electrostatic machine (a large device for making sparks) and a Leyden jar (a device used to store static electricity), he began to experiment with muscular stimulation by electrical means. His notebooks indicate that, from the early 1780s, animal electricity remained his major field of investigation. Numerous ingenious observations and experiments have been credited to him; in 1786, for example, he obtained muscular contraction in a frog by touching its nerves with a pair of scissors during an electrical storm. He also observed the legs of a skinned frog kick when a scalpel touched a lumbar nerve of the animal while an electrical machine was activated.

Galvani assured himself by further experiments that the twitching was, in fact, related to the electrical action. He also elicited twitching without the aid of the electrostatic machine by pressing a copper hook into a frog's spinal cord and hanging the hook on an iron railing. Although twitching could occur during a lightning storm or with the aid of an electrostatic machine, it also occurred with only a metallic contact between leg muscles and nerves leading to them. A metallic arc connecting the two tissues could therefore be a substitute for the electrostatic machine.

ELECTRICAL NATURE OF NERVE IMPULSE

Galvani delayed the announcement of his findings until 1791, when he published his essay *De Viribus Electricitatis in Motu Musculari Commentarius (Commentary on the Effect of Electricity on Muscular Motion)*. He concluded that animal tissue contained a heretofore neglected innate, vital force, which he termed "animal electricity," which activated nerve and muscle when spanned by metal probes. He believed that this new force was a form of electricity in addition to the "natural" form that is produced by lightning or by the electric eel and torpedo ray and to the "artificial" form that is produced by friction (i.e., static electricity). He considered the brain to be the most important organ for the secretion of this "electric fluid" and the nerves to be conductors of the fluid to the nerve and muscle, the tissues of which act as did the outer and inner surfaces of the Leyden jar. The flow of this electric fluid provided a stimulus for the irritable muscle fibres, according to his explanation.

Galvani's scientific colleagues generally accepted his views, but Alessandro Volta, the outstanding professor of physics at the University of Pavia, was not convinced by the analogy between the muscle and the Leyden jar. Deciding that the frog's legs served only as an indicating electroscope, he held that the contact of dissimilar metals was the true source of stimulation; he referred to the electricity so generated as "metallic electricity" and decided that the muscle, by contracting when touched by metal, resembled the action of an electroscope. Furthermore, Volta said that, if two dissimilar metals in contact both touched a muscle, agitation would also occur and increase with the dissimilarity of the metals. Thus Volta rejected the idea of an "animal electric fluid," replying that the frog's legs responded to differences in metal temper, composition, and bulk. Galvani refuted this by obtaining muscular action with two pieces of the same material. Galvani's gentle nature and Volta's high principles precluded any harshness between them. Volta, who coined the term galvanism, said of Galvani's work that "it contains one of the most beautiful and most surprising discoveries."

In retrospect, Galvani and Volta are both seen to have been partly right and partly wrong. Galvani was correct in attributing muscular contractions to an electrical stimulus but wrong in identifying it as an "animal electricity." Volta correctly denied the existence of an "animal electricity" but was wrong in implying that every electrophysiological effect requires two different metals as sources of current.

Galvani, shrinking from the controversy over his discovery, continued his work as teacher, obstetrician, and surgeon, treating both wealthy and needy without regard to fee. In 1794 he offered a defense of his position in an anonymous book, *Dell'uso e dell'attività dell'arco conduttore nella contrazione dei muscoli* ("On the Use and Activity of the Conductive Arch in the Contraction of Muscles"), the supplement of which described muscular contraction without the need of any metal. He caused a muscle to contract by touching the exposed muscle of one frog with a nerve of another and thus established for the first time that bioelectric forces exist within living tissue.

Galvani provided the major stimulus for Volta to discover a source of constant current electricity; this was the voltaic pile, or a battery, with its principles of operation combined from chemistry and physics. This discovery led to the subsequent age of electric power. Moreover, Galvani opened the way to new research in the physiology of muscle and nerve and to the entire subject of electrophysiology.

SIR WILLIAM HERSCHEL

(b. Nov. 15, 1738, Hanover, Ger.—d. Aug. 25, 1822, Slough, Buckinghamshire, Eng.)

German-born British astronomer Sir William Herschel was the founder of sidereal astronomy for the systematic observation of the heavens. He discovered the planet Uranus, hypothesized that nebulae are composed of stars, and developed a theory of stellar evolution. He was knighted in 1816.

DISCOVERY OF URANUS

The intellectual curiosity that Herschel acquired from his father led him from the practice to the theory of music, which he studied in Robert Smith's *Harmonics*. From this book he turned to Smith's *A Compleat System of Opticks*, which introduced him to the techniques of telescope construction. Herschel soon began to grind his own mirrors. They were ground from metal disks of copper, tin, and antimony in various proportions. He later produced large mirrors of superb quality—his telescopes proved far superior even to those used at the Greenwich Observatory. He also made his own eyepieces, the strongest with a magnifying power of 6,450 times. Herschel's largest instrument, too cumbersome for regular use, had a mirror made of speculum metal, with a diameter of 122 centimetres (48 inches) and a focal length of 12 metres (40 feet). Completed in 1789, it became one of the technical wonders of the 18th century.

In 1781, during his third and most complete survey of the night sky, Herschel came upon an object that he realized was not an ordinary star. It proved to be the planet Uranus, the first planet to be discovered since prehistoric times. Herschel became famous almost overnight. His friend Dr. William Watson, Jr., introduced him to the Royal Society of London, which awarded him the Copley Medal for the discovery of Uranus, and elected him a Fellow. He was subsequently appointed as an astronomer to George III.

Herschel's big telescopes were ideally suited to study the nature of nebulae, which appear as luminous patches in the sky. Some astronomers thought they were nothing more than clusters of innumerable stars the light of which blends to form a milky appearance. Others held that some nebulae were composed of a luminous fluid. However, Herschel found that his most powerful telescope could resolve into stars several nebulae that appeared "milky" to less well equipped observers. He was convinced that other nebulae would eventually be resolved into individual stars with more powerful instruments. This encouraged him to argue in 1784 and 1785 that all nebulae were formed of stars and that there was no need to postulate the existence of a mysterious luminous fluid to explain the observed facts. Nebulae that could not yet be resolved must be very distant systems, he maintained; and, since they seem large to the observer, their true size must indeed be vast—possibly larger even than the star system of which the Sun is a member. By this reasoning, Herschel was led to postulate the existence of what later were called "island universes" of stars.

THEORY OF THE EVOLUTION OF STARS

In order to interpret the differences between these star clusters, Herschel emphasized their relative densities by contrasting a cluster of tightly packed stars with others in which the stars were widely scattered. These formations showed that attractive forces were at work. In other words, a group of widely scattered stars was at an earlier stage of its development than one whose stars were tightly packed. Thus, Herschel made change in time, or evolution, a fundamental explanatory concept in astronomy.

In 1785 Herschel developed a cosmogony—a theory concerning the origin of the universe: the stars originally were scattered throughout infinite space, in which attractive forces gradually organized them into even more fragmented and tightly packed clusters. Turning then to the system of stars of which the Sun is part, he sought to determine its shape on the basis of two assumptions: (1) that with his telescope he could see all the stars in the system, and (2) that within the system the stars are regularly spread out. Both of these assumptions he subsequently had to abandon. But in his studies he gave the first major example of the usefulness of stellar statistics in that he could count the stars and interpret this data in terms of the extent in space of the Galaxy's star system.

Theory of the Structure of Nebulae

On Nov. 13, 1790, Herschel observed a remarkable nebula, which he was forced to interpret as a central star surrounded by a cloud of "luminous fluid." This discovery contradicted his earlier views. Hitherto Herschel had reasoned that many nebulae that he was unable to resolve (separate into distinct stars), even with his best telescopes, might be distant "island universes" (such objects are now known as galaxies). He was able, however, to adapt his earlier theory to this new evidence by concluding that the central star he had observed was condensing out of the surrounding cloud under the forces of gravity. In 1811 he extended his cosmogony backward in time to the stage when stars had not yet begun to form out of the fluid.

In dealing with the structural organization of the heavens, Herschel assumed that all stars were equally bright, so that differences in apparent brightness are an index only of differences in distances. Throughout his career he stubbornly refused to acknowledge the accumulating evidence that contradicted this assumption. Herschel's labours through 20 years of systematic sweeps for nebulae (1783–1802) resulted in three catalogs listing 2,500 nebulae and star clusters that he substituted for the 100 or so milky patches previously known. He also cataloged 848 double stars—pairs of stars that appear close together in space, and measurements of the comparative brightness of stars. He observed that double stars did not occur by chance as a result of random scattering of stars in space but that they actually revolved about each other. His 70 published papers include not only studies of the motion of the solar system through space and the announcement in 1800 of the discovery of infrared rays but also a succession of detailed investigations of the planets and other members of the solar system.

ANTOINE-LAURENT LAVOISIER
(b. Aug. 26, 1743, Paris, France—d. May 8, 1794, Paris)

Antoine-Laurent Lavoisier was a prominent French chemist and leading figure in the 18th-century chemical revolution who developed an experimentally based theory of the chemical reactivity of oxygen and coauthored the modern system for naming chemical substances. Having also served as a leading financier and public administrator before the French Revolution, he was executed with other financiers during the revolutionary terror.

PNEUMATIC CHEMISTRY

The chemistry Lavoisier studied as a student was not a subject particularly noted for conceptual clarity or theoretical rigour. Although chemical writings contained considerable information about the substances chemists studied, little agreement existed upon the precise composition of chemical elements or between explanations of changes in composition. Many natural philosophers still viewed the four elements of Greek natural philosophy—earth, air, fire, and water—as the primary substances of all matter. Chemists like Lavoisier focused their attention upon analyzing "mixts" (i.e., compounds), such as the salts formed when acids combine with alkalis. They hoped that by first identifying the properties of simple substances they would then be able to construct theories to explain the properties of compounds.

Pneumatic chemistry was a lively subject at the time Lavoisier became interested in a particular set of problems that involved air: the linked phenomena of combustion, respiration, and what 18th-century chemists called calcination (the change of metals to a powder [calx], such as that obtained by the rusting of iron).

CONSERVATION OF MASS

The assertion that mass is conserved in chemical reactions was an assumption of Enlightenment investigators rather than a discovery revealed by their experiments. Lavoisier believed that matter was neither created nor destroyed in chemical reactions, and in his experiments he sought to demonstrate that this belief was not violated. Still he had difficulty proving that his view was universally valid. His insistence that chemists accepted this assumption as a law was part of his larger program for raising chemistry to the investigative standards and causal explanation found in contemporary experimental physics.

While other chemists were also looking for conservation principles capable of explaining chemical reactions, Lavoisier was particularly intent on collecting and weighing all the substances involved in the reactions he studied. His success in the many elaborate experiments he conducted was in large part due to his independent wealth, which enabled him to have expensive apparatus built to his design, and to his ability to recruit and direct talented research associates. Today the conservation of mass is still sometimes taught as "Lavoisier's law," which is indicative of his success in making this principle a foundation of modern chemistry.

PHLOGISTON THEORY

After being elected a junior member of the Academy of Sciences, Lavoisier began searching for a field of research in which he could distinguish himself. Chemists had long recognized that burning, like breathing, required air, and they also knew that iron rusts only upon exposure to air. Noting that burning gives off light and heat, that warm-blooded animals breathe, and that ores are turned into metals in a furnace, they concluded that fire was the key causal element behind these chemical reactions. The Enlightenment German chemist Georg Ernst Stahl provided a well-regarded explanation of these phenomena. Stahl hypothesized that a common "fiery substance" he called phlogiston was released during combustion, respiration, and calcination, and that it was absorbed when these processes were reversed. Although plausible, this theory raised a number of problems for those who wished to explain chemical reactions in terms of substances that could be isolated and measured.

In the early stages of his research Lavoisier regarded the phlogiston theory as a useful hypothesis, but he sought ways either to solidify its firm experimental foundation or to replace it with an experimentally sound theory of combustion. In the end his theory of oxygenation replaced the phlogiston hypothesis, but it took Lavoisier many years and considerable help from others to reach this goal.

OXYGEN THEORY OF COMBUSTION

The oxygen theory of combustion resulted from a demanding and sustained campaign to construct an experimentally grounded chemical theory of combustion, respiration, and calcination. Lavoisier's research in the early 1770s focused upon weight gains and losses in calcination. It was known that when metals slowly changed into powders (calxes), as was observed in the rusting of iron, the calx actually weighed more than the original metal, whereas when the calx was "reduced" to a metal, a loss of weight occurred.

The phlogiston theory did not account for these weight changes, for fire itself could not be isolated and weighed. Lavoisier hypothesized that it was probably the fixation and release of air, rather than fire, that caused the observed gains and losses in weight. This idea set the course of his research for the next decade.

Along the way, he encountered related phenomena that had to be explained. Mineral acids, for instance, were made by roasting a mineral such as sulfur in fire and then mixing the resultant calx with water. Lavoisier had initially conjectured that the sulfur combined with air in the fire and that the air was the cause of acidity. However, it was not at all obvious just what kind of air made sulfur acidic. The problem was further complicated by the concurrent discovery of new kinds of airs within the atmosphere. British pneumatic chemists made most of these discoveries, with Joseph Priestley leading the effort.

And it was Priestley, despite his unrelenting adherence to the phlogiston theory, who ultimately helped Lavoisier unravel the mystery of oxygen. Priestley isolated oxygen in August 1774 after recognizing several properties that distinguished it from atmospheric air. In Paris at the same time, Lavoisier and his colleagues were experimenting with a set of reactions identical to those that Priestley was studying, but they failed to notice the novel properties of the air they collected. Priestley visited Paris later that year and at a dinner held in his honour at the Academy of Sciences informed his French colleagues about the properties of this new air. Lavoisier, who was familiar with Priestley's research and held him in high regard, hurried back to his laboratory, repeated the experiment, and found that it produced precisely the kind of air he needed to complete his theory. He called the gas that was produced oxygen, the generator of acids. Isolating oxygen allowed him to explain both the quantitative and qualitative changes that occurred in combustion, respiration, and calcination.

The Chemical Revolution

In the canonical history of chemistry Lavoisier is celebrated as the leader of the 18th-century chemical revolution and consequently one of the founders of modern chemistry. Lavoisier was fortunate in having made his contributions to the chemical revolution before the disruptions of political revolution. By 1785 his new theory of combustion was gaining support, and the campaign to reconstruct chemistry according to its precepts began. One tactic to enhance the wide acceptance of his new theory was to propose a related method of naming chemical substances.

In 1787 Lavoisier and three prominent colleagues published a new nomenclature of chemistry, and it was soon widely accepted, thanks largely to Lavoisier's eminence and the cultural authority of Paris and the Academy of Sciences. Its fundamentals remain the method of chemical nomenclature in use today. Two years later Lavoisier published a programmatic *Traité élémentaire de chimie* (*Elementary Treatise on Chemistry*) that described the precise methods chemists should employ when investigating, organizing, and explaining their subjects. It was a worthy culmination of a determined and largely successful program to reinvent chemistry as a modern science.

PIERRE-SIMON LAPLACE

(b. March 23, 1749, Beaumount-en-Auge, Normandy, France — d. March 5, 1827, Paris)

Pierre-Simon, marquis de Laplace was a French mathematician, astronomer, and physicist and is best known for his investigations into the stability of the solar system. Laplace successfully accounted for all the observed deviations of the planets from their theoretical orbits by applying Sir Isaac Newton's theory of gravitation to the solar system, and he developed a conceptual view of evolutionary change in the structure of the solar system. He also demonstrated the usefulness of probability for interpreting scientific data.

Laplace was the son of a peasant farmer. Little is known of his early life except that he quickly showed his mathematical ability at the military academy at Beaumont. In 1766 Laplace entered the University of Caen, but he left for Paris the next year, apparently without taking a degree. He arrived with a letter of recommendation to the mathematician Jean d'Alembert, who helped him secure a professorship at the École Militaire, where he taught from 1769 to 1776.

In 1773 he began his major lifework—applying Newtonian gravitation to the entire solar system—by taking up a particularly troublesome problem: why Jupiter's orbit appeared to be continuously shrinking while Saturn's continually expanded. The mutual gravitational interactions within the solar system were so complex that mathematical solution seemed impossible; indeed, Newton had concluded that divine intervention was periodically required to preserve the system in equilibrium. Laplace announced the invariability of planetary mean motions (average angular velocity). This discovery in 1773, the first and most important step in establishing the stability of the solar system, was the most important advance in physical astronomy since Newton. It won him associate membership in the French Academy of Sciences the same year.

Applying quantitative methods to a comparison of living and nonliving systems, Laplace and the chemist Antoine-Laurent Lavoisier in 1780, with the aid of an ice calorimeter that they had invented, showed respiration to be a form of combustion. Returning to his astronomical investigations with an examination of the entire subject of planetary perturbations—mutual gravitational effects— Laplace in 1786 proved that the eccentricities and inclinations of planetary orbits to each other will always remain small, constant, and self-correcting. The effects of perturbations were therefore conservative and periodic, not cumulative and disruptive.

During 1784–85 Laplace worked on the subject of attraction between spheroids; in this work the potential function of later physics can be recognized for the first time. Laplace explored the problem of the attraction of any spheroid upon a particle situated outside or upon its surface. Through his discovery that the attractive force of a mass upon a particle, regardless of direction, can be obtained directly by differentiating a single function, Laplace laid the mathematical foundation for the scientific study of heat, magnetism, and electricity.

Laplace removed the last apparent anomaly from the theoretical description of the solar system in 1787 with the announcement that lunar acceleration depends on the eccentricity of the Earth's orbit. Although the mean motion of the Moon around the Earth depends mainly on the gravitational attraction between them, it is slightly diminished by the pull of the Sun on the Moon. This solar action depends, however, on changes in the eccentricity of the Earth's orbit resulting from perturbations by the other planets. As a result, the Moon's mean motion is accelerated as long as the Earth's orbit tends to become more circular; but, when the reverse occurs, this motion is retarded. The inequality is therefore not truly cumulative, Laplace concluded, but is of a period running into millions of years. The last threat of instability thus disappeared from the theoretical description of the solar system.

In 1796 Laplace published *Exposition du système du monde* (*The System of the World*), a semipopular treatment of his work in celestial mechanics and a model of French prose. The book included his "nebular hypothesis"—attributing the origin of the solar system to cooling and contracting of a gaseous nebula—which strongly influenced future thought on planetary origin. His *Traité de mécanique céleste* (*Celestial Mechanics*), appearing in five volumes between 1798 and 1827, summarized the results obtained by his mathematical development and application of the law of gravitation. He offered a complete mechanical interpretation of the solar system by devising methods for calculating the motions of the planets and their satellites and their perturbations, including the resolution of tidal problems. The book made him a celebrity.

In 1814 Laplace published a popular work for the general reader, *Essai philosophique sur les probabilités* (*A Philosophical Essay on Probability*). This work was the introduction to the second edition of his comprehensive and important *Théorie analytique des probabilités* (*Analytic Theory of Probability*), first published in 1812, in which he described many of the tools he invented for mathematically predicting the probabilities that particular events will occur in nature. He applied his theory not only to the ordinary problems of chance but also to the inquiry into the causes of phenomena, vital statistics, and future events, while emphasizing its importance for physics and astronomy. The book is notable also for including a special case of what became known as the central limit theorem. Laplace proved that the distribution of errors in large data samples from astronomical observations can be approximated by a Gaussian or normal distribution.

Probably because he did not hold strong political views and was not a member of the aristocracy, he escaped imprisonment and execution during the French Revolution. Laplace was president of the Board of Longitude, aided in the organization of the metric system, helped found the scientific Society of Arcueil, and was created a marquis. He served for six weeks as minister of the interior under Napoleon, who famously reminisced that Laplace "carried the spirit of the infinitesimal into administration."

EDWARD JENNER

(b. May 17, 1749, Berkeley, Gloucestershire, Eng.—d. Jan. 26, 1823, Berkeley)

English surgeon Edward Jenner is best known as the discoverer of vaccination for smallpox. Jenner lived at a time when the patterns of British medical practice and education were undergoing gradual change. During this time, the division between the trained physicians and the apothecaries or surgeons—who acquired their medical knowledge through apprenticeship rather than through academic work—was becoming less sharp, and hospital work was becoming much more important.

Jenner attended grammar school and at the age of 13 was apprenticed to a nearby surgeon. In the following eight years Jenner acquired a sound knowledge of medical and surgical practice. On completing his apprenticeship at the age of 21, he went to London and became the house pupil of John Hunter, who was on the staff of St. George's Hospital and was one of the most prominent surgeons in London. Even more important, however, he was an anatomist, biologist, and experimentalist of the first rank; not only did he collect biological specimens, but he also concerned himself with problems of physiology and function.

The firm friendship that grew between the two men lasted until Hunter's death in 1793. From no one else could Jenner have received the stimuli that so confirmed his natural bent—a catholic interest in biological phenomena, disciplined powers of observation, sharpening of critical faculties, and a reliance on experimental investigation. From Hunter, Jenner received the characteristic advice, "Why think [i.e., speculate]—why not try the experiment?"

In addition to his training and experience in biology, Jenner made progress in clinical surgery. After studying in London from 1770 to 1773, he returned to country practice in Berkeley and enjoyed substantial success. He was capable, skillful, and popular. In addition to practicing medicine, he joined two medical groups for the promotion of medical knowledge and wrote occasional medical papers. He played the violin in a musical club, wrote light verse, and, as a naturalist, made many observations, particularly on the nesting habits of the cuckoo and on bird migration. He also collected specimens for Hunter; many of Hunter's letters to Jenner have been preserved, but Jenner's letters to Hunter have unfortunately been lost. After one disappointment in love in 1778, Jenner married in 1788.

Smallpox was widespread in the 18th century, and occasional outbreaks of special intensity resulted in a very high death rate. The disease, a leading cause of death at the time, respected no social class, and disfigurement was not uncommon in patients who recovered. The only means of combating smallpox was a primitive form of vaccination called variolation—intentionally infecting a healthy person with the "matter" taken from a patient sick with a mild attack of the disease. The practice, which originated in China and India, was based on two distinct concepts: first, that one attack of smallpox effectively protected against any subsequent attack and, second, that a person deliberately infected with a mild case of the disease would safely acquire such protection. It was, in present-day terminology, an "elective" infection—i.e., one given to a person in good health. Unfortunately, the transmitted disease did not always remain mild, and mortality sometimes occurred. Furthermore, the inoculated person could disseminate the disease to others and thus act as a focus of infection.

Jenner had been impressed by the fact that a person who had suffered an attack of cowpox—a relatively harmless disease that could be contracted from cattle—could not take the smallpox—i.e., could not become infected whether by accidental or intentional exposure to smallpox. Pondering this phenomenon, Jenner concluded that cowpox not only protected against smallpox but could be transmitted from one person to another as a deliberate mechanism of protection.

The story of the great breakthrough is well known. In May 1796 Jenner found a young dairymaid, Sarah Nelmes, who had fresh cowpox lesions on her hand. On May 14, using matter from Sarah's lesions, he inoculated an eight-year-old boy, James Phipps, who had never had smallpox. Phipps became slightly ill over the course of the next 9 days but was well on the 10th. On July 1 Jenner inoculated the boy again, this time with smallpox matter. No disease developed; protection was complete. In 1798 Jenner, having added further cases, published privately a slender book entitled *An Inquiry into the Causes and Effects of the Variolae Vaccinae.* The procedure spread rapidly to America and the rest of Europe and soon was carried around the world.

Despite errors and occasional chicanery, the death rate from smallpox plunged. Jenner received worldwide recognition and many honours, but he made no attempt to enrich himself through his discovery and actually devoted so much time to the cause of vaccination that his private practice and personal affairs suffered severely. Parliament voted him a sum of £10,000 in 1802 and a further sum of £20,000 in 1806. Jenner not only received honours but also aroused opposition and found himself subjected to attacks and calumnies, despite which he continued his activities on behalf of vaccination. His wife, ill with tuberculosis, died in 1815, and Jenner retired from public life.

JOHN DALTON

(b. Sept. 5 or 6, 1766, Eaglesfield, Cumberland, Eng.—d. July 27, 1844, Manchester)

English meteorologist and chemist John Dalton was a pioneer in the development of modern atomic theory.

EARLY SCIENTIFIC CAREER

In 1793 Dalton published a collection of essays, *Meteorological Observations and Essays*, on meteorologic topics based on his own observations together with those of his friends John Gough and Peter Crosthwaite. It created little stir at first but contained original ideas that, together with Dalton's more developed articles, marked the transition of meteorology from a topic of general folklore to a serious scientific pursuit.

Dalton upheld the view, against contemporary opinion, that the atmosphere was a physical mixture of approximately 80 percent nitrogen and 20 percent oxygen rather than being a specific compound of elements. He measured the capacity of the air to absorb water vapour and the variation of its partial pressure with temperature. He defined partial pressure in terms of a physical law whereby every constituent in a mixture of gases exerted the same pressure it would have if it had been the only gas present. One of Dalton's contemporaries, the British scientist John Frederic Daniell, later hailed him as the "father of meteorology."

Soon after the publication of the essays, Dalton wrote a description of the defect he had discovered in his own and his brother's vision. This paper was the first publication on colour blindness, which for some time thereafter was known as Daltonism.

ATOMIC THEORY

By far Dalton's most influential work in chemistry was his atomic theory. Attempts to trace precisely how Dalton developed this theory have proved futile; even Dalton's own recollections on the subject are incomplete. He based his theory of partial pressures on the idea that only like atoms in a mixture of gases repel one another, whereas unlike atoms appear to react indifferently toward each other. This conceptualization explained why each gas in a mixture behaved independently. Although this view was later shown to be erroneous, it served a useful purpose in allowing him to abolish the idea, held by many previous atomists from the Greek philosopher Democritus to the 18th-century mathematician and astronomer Ruggero Giuseppe Boscovich, that atoms of all kinds of matter are alike. Dalton claimed that atoms of different elements vary in size and mass, and indeed this claim is the cardinal feature of his atomic theory. He focused upon determining the relative masses of each different kind of atom, a process that could be accomplished, he claimed, only by considering the number of atoms of each element present in different chemical compounds.

Although Dalton had taught chemistry for several years, he had not yet performed actual research in this field. In a memoir read to the Manchester Literary and Philosophical Society on Oct. 21, 1803, he claimed: "An inquiry into the relative weights of the ultimate particles of bodies is a subject, as far as I know, entirely new; I have lately been prosecuting this inquiry with remarkable success." He described his method of measuring the masses of various elements, including hydrogen, oxygen, carbon, and nitrogen, according to the way they combined with fixed masses of each other. If such measurements were to be meaningful, the elements had to combine in fixed proportions. His measurements, crude as they were, allowed him to formulate the Law of Multiple Proportions: When two elements form more than one compound, the masses of one element that combine with a fixed mass of the other are in a ratio of small whole numbers. Thus, taking the elements as A and B, various combinations between them naturally occur according to the mass ratios $A:B = x:y$ or $x:2y$ or $2x:y$, and so on. Different compounds were formed by combining atomic building blocks of different masses. As the Swedish chemist Jöns Jacob Berzelius wrote to Dalton: "The law of multiple proportions is a mystery without the atomic theory." And Dalton provided the basis for this theory.

The problem remained, however, that a knowledge of ratios was insufficient to determine the actual number of elemental atoms in each compound. For example, methane was found to contain twice as much hydrogen as ethylene. Following Dalton's rule of "greatest simplicity," namely, that AB is the most likely combination for which he found a meretricious justification in the geometry of close-packed spheres, he assigned methane a combination of one carbon and two hydrogen atoms and ethylene a combination of one carbon and one hydrogen atom. This is now known to be incorrect because the methane molecule is chemically symbolized as CH_4 and the ethylene molecule as C_2H_4. Nevertheless, Dalton's atomic theory triumphed over its weaknesses because his foundational argument was correct. However, overcoming the defects of Dalton's theory was a gradual process, finalized in 1858 only after the Italian chemist Stanislao Cannizzaro pointed out the utility of Amedeo Avogadro's hypothesis in determining molecular masses. Since then, chemists have shown the theory of Daltonian atomism to be a key factor under-lying further advances in their field. Organic chemistry in particular progressed rapidly once Dalton's theory gained acceptance. Dalton's atomic theory earned him the sobri-quet "father of chemistry."

GEORGES CUVIER

(b. Aug. 23, 1769, Montbéliard, France—d. May 13, 1832, Paris)

French zoologist and statesman Baron Georges Cuvier established the sciences of comparative anatomy and paleontology. From 1784 to 1788 Cuvier attended the Académie Caroline (Karlsschule) in Stuttgart, Ger., where he studied comparative anatomy and learned to dissect. After graduation Cuvier served in 1788–95 as a tutor, dur-ing which time he wrote original studies of marine invertebrates, particularly the mollusks. His notes were sent to Étienne Geoffroy Saint-Hilaire, a professor of zoology at the Museum of Natural History in Paris, and at Geoffroy's urging Cuvier joined the staff of the museum. For a time the two scientists collaborated, and in 1795 they jointly published a study of mammalian classification, but their views eventually diverged.

Cuvier remained at the museum and continued his research in comparative anatomy. His first result, in 1797, was *Tableau élémentaire de l'histoire naturelle des animaux* ("Elementary Survey of the Natural History of Animals"), a popular work based on his lectures. In 1800–05, he pub-lished his *Leçons d'anatomie comparée* ("Lessons on Comparative Anatomy"). In this work, based also on his lectures at the museum, he put forward his principle of the "correlation of parts," according to which the anatom-ical structure of every organ is functionally related to all other organs in the body of an animal, and the functional and structural characteristics of organs result from their interaction with their environment. Moreover, according to Cuvier, the functions and habits of an animal determine its anatomical form, in contrast to Geoffroy, who held the reverse theory—that anatomical structure preceded and made necessary a particular mode of life.

Cuvier also argued that the anatomical characteristics distinguishing groups of animals are evidence that species had not changed since the Creation. Each species is so well coordinated, functionally and structurally, that it could not survive significant change. He further maintained that each species was created for its own special purpose and each organ for its special function. In denying evolution, Cuvier disagreed with the views of his colleague Jean-Baptiste Lamarck, who published his theory of evolution in 1809, and eventually also with Geoffroy, who in 1825 published evidence concerning the evolution of crocodiles.

While continuing his zoological work at the museum, Cuvier served as imperial inspector of public instruction and assisted in the establishment of French provincial universities. For these services he was granted the title "chevalier" in 1811. He also wrote the *Rapport historique sur les progrès des sciences naturelles depuis 1789, et sur leur état actuel* ("Historical Report on the Progress of the Sciences"), published in 1810. These publications are lucid expositions of the European science of his time.

Meanwhile, Cuvier also applied his views on the correlation of parts to a systematic study of fossils that he had excavated. He reconstructed complete skeletons of unknown fossil quadrupeds. These constituted astonishing new evidence that whole species of animals had become extinct. Furthermore, he discerned a remarkable sequence in the creatures he exhumed. The deeper, more remote strata contained animal remains—giant salamanders, flying reptiles, and extinct elephants—that were far less similar to animals now living than those found in the more recent strata. He summarized his conclusions, first in 1812 in his *Recherches sur les ossements fossiles de quadrupèdes* ("Researches on the Bones of Fossil Vertebrates"), which included the essay "Discours préliminaire" ("Preliminary Discourse"), as well as in the expansion of this essay in book form in 1825, *Discours sur les révolutions de la surface du globe* ("Discourse on the Revolutions of the Globe").

Cuvier's work gave new prestige to the old concept of catastrophism according to which a series of "revolutions," or catastrophes—sudden land upheavals and floods—had destroyed entire species of organisms and carved out the present features of the Earth. He believed that the area laid waste by these spectacular paroxysms, of which Noah's flood was the most recent and dramatic, was sometimes repopulated by migration of animals from an area that had been spared. Catastrophism remained a major geologic doctrine until it was shown that slow changes over long periods of time could explain the features of the Earth.

In 1817 Cuvier published *Le Règne animal distribué d'après son organisation* ("The Animal Kingdom, Distributed According to Its Organization"), which, with its many subsequent editions, was a significant advance over the systems of classification established by Linnaeus. Cuvier showed that animals possessed so many diverse anatomical traits that they could not be arranged in a single linear system. Instead, he arranged animals into four large groups of animals (vertebrates, mollusks, articulates, and radiates), each of which had a special type of anatomical organization. All animals within the same group were classified together, as he believed they were all modifications of one particular anatomical type. Although his classification is no longer used, Cuvier broke away from the 18th-century idea that all living things were arranged in a continuous series from the simplest up to man.

Cuvier's lifework may be considered as marking a transition between the 18th-century view of nature and the view that emerged in the last half of the 19th century as a result of the doctrine of evolution. By rejecting the 18th-century method of arranging animals in a continuous series in favour of classifying them in four separate groups, he raised the key question of why animals were anatomically different. Although Cuvier's doctrine of catastrophism did not last, he did set the science of palaeontology on a firm, empirical foundation. He did this by introducing fossils into zoological classification, showing the progressive relation between rock strata and their fossil remains, and by demonstrating, in his comparative anatomy and his reconstructions of fossil skeletons, the importance of functional and anatomical relationships.

ALEXANDER VON HUMBOLDT
(b. Sept. 14, 1769, Berlin, Ger.—d. May 6, 1859, Berlin)

German naturalist and explorer Alexander von Humboldt was a major figure in the classical period of physical geography and biogeography—areas of science now included in the earth sciences and ecology. With his book *Kosmos* he made a valuable contribution to the popularization of science. The Humboldt Current off the west coast of South America was named after him.

EXPEDITION TO SOUTH AMERICA

The conviction had grown in Humboldt that his real aim in life was scientific exploration, and in 1797 he set himself to acquiring a thorough knowledge of the systems of geodetic, meteorological, and geomagnetic measurements. He obtained permission from the Spanish government to visit the Spanish colonies in Central and South America.

Completely shut off from the outside world, these colonies offered enormous possibilities to a scientific explorer. Humboldt's social standing assured him of access to official circles, and in the Spanish prime minister Mariano de Urquijo he found an enlightened man who supported his application to the king for a royal permit. In the summer of 1799 he set sail from Marseille accompanied by the French botanist Aimé Bonpland, whom he had met in Paris, then the liveliest scientific centre in Europe. The estate he had inherited at the death of his mother enabled Humboldt to finance the expedition entirely out of his own pocket. Humboldt and Bonpland spent five years, from 1799 to 1804, in Central and South America, covering more than 6,000 miles (9,650 kilometres) on foot, on horseback, and in canoes. It was a life of great physical exertion and serious deprivation.

Starting from Caracas, they travelled south through grasslands and scrublands until they reached the banks of the Apure, a tributary of the Orinoco River. They continued their journey on the river by canoe as far as the Orinoco. Following its course and that of the Casiquiare, they proved that the Casiquiare River formed a connection between the vast river systems of the Amazon and the Orinoco. For three months Humboldt and Bonpland moved through dense tropical forests, tormented by clouds of mosquitoes and stifled by the humid heat. Their provisions were soon destroyed by insects and rain; the lack of food finally drove them to subsist on ground-up wild cacao beans and river water.

After a short stay in Cuba, Humboldt and Bonpland returned to South America for an extensive exploration of the Andes. From Bogotá to Trujillo, Peru, they wandered over the Andean Highlands—following a route now traversed by the Pan-American Highway, in their time a series of steep, rocky, and often very narrow paths. They climbed

a number of peaks, including all the volcanoes in the surroundings of Quito, Ecuador; Humboldt's ascent of
Chimborazo (20,702 feet [6,310 metres]) to a height of
19,286 feet (5,878 metres), but short of the summit,
remained a world mountain-climbing record for nearly 30
years. All these achievements were carried out without
the help of modern mountaineering equipment, without
ropes, crampons, or oxygen supplies; hence, Humboldt
and Bonpland suffered badly from mountain sickness. But
Humboldt turned his discomfort to advantage: he became
the first person to ascribe mountain sickness to lack of
oxygen in the rarefied air of great heights. He also studied
the oceanic current off the west coast of South America
that was originally named after him but is now known as
the Peru Current.

In the spring of 1803, the two travellers sailed from
Guayaquil to Acapulco, Mex., where they spent the last
year of their expedition in a close study of this most developed and highly civilized part of the Spanish colonies.
After a short stay in the United States, where Humboldt
was received by President Jefferson, they sailed for France.
Humboldt and Bonpland returned with an immense
amount of information. In addition to a vast collection of
new plants, there were determinations of longitudes and
latitudes, measurements of the components of the Earth's
geomagnetic field, and daily observations of temperatures
and barometric pressure, as well as statistical data on the
social and economic conditions of Mexico.

PROFESSIONAL LIFE IN PARIS

The years from 1804 to 1827 Humboldt devoted to publication of the data accumulated on the South American
expedition. With the exception of brief visits to Berlin, he
lived in Paris during this important period of his life. There

he found not only collaborators among the French scientists—the greatest of his time—but engravers for his maps and illustrations and publishers for printing the 30 volumes into which the scientific results of the expedition were distilled. Of great importance were the meteorological data, with an emphasis on mean daily and nightly temperatures, and Humboldt's representation on weather maps of isotherms (lines connecting points with the same mean temperature) and isobars (lines connecting points with the same barometric pressure for a given time or period)—all of which helped lay the foundation for the science of comparative climatology.

Even more important were his pioneering studies on the relationship between a region's geography and its flora and fauna, and, above all, the conclusions he drew from his study of the Andean volcanoes concerning the role played by eruptive forces and metamorphosis in the history and ongoing development of the Earth's crust. Lastly, his *Political Essay on the Kingdom of New Spain* contained a wealth of material on the geography and geology of Mexico, including descriptions of its political, social, and economic conditions, and also extensive population statistics.

During his years in Paris, Humboldt had the ability to cultivate deep and long-lasting friendships with well-known scientists, such as the renowned physicist and astronomer François Arago, and to evoke respect and admiration from the common man, an ability that reflected his generosity, humanity, and vision of what science could do. He was, moreover, always willing and anxious to assist young scientists at the beginning of their careers. Such men as the German chemist Justus von Liebig and the Swiss-born zoologist Louis Agassiz owed to Humboldt the means to continue their studies and embark on an academic career. The best proof of his wide interests and affectionate nature lies in his voluminous correspondence: about 8,000 letters remain.

LATER YEARS

In 1827 Humboldt had to return to Berlin, where the King impatiently demanded his presence at court. In 1829 Humboldt was given the opportunity to visit Russia and Siberia. On the initiative of the Russian minister of finance, Count Yegor Kankrin, he was invited to visit the gold and platinum mines in the Urals. This expedition, lasting only one summer, was very different from the South American journey; the members, Humboldt and two young scientists, were accompanied throughout by an official guard, since they were guests of the Tsar. Humboldt and his companions had to endure tiresome receptions at the imperial court and in the homes of provincial governors. They travelled in carriages as far as the Altai Mountains and the Chinese frontier. The resulting geographical, geological, and meteorological observations, especially those regarding the Central Asian regions, were of great importance to the Western world, for Central Asia was then to a large degree unknown territory.

Even before his visit to Russia, he had returned to an investigation of a phenomenon that had aroused his interest in South America: the sudden fluctuations of the Earth's geomagnetic field—the so-called magnetic storms. With the help of assistants, he carried out observations of the movement of a magnetometer in a quiet garden pavilion in Berlin; but it had been clear to him for a number of years that, to discover whether these magnetic storms were of terrestrial or extraterrestrial origin, it would be necessary to set up a worldwide net of magnetic observatories. The German mathematician Carl Friedrich Gauss had already begun to organize simultaneous measurements of the magnetic field by several observatories in Germany, England, and Sweden.

In 1836 Humboldt, still interested in the problem, approached the Royal Society in London with the request that it establish an additional series of stations in the British possessions overseas. As a result, the British government provided the means for permanent observatories in Canada, South Africa, Australia, and New Zealand and equipped an Antarctic expedition. With the help of the mass of data produced by this international scientific collaboration, one of the first of its kind, the English geophysicist Sir Edward Sabine later succeeded in correlating the appearance of magnetic storms in the Earth's atmosphere with the periodically changing activity of sunspots, thus proving the extraterrestrial origin of the storms.

During the last 25 years of his life, Humboldt was chiefly occupied with writing *Kosmos*, one of the most ambitious scientific works ever published. Four volumes appeared during his lifetime. Written in a pleasant, literary style, *Kosmos* gives a generally comprehensible account of the structure of the universe as then known, at the same time communicating the scientist's excitement and aesthetic enjoyment at his discoveries. Humboldt had taken immense pains to discipline his inclination to discursiveness, which often gave his writing a certain lack of logical coherence. He was rewarded for his effort by the success of his book, which, within a few years, had been translated into nearly all European languages.

ANDRÉ-MARIE AMPÈRE

(b. Jan. 22, 1775, Lyon, France—d. June 10, 1836, Marseille)

French physicist André-Marie Ampère founded and named the science of electrodynamics, now known as electromagnetism. His name endures in everyday life in the ampere, the unit for measuring electric current.

EARLY LIFE

Ampère, who was born into a prosperous bourgeois family during the height of the French Enlightenment, personified the scientific culture of his day. His father, Jean-Jacques Ampère, was a successful merchant, and also an admirer of the philosophy of Jean-Jacques Rousseau, whose theories of education, as outlined in his treatise *Émile*, were the basis of Ampère's education. Rousseau argued that young boys should avoid formal schooling and pursue instead an "education direct from nature." Ampère's father actualized this ideal by allowing his son to educate himself within the walls of his well-stocked library. French Enlightenment masterpieces such as Georges-Louis Leclerc, comte de Buffon's *Histoire naturelle, générale et particulière* (begun in 1749) and Denis Diderot and Jean Le Rond d'Alembert's *Encyclopédie* (volumes added between 1751 and 1772) thus became Ampère's schoolmasters. In addition, he

André-Marie Ampère, detail of an oil painting by an unknown artist. The Mansell Collection

used his access to the latest mathematical books to begin teaching himself advanced mathematics at age 12. His mother was a devout woman, so Ampère was also initiated into the Catholic faith along with Enlightenment science.

The French Revolution (1787–99) that erupted during his youth was also formative. Ampère's father was called into public service by the new revolutionary government, becoming a justice of the peace in a small town near Lyon. Yet when the Jacobin faction seized control of the Revolutionary government in 1792, Jean-Jacques Ampère resisted the new political tides, and he was guillotined on Nov. 24, 1793, as part of the Jacobin purges of the period.

While the French Revolution brought these personal traumas, it also created new institutions of science that ultimately became central to André-Marie Ampère's professional success. Ampère's maturation corresponded with the transition to the Napoleonic regime in France, and he found new opportunities for success within the technocratic structures favoured by the new French emperor.

In 1802 Ampère produced *Considérations sur la théorie mathématique de jeu* ("Considerations on the Mathematical Theory of Games"), a treatise on mathematical probability that he sent to the Paris Academy of Sciences in 1803. In the following years Ampère engaged in a diverse array of scientific inquiries—writing papers and engaging in topics ranging from mathematics and philosophy to chemistry and astronomy. Such breadth was customary among the leading scientific intellectuals of the day.

FOUNDING OF ELECTROMAGNETISM

In 1820 Ampère's friend and eventual eulogist François Arago demonstrated before the members of the French Academy of Sciences the surprising discovery of Danish physicist Hans Christiaan Ørsted that a magnetic needle is deflected by an adjacent electric current. Ampère was well prepared to throw himself fully into this new line of research.

Ampère immediately set to work developing a mathematical and physical theory to understand the relationship between electricity and magnetism. Extending Ørsted's experimental work, Ampère showed that two parallel wires carrying electric currents repel or attract each other, depending on whether the currents flow in the same or opposite directions, respectively. He also applied mathematics in generalizing physical laws from these experimental results. Most important was the principle that came to be called Ampère's law, which states that the mutual action of two lengths of current-carrying wire is proportional to their lengths and to the intensities of their currents. Ampère also applied this same principle to magnetism, showing the harmony between his law and French physicist Charles Augustin de Coulomb's law of magnetic action. Ampère's devotion to, and skill with, experimental techniques anchored his science within the emerging fields of experimental physics.

Ampère also offered a physical understanding of the electromagnetic relationship, theorizing the existence of an "electrodynamic molecule" (the forerunner of the idea of the electron) that served as the constituent element of electricity and magnetism. Using this physical understanding of electromagnetic motion, Ampère developed a physical account of electromagnetic phenomena that was both empirically demonstrable and mathematically predictive. In 1827 Ampère published his magnum opus, *Mémoire sur la théorie mathématique des phénomènes électrodynamiques uniquement déduite de l'experience* (*Memoir on the Mathematical Theory of Electrodynamic Phenomena, Uniquely Deduced from Experience*), the work that coined the name of his new science, electrodynamics, and became known ever after as its founding treatise. In recognition of his contribution to the making of modern electrical science, an international convention signed in 1881 established the ampere as a standard unit of electrical measurement, along with the coulomb, volt, ohm, and watt, which are named, respectively, after Ampère's contemporaries Coulomb, Alessandro Volta of Italy, Georg Ohm of Germany, and James Watt of Scotland.

The 1827 publication of Ampère's synoptic *Mémoire* brought to a close his feverish work over the previous seven years on the new science of electrodynamics. The text also marked the end of his original scientific work. His health began to fail, and he died while performing a university inspection, decades before his new science was canonized as the foundation stone for the modern science of electromagnetism.

AMEDEO AVOGADRO

(b. Aug. 9, 1776, Turin, in the Kingdom of Sardinia and Piedmont—
d. July 9, 1856, Turin, Italy)

Italian mathematical physicist Amedeo Avogadro showed in what became known as Avogadro's law that, under controlled conditions of temperature and pressure, equal volumes of gases contain an equal number of molecules.

EDUCATION AND EARLY CAREER

The son of Filippo Avogadro, conte di Quaregna e Cerreto, a distinguished lawyer and senator in the Piedmont region of northern Italy, Avogadro graduated in jurisprudence in 1792 but did not practice law until after receiving his doctorate in ecclesiastical law four years later. In 1801 he became secretary to the prefecture of Eridano.

Beginning in 1800 Avogadro privately pursued studies in mathematics and physics, and he focused his early research on electricity. In 1804 he became a corresponding member of the Academy of Sciences of Turin, and in 1806 he was appointed to the position of demonstrator at the academy's college. Three years later he became professor of natural philosophy at the Royal College of Vercelli, a post he held until 1820 when he accepted the first chair of mathematical physics at the University of Turin. Due to civil disturbances in the Piedmont, the university was closed and Avogadro lost his chair in July 1822. The chair was reestablished in 1832 and offered to the French mathematical physicist Augustin-Louis Cauchy. A year later Cauchy left for Prague, and on Nov. 28, 1834, Avogadro was reappointed.

MOLECULAR HYPOTHESIS OF COMBINING GASES

Avogadro is chiefly remembered for his molecular hypothesis, first stated in 1811, in which he claimed that equal volumes of all gases at the same temperature and pressure contain the same number of molecules. He used this hypothesis further to explain the French chemist Joseph-Louis Gay-Lussac's law of combining volumes of gases (1808) by assuming that the fundamental units of elementary gases may actually divide during chemical reactions. It also allowed for the calculation of the molecular weights of gases relative to some chosen standard. Avogadro and his contemporaries typically used the density of hydrogen gas as the standard for comparison. Thus, the following relationship was shown to exist:

$$\frac{\text{Weight of 1 volume of gas or vapour}}{\text{Weight of 1 volume of hydrogen}} = \frac{\text{Weight of 1 molecule of gas or vapour}}{\text{Weight of 1 molecule of hydrogen}}$$

To distinguish between atoms and molecules of different kinds, Avogadro adopted terms including *molécule intégrante* (the molecule of a compound), *molécule constituante* (the molecule of an element), and *molécule élémentaire* (atom). Although his gaseous elementary molecules were predominantly diatomic, he also recognized the existence of monatomic, triatomic, and tetratomic elementary molecules.

In 1811 he provided the correct molecular formula for water, nitric and nitrous oxides, ammonia, carbon monoxide, and hydrogen chloride. Three years later he described the formulas for carbon dioxide, carbon disulfide, sulfur dioxide, and hydrogen sulfide. He also applied his hypothesis to metals and assigned atomic weights to 17 metallic elements based upon analyses of particular compounds that they formed. However, his references to *gaz métalliques* may have actually delayed chemists' acceptance of his ideas. In 1821 he offered the correct formula for alcohol (C_2H_6O) and for ether ($C_4H_{10}O$).

Priority over who actually introduced the molecular hypothesis of gases was disputed throughout much of the 19th century. Avogadro's claim rested primarily upon his repeated statements and applications. Others attributed this hypothesis to the French natural philosopher André-Marie Ampère, who published a similar idea in 1814. Many factors account for the fact that Avogadro's hypothesis was generally ignored until after his death. First, the distinction between atoms and molecules was not generally understood. Furthermore, as similar atoms were thought to repel one another, the existence of polyatomic elementary molecules seemed unlikely.

Avogadro also mathematically represented his findings in ways more familiar to physicists than to chemists. Consider, for example, his proposed relationship between the specific heat of a compound gas and its chemical constituents:

$$c^2 = p_1 c_1^{\ 2} + p_2 c_2^{\ 2} + \text{etc.}$$

(Here c, c_1, c_2, etc., represent the specific heats at constant volume of the compound gas and its constituents; p_1, p_2, etc., represent the numbers of molecules of each component in the reaction). Based upon experimental evidence, Avogadro determined that the specific heat of a gas at constant volume was proportional to the square root of its attractive power for heat. In 1824 he calculated the "true affinity for heat" of a gas by dividing the square of its specific heat by its density. The results ranged from 0.8595 for oxygen to 10.2672 for hydrogen, and the numerical order of the affinities coincided with the electrochemical series, which listed the elements in the order of their chemical reactivities. Mathematically dividing an element's affinity for heat by that of his selected standard, oxygen, resulted in what he termed the element's "affinity number." Between 1843 and his retirement in 1850, Avogadro wrote four memoirs on atomic volumes and designated affinity numbers for the elements using atomic volumes according to a method "independent of all chemical considerations"—a claim that held little appeal for chemists.

LEGACY

Avogadro's minimal contact with prominent scientists and his habit of citing his own results increased his isolation. Although he argued in 1845 that his molecular hypothesis for determining atomic weights was widely accepted, considerable confusion still existed over the concept of atomic weights at that time. Avogadro's hypothesis began to gain broad appeal among chemists only after his compatriot and fellow scientist Stanislao Cannizzaro demonstrated its value in 1858, two years after Avogadro's death. Many of Avogadro's pioneering ideas and methods anticipated later developments in physical chemistry. His hypothesis is now regarded as a law, and the value known as Avogadro's number ($6.02214179 \times 10^{23}$), the number of molecules in a gram molecule, or mole, of any substance, has become a fundamental constant of physical science.

JOSEPH-LOUIS GAY-LUSSAC

(b. Dec. 6, 1778, Saint-Léonard-de-Noblat, France—d. May 9, 1850, Paris)

French chemist and physicist Joseph-Louis Gay-Lussac pioneered investigations into the behaviour of gases, established new techniques for analysis, and made notable advances in applied chemistry.

SEARCHING FOR LAWS OF NATURE

In 1801 Gay-Lussac became involved in experiments on capillarity in order to study short-range forces. Gay-Lussac's first publication (1802), however, was on the thermal expansion of gases. To ensure more accurate experimental results, he used dry gases and pure mercury. He concluded from his experiments that all gases expand equally over the temperature range 0–100 °C (32–212 °F). This law, usually (and mistakenly) attributed to French physicist J.-A.-C. Charles as "Charles's law," was the first of several regularities in the behaviour of matter that Gay-Lussac established.

Of the laws Gay-Lussac discovered, he remains best known for his law of the combining volumes of gases (1808). He had previously (1805) established that hydrogen and oxygen combine by volume in the ratio 2:1 to form water. Later experiments with boron trifluoride and ammonia produced spectacularly dense fumes and led him to investigate similar reactions, such as that between hydrogen chloride and ammonia, which combine in equal volumes to form ammonium chloride. Further study enabled him to generalize about the behaviour of all gases. Gay-Lussac's approach to the study of matter was consistently volumetric rather than gravimetric, in contrast to that of his English contemporary John Dalton.

Another example of Gay-Lussac's fondness for volumetric ratios appeared in an 1810 investigation into the composition of vegetable substances performed with his friend Louis-Jacques Thenard. Together they identified a class of substances (later called carbohydrates) including sugar and starch that contained hydrogen and oxygen in the ratio of 2:1. They announced their results in the form of three laws, according to the proportion of hydrogen and oxygen contained in the substances.

OTHER RESEARCHES

As a young man, Gay-Lussac participated in dangerous exploits for scientific purposes. In 1804 he ascended in a hydrogen balloon with Jean-Baptiste Biot in order to investigate the Earth's magnetic field at high altitudes and to study the composition of the atmosphere. They reached an altitude of 4,000 metres (about 13,000 feet). In a following solo flight, Gay-Lussac reached 7,016 metres (more than 23,000 feet), thereby setting a record for the highest balloon flight that remained unbroken for a half-century. In 1805–06, amid the Napoleonic wars, Gay-Lussac embarked upon a European tour with the Prussian explorer Alexander von Humboldt.

In 1807 Gay-Lussac published an important study of the heating and cooling produced by the compression and expansion of gases. This was later to have significance for the law of conservation of energy.

RIVALRY WITH DAVY

When Gay-Lussac and his colleague Louis-Jacques Thenard heard of the English chemist Humphry Davy's isolation of the newly discovered reactive metals sodium and potassium by electrolysis in 1807, they worked to produce even larger quantities of the metals by chemical means and tested their reactivity in various experiments. Notably they isolated the new element boron. They also studied the effect of light on reactions between hydrogen and chlorine, though it was Davy who demonstrated that the latter gas was an element.

Rivalry between Gay-Lussac and Davy reached a climax over the iodine experiments Davy carried out during an extraordinary visit to Paris in November 1813, at a time when France was at war with Britain. Both chemists claimed priority over discovering iodine's elemental nature. Although Davy is typically given credit for this discovery, most of his work was hurried and incomplete. Gay-Lussac presented a much more complete study of iodine in a long memoir presented to the National Institute on Aug. 1, 1814, and subsequently published in the *Annales de chimie*. In 1815 Gay-Lussac experimentally demonstrated that prussic acid was simply hydrocyanic acid, a compound of carbon, hydrogen, and nitrogen, and he also isolated the compound cyanogen [$(CN)_2$ or C_2N_2]. His analyses of prussic acid and hydriodic acid (HI) necessitated a modification of Antoine-Laurent Lavoisier's theory that oxygen was present in all acids.

APPLIED SCIENCE

Beginning in 1816, Gay-Lussac served in a wide array of appointments, attesting to the value his contemporaries placed upon applying chemistry toward solving social and economic concerns. Among his more lucrative positions was his 1829 appointment as director of the assay department at the Paris Mint, for which he developed a precise and accurate method for the assaying of silver.

Gay-Lussac was a key figure in the development of the new science of volumetric analysis. Previously a few crude trials had been carried out to estimate the strength of chlorine solutions in bleaching, but Gay-Lussac introduced a scientific rigour to chemical quantification and devised important modifications to apparatuses. In a paper on commercial soda (sodium carbonate, 1820), he identified the weight of a sample required to neutralize a given amount of sulfuric acid, using litmus as an indicator. He went on to estimate the strength of bleaching powder (1824), using a solution of indigo to signify when the reaction was complete. In his publications are found the first use of the chemical terms *burette*, *pipette*, and *titrate*. The principles of volumetric analysis could be established only through Gay-Lussac's theoretical and practical genius but, once established, the analysis itself could be carried out by a junior assistant with brief training. Gay-Lussac published an entire series of *Instructions* on subjects ranging from the estimation of potash (1818) to the construction of lightning conductors. Among the most influential *Instructions* was his estimation of silver in solution (1832), which he titrated with a solution of sodium chloride of known strength. This method was later employed at the Royal Mint.

SIR HUMPHRY DAVY

(b. Dec. 17, 1778, Penzance, Cornwall, Eng.—d. May 29, 1829, Geneva, Switz.)

English chemist Sir Humphry Davy discovered several chemical elements (including sodium and potassium) and compounds, invented the miner's safety lamp, and became one of the greatest exponents of the scientific method.

EARLY CAREER

Early in his career Davy formed strongly independent views on topics of the moment, such as the nature of heat, light, and electricity and the chemical and physical doctrines of Antoine-Laurent Lavoisier. In his small private laboratory, he prepared and inhaled nitrous oxide (laughing gas), in order to test a claim that it was the "principle of contagion," that is, caused diseases. Davy subsequently investigated the composition of the oxides and acids of nitrogen, as well as ammonia, and persuaded his scientific and literary friends to report the effects of inhaling nitrous oxide. He nearly lost his own life inhaling water gas, a mixture of hydrogen and carbon monoxide sometimes used as fuel. The account of his work, published as *Researches, Chemical and Philosophical* (1800), immediately established his reputation.

In 1801 Davy moved to London, where he delivered lectures and furthered his researches on voltaic cells, early forms of electric batteries. His carefully prepared and rehearsed lectures rapidly became important social functions and added greatly to the prestige of science. In 1802 he conducted special studies of tanning: he found catechu, the extract of a tropical plant, as effective as and cheaper than the usual oak extracts, and his published account was long used as a tanner's guide.

In 1803 Davy was admitted a fellow of the Royal Society and an honorary member of the Dublin Society and delivered the first of an annual series of lectures before the board of agriculture. This led to his *Elements of Agricultural Chemistry* (1813), the only systematic work available for many years. For his researches on voltaic cells, tanning, and mineral analysis, he received the Copley Medal in 1805. He was elected secretary of the Royal Society in 1807.

MAJOR DISCOVERIES

Davy early concluded that the production of electricity in simple electrolytic cells resulted from chemical action and that chemical combination occurred between substances of opposite charge. He therefore reasoned that electrolysis, the interactions of electric currents with chemical compounds, offered the most likely means of decomposing all substances to their elements. These views were explained in 1806 in his lecture "On Some Chemical Agencies of Electricity," for which, despite the fact that England and France were at war, he received the Napoleon Prize from the Institut de France (1807). This work led directly to the isolation of sodium and potassium from their compounds (1807) and of the alkaline-earth metals from theirs (1808). He also discovered boron (by heating borax with potassium), hydrogen telluride, and hydrogen phosphide

Sir Humphry Davy, detail of an oil painting after Sir Thomas Lawrence; in the National Portrait Gallery, London. Courtesy of the National Portrait Gallery, London

(phosphine). He showed the correct relation of chlorine to hydrochloric acid and the untenability of the earlier name (oxymuriatic acid) for chlorine; this negated Lavoisier's theory that all acids contained oxygen. He explained the bleaching action of chlorine (through its liberation of oxygen from water) and discovered two of its oxides (1811 and 1815), but his views on the nature of chlorine were disputed. He was not aware that chlorine is a chemical element, and experiments designed to reveal oxygen in chlorine failed.

Davy later published the first part of the *Elements of Chemical Philosophy*, which contained much of his own work; his plan was too ambitious, however, and nothing further appeared. Its completion, according to a Swedish chemist, J.J. Berzelius, would have "advanced the science of chemistry a full century."

Davy conducted a number of other studies as well. He investigated the substance "X" (later called iodine), whose properties and similarity to chlorine he quickly discovered, and he analyzed many specimens of classical pigments and proved that diamond is a form of carbon. Davy also investigated the conditions under which mixtures of firedamp and air explode. This led to the invention of the miner's safety lamp and to subsequent researches on flame.

After being created a baronet in 1818, he again went to Italy, where he had been years earlier, inquiring into volcanic action and trying unsuccessfully to find a way of unrolling the papyri found at Herculaneum. During the 1820s, he examined magnetic phenomena caused by electricity and electrochemical methods for preventing saltwater corrosion of copper sheathing on ships by means of iron and zinc plates. Though the protective principles were made clear, considerable fouling occurred, and the method's failure greatly vexed him. His Bakerian lecture for 1826, "On the Relation of Electrical and Chemical Changes," contained his last known thoughts on electrochemistry and earned him the Royal Society's Royal Medal.

In the last months of his life, Davy wrote a series of dialogues, which were published posthumously as *Consolations in Travel, or the Last Days of a Philosopher* (1830).

JÖNS JACOB BERZELIUS

(b. Aug. 20, 1779, near Linköping, Sweden — d. Aug. 7, 1848, Stockholm)

Jöns Jacob Berzelius was one of the founders of modern chemistry. He is especially noted for his determination of atomic weights, the development of modern chemical symbols, his electrochemical theory, the discovery and isolation of several elements, the development of classical analytical techniques, and his investigation of isomerism and catalysis, phenomena that owe their names to him. He was a strict empiricist and insisted that any new theory be consistent with the sum of chemical knowledge.

ELECTROCHEMICAL DUALISM

Berzelius is best known for his system of electrochemical dualism. The electrical battery, invented in 1800 by Alessandro Volta and known as the voltaic pile, provided the first experimental source of current electricity. In 1803 Berzelius demonstrated, as did the English chemist Humphry Davy at a slightly later date, the power of the voltaic pile to decompose chemicals into pairs of electrically opposite constituents. For example, water decomposed into electropositive hydrogen and electronegative oxygen, whereas salts degraded into electronegative acids and electropositive bases. Based upon this evidence, Berzelius revised and generalized the acid/base chemistry chiefly promoted by Lavoisier. For Berzelius, all chemical compounds contained two electrically opposing constituents, the acidic, or electronegative, and the basic, or electropositive. Furthermore, according to Berzelius, all chemicals, whether natural or artificial, mineral or organic, could be distinguished and specified qualitatively by identifying their electrically opposing constituents.

STOICHIOMETRY

In addition to his qualitative specification of chemicals, Berzelius investigated their quantitative relationships as well. As early as 1806, he began to prepare an up-to-date Swedish chemistry textbook and read widely on the subject of chemical combination. Finding little information on the subject, he decided to undertake further investigations. His teaching interests focused his attention upon inorganic chemistry. Around 1808 he launched what became a vast and enduring program in the laboratory analysis of inorganic matter. To this end, he created most of his apparatuses, prepared his own reagents, and established the atomic weights of the elements, the formulas of their oxides, sulfides, and salts, and the formulas of virtually all known inorganic compounds.

Berzelius's experiments led to a more complete depiction of the principles of chemical combining proportions, an area of investigation that the German chemist Jeremias Benjamin Richter named "stoichiometry" in 1792. Berzelius was able to establish the quantitative specificity by which substances combined. He reported his analytical results in a series of famous publications, most prominently his *Essai sur la théorie des proportions chimiques et sur l'influence chimique de l'électricité* (1819; "Essay on the Theory of Chemical Proportions and on the Chemical Influence of Electricity"), and the atomic weight tables that appeared in the 1826 German translation of his *Lärbok i kemien* (*Textbook of Chemistry*).

ATOMISM AND NOMENCLATURE

The project of specifying substances had several important consequences. In order to establish and display the laws of stoichiometry, Berzelius invented and perfected more exacting standards and techniques of analysis. His generalization of the older acid/base chemistry led him to extend chemical nomenclature that Lavoisier had introduced to cover the bases (mostly metallic oxides), a change that allowed Berzelius to name any compound consistently with Lavoisier's chemistry. For this purpose, Berzelius created a Latin template for translation into diverse vernacular languages.

The project of specifying substances also led Berzelius to develop a new system of notation that could portray the composition of any compound both qualitatively (by showing its electrochemically opposing ingredients) and quantitatively (by showing the proportions in which the ingredients were united). His system abbreviated the Latin names of the elements with one or two letters and applied superscripts to designate the number of atoms of each element present in both the acidic and basic ingredient. In his own work, however, Berzelius preferred to indicate the proportions of oxygen with dots placed over the letters of the oxidized elements, but most chemists rejected that practice. Instead, they followed Berzelius's younger German colleagues, who replaced his superscripts with subscripts and thus created the system still used today. Berzelius's new nomenclature and notation were prominently displayed in his 1819 *Essai*.

MINERALOGY

Berzelius applied his analytical method to two primary areas, mineralogy and organic chemistry. Mineralogy had long stimulated Berzelius's analytical interest. Berzelius himself discovered several new elements, including cerium (1803) and thorium (1828), in samples of naturally occurring minerals, and his students discovered lithium, vanadium, lanthanum, didymium (later resolved into praseodymium and neodymium), erbium (later resolved into erbium, ytterbium, scandium, holmium, and thulium), and terbium. Berzelius also discovered selenium (1818), though this element was isolated in the mud resulting from the manufacture of sulfuric acid rather than from a mineral sample.

In 1813 Berzelius received a mineral collection from a visiting British physician, William MacMichael, that prompted him to take up the analysis and classification of minerals. His major contribution, reported in 1814, was recognizing that silica, formerly seen as a base, frequently served as the electronegative or acidic constituent of minerals and that the traditional mineralogical class of "earths" could be reduced primarily to silicate salts. Distinguishing mineral species therefore demanded a knowledge of the stoichiometry of complex silicates, a conviction that led Berzelius in 1815 to develop his dualistic doctrine, which now anticipated a dualistic structure for substances formerly seen as "triple salts" and for other complex minerals.

Many remaining problems in the specification of minerals were resolved by the law of isomorphism, the recognition that chemically similar substances possess similar crystal forms, discovered in 1818 by the German chemist Eilhardt Mitscherlich. Berzelius had provided both the patronage and the foundational concepts for

Mitscherlich's own career. Ultimately, Berzelius transformed the field and established a flourishing tradition of chemical mineralogy.

ORGANIC CHEMISTRY

Organic chemistry also posed problems in the discrimination between substances. In 1814 Berzelius again turn his attention to organic analysis. At this point, he isolated stoichiometric compounds and worked to determine their elemental constituents. Berzelius argued that, despite differences between organic and inorganic matter, organic compounds could be assigned a dualistic composition and therefore could be specified in the same manner as inorganic ones. The application of his precept that organic chemistry could be understood in terms of the principles that govern inorganic chemistry reached its zenith in the 1830s, especially as it was embodied in the older theory of radicals. However, it was also at this time that younger chemists discovered phenomena such as chlorine substitution and began to recast inorganic chemistry in the light of organic substances.

A MAN OF INFLUENCE

Among Berzelius's other accomplishments were his improvements of laboratory apparatuses and techniques used for chemical and mineral analysis, especially solvent extraction, elemental analysis, quantitative wet chemistry, and qualitative mineral analysis. Berzelius also characterized and named two new concepts: "isomerism," in which chemically diverse substances possess the same composition; and "catalysis," in which certain chemical reactions are facilitated by the presence of substances that are themselves unaffected. He also coined the term *protein* while attempting to apply a dualistic organic chemistry to the constituents of living things.

JOHN JAMES AUDUBON

(b. April 26, 1785, Les Cayes, Saint-Domingue, West Indies [now in Haiti]—d. Jan. 27, 1851, New York, N.Y., U.S.)

John James Audubon, whose original name was Fougère Rabin, or Jean Rabin, was an ornithologist, artist, and naturalist who became particularly well known for his drawings and paintings of North American birds. The illegitimate son of a French merchant, planter, and slave trader and a Creole woman of Saint-Domingue, Audubon and his illegitimate half-sister (who was also born in the West Indies) were legalized by adoption in 1794, five years after their father returned to France.

Young Audubon developed an interest in drawing birds during his boyhood in France. At age 18 he was sent to the United States in order to avoid conscription and to enter business. He began his study of North American birds at that time; this study would eventually lead him from Florida to Labrador, Can. With Frederick Rozier, Audubon attempted to operate a mine, then a general store. The latter venture they attempted first in Louisville, Ky., later in Henderson, Ky., but the partnership was dissolved after they failed utterly. Audubon then attempted some business ventures in partnership with his brother-in-law; these, too, failed. By 1820 he had begun to take what jobs he could to provide a living and to concentrate on his steadily growing interest in drawing birds; he worked for a time as a taxidermist, later making portraits and teaching drawing, while his wife worked as a governess.

By 1824 he began to consider publication of his bird drawings, but he was advised to seek a publisher in Europe, where he would find better engravers and greater interest in his subject. In 1826 he went to Europe in search of patrons and a publisher. He was well received in Edinburgh and, after the king subscribed for his books, in London as well. The engraver Robert Havell of London undertook publication of his illustrations as *The Birds of America*, 4 vol. (435 hand-coloured plates, 1827–38). William MacGillivray helped write the accompanying text, *Ornithological Biography*, 5 vol. (octavo, 1831–39), and *A Synopsis of the Birds of North America*, 1 vol. (1839), which serves as an index. Until 1839 Audubon divided his time between Europe and the United States, gathering material, completing illustrations, and financing publication through subscription. His reputation established, Audubon then settled in New York City and prepared a smaller edition of his *Birds of America*, 7 vol. (octavo, 1840–44), and a new work, *Viviparous Quadrupeds of North America*, 3 vol. (150 plates, 1845–48), and the accompanying text (3 vol., 1846–53), completed with the aid of his sons and the naturalist John Bachman.

Critics of Audubon's work have pointed to certain fanciful (or even impossible) poses and inaccurate details, but few argue with their excellence as art. To many, Audubon's work far surpasses that of his contemporary (and more scientific) fellow ornithologist, Alexander Wilson.

MICHAEL FARADAY

(b. Sept. 22, 1791, Newington, Surrey, Eng.—d. Aug. 25, 1867, Hampton Court)

English physicist and chemist Michael Faraday is known for his many experiments that contributed greatly to the understanding of electromagnetism. Faraday, who became one of the greatest scientists of the 19th century, began his career as a chemist. He wrote a manual of practical chemistry that reveals his mastery of the technical aspects of his art, discovered a number of new organic compounds, among them benzene, and was the first to liquefy a "permanent" gas (i.e., one that was believed to be incapable of liquefaction). His major contribution, however, was in the field of electricity and magnetism. He was the first to produce an electric current from a magnetic field, invented the first electric motor and dynamo, demonstrated the relation between electricity and chemical bonding, discovered the effect of magnetism on light, and discovered and named diamagnetism, the peculiar behaviour of certain substances in strong magnetic fields. He provided the experimental, and a good deal of the theoretical, foundation upon which James Clerk Maxwell erected classical electromagnetic field theory.

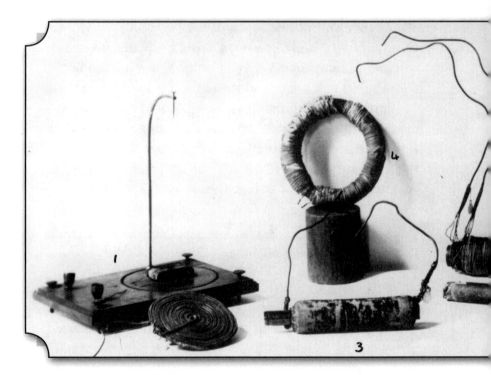

Depicted are of the tools used by physicist Michael Farady. From left to right: an astatic galvanometer, an indictator coil, a solenoid, a compound helix, and the first apparatus for an electromagnetic spark. Hulton Archive/Getty Images

EARLY CAREER

Faraday began his scientific career as Sir Humphry Davy's laboratory assistant. When Faraday joined Davy in 1812, Davy was in the process of revolutionizing the chemistry of the day. Davy's ideas were influenced by an atomic theory that was also to have important consequences for Faraday's thought. This theory, proposed in the 18th century by Ruggero Giuseppe Boscovich, argued that atoms were mathematical points surrounded by alternating fields of attractive and repulsive forces. One property of such atoms is that they can be placed under considerable strain, or tension, before the "bonds" holding them together are broken. These strains were to be central to Faraday's ideas about electricity.

Faraday's work under Davy came to an end in 1820. There followed a series of discoveries that astonished the scientific world. Faraday achieved his early renown as a chemist. In 1820 he produced the first known compounds of carbon and chlorine, C_2Cl_6 and C_2Cl_4. These compounds were produced by substituting chlorine for hydrogen in "olefiant gas" (ethylene), the first substitution reactions induced. In 1825, as a result of research on illuminating gases, Faraday isolated and described benzene. In the 1820s he also conducted investigations of steel alloys, helping to lay the foundations for scientific metallurgy and metallography. While completing an assignment from the Royal Society of London to improve the quality of optical glass for telescopes, he produced a glass of very high refractive index that was to lead him, in 1845, to the discovery of diamagnetism.

By the 1820s André-Marie Ampère had shown that magnetic force apparently was a circular one, producing in effect a cylinder of magnetism around a wire carrying an electric current. No such circular force had ever before been observed, and Faraday was the first to understand what it implied. If a magnetic pole could be isolated, it ought to move constantly in a circle around a current-carrying wire. Faraday's ingenuity and laboratory skill enabled him to construct an apparatus that confirmed this conclusion. This device, which transformed electrical energy into mechanical energy, was the first electric motor.

On Aug. 29, 1831, Faraday wound a thick iron ring on one side with insulated wire that was connected to a battery. He then wound the opposite side with wire connected to a galvanometer. What he expected was that a "wave" would be produced when the battery circuit was closed and that the wave would show up as a deflection of the galvanometer in the second circuit. He closed the primary circuit and, to his delight and satisfaction, saw the galvanometer needle jump. A current had been induced in the secondary coil by one in the primary. When he opened the circuit, however, he was astonished to see the galvanometer jump in the opposite direction. Somehow, turning off the current also created an induced current in the secondary circuit, equal and opposite to the original current. This phenomenon led Faraday to propose what he called the "electrotonic" state of particles in the wire, which he considered a state of tension.

In the fall of 1831 Faraday attempted to determine just how an induced current was produced. He discovered that when a permanent magnet was moved in and out of a coil of wire a current was induced in the coil. Magnets, he knew, were surrounded by forces that could be made visible by the simple expedient of sprinkling iron filings on a card held over them. Faraday saw the "lines of force" thus revealed as lines of tension in the medium, namely air, surrounding the magnet, and he soon discovered the law determining the production of electric currents by magnets: the magnitude of the current was dependent upon the number of lines of force cut by the conductor in unit time. He immediately realized that a continuous current could be produced by rotating a copper disk between the poles of a powerful magnet and taking leads off the disk's rim and centre. This was the first dynamo. It was also the direct ancestor of electric motors, for it was only necessary to reverse the situation, to feed an electric current to the disk, to make it rotate.

THEORY OF ELECTROCHEMISTRY

In 1832 Faraday began what promised to be a rather tedious attempt to prove that all electricities had precisely the same properties and caused precisely the same effects. The key effect was electrochemical decomposition. Voltaic and electromagnetic electricity posed no problems, but static electricity did. As Faraday delved deeper into the problem, he made two startling discoveries. First, electrical force did not, as had long been supposed, act at a distance upon chemical molecules to cause them to dissociate. It was the passage of electricity through a conducting liquid medium that caused the molecules to dissociate, even when the electricity merely discharged into the air and did not pass into a "pole" or "centre of action" in a voltaic cell. Second, the amount of the decomposition was found to be related in a simple manner to the amount of electricity that passed through the solution.

These findings led Faraday to a new theory of electrochemistry. The electric force, he argued, threw the molecules of a solution into a state of tension (his electrotonic state). When the force was strong enough to distort the fields of forces that held the molecules together so as to permit the interaction of these fields with neighbouring particles, the tension was relieved by the migration of particles along the lines of tension, the different species of atoms migrating in opposite directions. The amount of electricity that passed, then, was clearly related to the chemical affinities of the substances in solution. These experiments led directly to Faraday's two laws of electrochemistry: (1) The amount of a substance deposited on each electrode of an electrolytic cell is directly proportional to the quantity of electricity passed through the cell. (2) The quantities of different elements deposited by a given amount of electricity are in the ratio of their chemical equivalent weights.

Faraday's work on electrochemistry provided him with an essential clue for the investigation of static electrical induction. Since the amount of electricity passed through the conducting medium of an electrolytic cell determined the amount of material deposited at the electrodes, why should not the amount of electricity induced in a nonconductor be dependent upon the material out of which it was made? In short, why should not every material have a specific inductive capacity? Every material does, and Faraday was the discoverer of this fact.

By 1839 Faraday was able to bring forth a new and general theory of electrical action. Electricity, whatever it was, caused tensions to be created in matter. When these tensions were rapidly relieved (i.e., when bodies could not take much strain before "snapping" back), then what occurred was a rapid repetition of a cyclical buildup, breakdown, and buildup of tension that, like a wave, was passed along the substance. Such substances were called conductors. In electrochemical processes the rate of buildup and breakdown of the strain was proportional to the chemical affinities of the substances involved, but again the current was not a material flow but a wave pattern of tensions and their relief. Insulators were simply materials whose particles could take an extraordinary amount of strain before they snapped. Electrostatic charge in an isolated insulator was simply a measure of this accumulated strain. Thus, all electrical action was the result of forced strains in bodies.

LATER LIFE

Since the very beginning of his scientific work, Faraday had believed in what he called the unity of the forces of nature. By this he meant that all the forces of nature were but manifestations of a single universal force and ought, therefore, to be convertible into one another. In 1846 he made public some of his speculations in a lecture titled "Thoughts on Ray Vibrations." Specifically referring to point atoms and their infinite fields of force, he suggested that the lines of electric and magnetic force associated with these atoms might, in fact, serve as the medium by which light waves were propagated.

In 1845 Faraday tackled the problem of his hypothetical electrotonic state. He passed a beam of plane-polarized light through the optical glass of high refractive index and then turned on an electromagnet so that its lines of force ran parallel to the light ray. The plane of polarization was rotated, indicating a strain in the molecules of the glass. But Faraday again noted an unexpected result. When he changed the direction of the ray of light, the rotation remained in the same direction, a fact that Faraday correctly interpreted as meaning that the strain was not in the molecules of the glass but in the magnetic lines of force. The direction of rotation of the plane of polarization depended solely upon the polarity of the lines of force; the glass served merely to detect the effect.

By 1850 Faraday had evolved a radically new view of space and force. Space was not "nothing," the mere location of bodies and forces, but a medium capable of supporting the strains of electric and magnetic forces. The energies of the world were not localized in the particles from which these forces arose but rather were to be found in the space surrounding them. Thus was born field theory. As Maxwell later freely admitted, the basic ideas for his mathematical theory of electrical and magnetic fields came from Faraday; his contribution was to mathematize those ideas in the form of his classical field equations.

SIR CHARLES LYELL

(b. Nov. 14, 1797, Kinnordy, Forfarshire, Scot.—d. Feb. 22, 1875, London, Eng.)

Scottish geologist Sir Charles Lyell was largely responsible for the general acceptance of the view that all features of the Earth's surface are produced by physical, chemical, and biological processes through long periods of geological time. The concept was called uniformitarianism (initially set forth by James Hutton). Lyell's achievements laid the foundations for evolutionary biology as well as for an understanding of the Earth's development. He was knighted in 1848 and made a baronet in 1864.

NEW APPROACH TO GEOLOGY

In the 1820s Lyell was rapidly developing new principles of reasoning in geology and began to plan a book which would stress that there are natural (as opposed to supernatural) explanations for all geologic phenomena, that the ordinary natural processes of today and their products do not differ in kind or magnitude from those of the past, and that the Earth must therefore be very ancient because these everyday processes work so slowly. With the ambitious young geologist Roderick Murchison, he explored districts in France and Italy where proof of his principles could be sought. From northern Italy Lyell went south alone to Sicily. Poor roads and accommodations made travel difficult, but in the region around Mt. Etna he found striking confirmation of his belief in the adequacy of natural causes to explain the features of the Earth and in the great antiquity even of such a recent feature as Etna itself.

The results of this trip, which lasted from May 1828 until February 1829, far exceeded Lyell's expectations. Returning to London, he set to work immediately on his book, *Principles of Geology*, the first volume of which was published in July 1830. Lyell finished the second volume of *Principles of Geology* in December 1831 and the third and final volume in April 1833. His steady work was relieved by occasional social or scientific gatherings and a trip to a volcanic district in Germany.

SCIENTIFIC EMINENCE

In 1838 Lyell's *Elements of Geology* was published, which described European rocks and fossils from the most recent, Lyell's specialty, to the oldest then known. Like *Principles of Geology*, this well-illustrated work was periodically enlarged and updated.

In 1841 Lyell accepted an invitation to lecture and travel for a year in North America, returning again for nine months in 1845–46 and for two short visits in the 1850s. During these travels, Lyell visited nearly every part of the United States east of the Mississippi River and much of eastern Canada, seeing almost all of the important geological "monuments" along the way, including Niagara Falls. Lyell was amazed at the comparative ease of travel, and he often praised the speed and comfort of the new railroads and steamships. Lyell wrote enthusiastic and informative books, in 1845 and 1849, about each of his two long visits to the New World.

In the 1840s Lyell became more widely known outside the scientific community. He studied the prevention of mine disasters with the English physicist Michael Faraday in 1844, served as a commissioner for the Great Exhibition in 1851–52, and in the same year helped to begin educational reform at Oxford University—he had long objected to church domination of British colleges. In the winter of 1854 he travelled to Madeira to study the origin of the island itself and its curious fauna and flora. After exhaustive restudy carried out on muleback in 1858, he proved conclusively that Mt. Etna had been built up by repeated small eruptions rather than by a cataclysmic upheaval as some geologists still insisted.

In 1859 publication of Darwin's *Origin of Species* gave new impetus to Lyell's work. Although Darwin drew heavily on Lyell's *Principles of Geology* both for style and content, Lyell had never shared Darwin's belief in evolution. But reading the *Origin of Species* triggered studies that culminated in publication of *The Geological Evidence of the Antiquity of Man* in 1863, in which Lyell tentatively accepted evolution by natural selection. Only during completion of a major revision of the *Principles of Geology* in 1865 did he fully adopt Darwin's conclusions, however, adding powerful arguments of his own that won new adherents to Darwin's theory.

LOUIS AGASSIZ

(b. May 28, 1807, Motier, Switz.—d. Dec. 14, 1873, Cambridge, Mass., U.S.)

Swiss-born U.S. naturalist, geologist, and teacher Louis Agassiz made revolutionary contributions to the study of natural science with landmark work on glacier activity and extinct fishes. He achieved lasting fame through his innovative teaching methods, which altered the character of natural science education in the United States.

EARLY CAREER

Agassiz's interest in ichthyology began with his study of an extensive collection of Brazilian fishes, mostly from the Amazon River, which had been collected in 1819 and 1820 by two eminent naturalists at Munich. The classification of these species was begun by one of the collectors in 1826, and when he died the collection was turned over to Agassiz. The work was completed and published in 1829 as *Selecta Genera et Species Piscium*. The study of fish forms became henceforth the prominent feature of his research. In 1830 he issued a prospectus of a *History of the Fresh Water Fishes of Central Europe*, printed in parts from 1839 to 1842.

The year 1832 proved the most significant in Agassiz's early career because it took him first to Paris, then the centre of scientific research, and later to Neuchâtel, Switz., where he spent many years of fruitful effort. Already Agassiz had become interested in the rich stores of the extinct fishes of Europe, especially those of Glarus in Switzerland and of Monte Bolca near Verona, of which, at that time, only a few had been critically studied. As early as 1829 Agassiz planned a comprehensive and critical study of these fossils and spent much time gathering material wherever possible. His epoch-making work, *Recherches sur les poissons fossiles*, appeared in parts from 1833 to 1843. In it, the number of named fossil fishes was raised to more than 1,700. The great importance of this fundamental work rests on the impetus it gave to the study of extinct life itself. Turning his attention to other extinct animals found with the fishes, Agassiz published in 1838–42 two volumes on the fossil echinoderms of Switzerland, and later (1841–42) his *Études critiques sur les mollusques fossiles*.

From 1832 to 1846 Agassiz worked on his *Nomenclator Zoologicus*, a catalog with references of all the names applied to genera of animals from the beginning of scientific nomenclature, a date since fixed at Jan. 1, 1758. However, in 1836 Agassiz began a new line of studies: the movements and effects of the glaciers of Switzerland. In 1840 he published his *Études sur les glaciers*, in some respects his most important work. In it, Agassiz showed that at a geologically recent period Switzerland had been covered by one vast ice sheet. His final conclusion was that "great sheets of ice, resembling those now existing in Greenland, once covered all the countries in which unstratified gravel (boulder drift) is found."

ACTIVITIES IN THE UNITED STATES

In 1846 Agassiz visited the United States for the general purpose of studying natural history and geology there but more specifically to give a course of lectures at the Lowell Institute in Boston. In 1847 he accepted a professorship of zoology at Harvard University. In the United States his chief volumes of scientific research were the following: *Lake Superior* (1850); *Contributions to the Natural History of the United States* (1857–62), in four quarto volumes, the most notable being on the embryology of turtles; and the *Essay on Classification* (1859), a brilliant publication, which, however, failed to grasp the fact that zoology was moving away from the doctrine of special creation toward the doctrine of evolution.

Besides these extensive contributions there appeared a multitude of short papers on natural history and especially on the fishes of the U.S. His two expeditions of most importance were, first, to Brazil in 1865 and, second, to California in 1871, the former trip involving both shores of

South America. *A Journey in Brazil* (1868), written by Mrs. Agassiz and himself, gives an account of their experiences. His most important paper on U.S. fishes dealt with the group of viviparous surf fishes of California.

Agassiz's method as teacher was to give contact with nature rather than information. He discouraged the use of books except in detailed research. The result of his instruction at Harvard was a complete revolution in the study of natural history in the U.S. The purpose of study was not to acquire a category of facts from others but to be able, through active contact with the natural world, to gather the needed facts. As a result of his activities, every notable teacher of natural history in the U.S. for the second half of the 19th century was a pupil either of Agassiz or of one of his students.

In the interests of better teaching and scientific enthusiasm, he organized in the summer of 1873 the Anderson School of Natural History at Penikese, an island in Buzzards Bay. This school, which had the greatest influence on science teaching in America, was run solely by Agassiz. After his death it vanished.

CHARLES DARWIN

(b. Feb. 12, 1809, Shrewsbury, Shropshire, Eng.—d. April 19, 1882, Downe, Kent)

English naturalist Charles Darwin developed the theory of evolution by natural selection, which became the foundation of modern evolutionary studies. An affable country gentleman, Darwin at first shocked religious Victorian society by suggesting that animals and humans shared a common ancestry. However, his nonreligious biology appealed to the rising class of professional scientists, and by the time of his death evolutionary imagery had spread through all of science, literature, and politics.

Darwin, himself an agnostic, was accorded the ultimate British accolade of burial in Westminster Abbey, London.

Darwin formulated his bold theory in private in 1837–39, after returning from a voyage around the world aboard HMS *Beagle*, but it was not until two decades later that he finally gave it full public expression in *On the Origin of Species* (1859), a book that has deeply influenced modern Western society and thought.

THE *BEAGLE* VOYAGE

Darwin embarked on the *Beagle* voyage on Dec. 27, 1831. The circumnavigation of the globe would be the making of Darwin. Five years of physical hardship and mental rigour, imprisoned within a ship's walls, offset by wide-open opportunities in the Brazilian jungles and the Andes Mountains, were to give Darwin a new seriousness. As a gentleman naturalist, he could leave the ship for extended periods, pursuing his own interests. As a result, he spent only 18 months of the voyage aboard the ship. Among the places Darwin visited on the voyage were the Cape Verde Islands, coastal regions of Brazil, Uruguay, and Argentina, and the Galapagos Islands.

On the last leg of the voyage Darwin finished his 770-page diary, wrapped up 1,750 pages of notes, drew up 12 catalogs of his 5,436 skins, bones, and carcasses—and still he wondered: Was each Galapagos mockingbird a naturally produced variety? Why did ground sloths become extinct? He sailed home with problems enough to last him a lifetime.

EVOLUTION BY NATURAL SELECTION

Following the voyage, Darwin became well known through his diary's publication as *Journal of Researches into the Geology and Natural History of the Various Countries Visited by H.M.S. Beagle* (1839). He also employed the best experts and published their descriptions of his specimens in his *Zoology of the Voyage of H.M.S. Beagle* (1838–43). Darwin drafted a 35-page sketch of his theory of natural selection in 1842 and expanded it in 1844, but he had no immediate intention of publishing it. In 1842, Darwin, increasingly shunning society, had moved his family to the isolated village of Downe, in Kent, at the "extreme edge of [the] world." (It was in fact only 16 miles [26 km] from central London.)

From 1846 to 1854, Darwin added to his credibility as an expert on species by pursuing a detailed study of all known barnacles. Intrigued by their sexual differentiation, he discovered that some females had tiny degenerate males clinging to them. This sparked his interest in the evolution of diverging male and female forms from an original hermaphrodite creature. Four monographs on such an obscure group made him a world expert. No longer could he be dismissed as a speculator on biological matters.

ON THE ORIGIN OF SPECIES

In the 1850s the changing social composition of science in England—typified by the rise of the freethinking biologist Thomas Henry Huxley—promised that Darwin's work would be well-received. Huxley, the philosopher Herbert Spencer, and other outsiders were opting for a secular nature in the rationalist *Westminster Review* and deriding the influence of "parsondom" (the influence of the church). Darwin had himself lost the last shreds of his belief in Christianity with the tragic death of his oldest daughter, Annie, from typhoid in 1851.

In 1854 Darwin solved his last major problem, the forking of genera to produce new evolutionary branches. He used an industrial analogy familiar from the Wedgwood factories, the division of labour: competition in nature's overcrowded marketplace would favour variants that could exploit different aspects of a niche. Species would diverge on the spot, like tradesmen in the same tenement.

In 1856 Darwin began writing a triple-volume book, tentatively called *Natural Selection*. Whereas in the 1830s Darwin had thought that species remained perfectly adapted until the environment changed, he now believed that every new variation was imperfect, and that perpetual struggle was the rule. He also explained the evolution of sterile worker bees in 1857. These could not be selected because they did not breed, so he opted for "family" selection (kin selection, as it is known today): the whole colony benefited from their retention.

Darwin had finished a quarter of a million words by June 18, 1858. That day he received a letter from Alfred Russel Wallace, an English socialist and specimen collector working in the Malay Archipelago, sketching a similar-looking theory. Darwin, fearing loss of priority, accepted a solution proposed by geologist Sir Charles Lyell and botanist Joseph Dalton Hooker: joint extracts from Darwin's and Wallace's works would be read at the Linnean Society on July 1, 1858. Darwin was away, sick, grieving for his tiny son who had died from scarlet fever, and thus he missed the first public presentation of the theory of natural selection.

Darwin hastily began an "abstract" of *Natural Selection*, which grew into a more accessible book, *On the Origin of Species by Means of Natural Selection, or the Preservation of Favoured Races in the Struggle for Life*. Suffering from a terrible bout of nausea, Darwin, now 50, was secreted away at a spa on the desolate Yorkshire moors when the book was sold to the trade on Nov. 22, 1859. He still feared the worst.

The book did distress his Cambridge patrons, but they were marginal to science now. However, radical Dissenters were sympathetic, as were the rising London biologists and geologists, even if few actually adopted Darwin's cost-benefit approach to nature. The newspapers drew the one conclusion that Darwin had specifically avoided: that humans had evolved from apes, and that Darwin was denying mankind's immortality. A sensitive Darwin, making no personal appearances, let Huxley, by now a good friend, manage this part of the debate. The pugnacious Huxley, who loved public argument as much as Darwin loathed it, had his own reasons for taking up the cause, and did so with enthusiasm. He wrote three reviews of *Origin of Species*, defended human evolution at the Oxford meeting of the British Association for the Advancement of Science in 1860 (when Bishop Samuel Wilberforce jokingly asked whether the

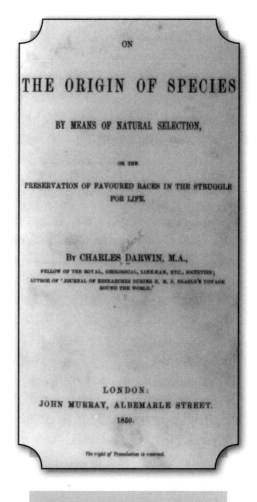

Title page of the 1859 edition of Charles Darwin's On the Origin of Species. *Library of Congress, Washington, D.C.*

apes were on Huxley's grandmother's or grandfather's side), and published his own book on human evolution, *Evidence as to Man's Place in Nature* (1863). What Huxley championed was Darwin's evolutionary naturalism, his nonmiraculous assumptions, which pushed biological science into previously taboo areas and increased the power of Huxley's professionals.

Huxley's reaction, with its enthusiasm for evolution and cooler opinion of natural selection, was typical. Natural selection received little support in Darwin's day. By contrast, evolution itself ("descent," Darwin called it—the word *evolution* would only be introduced in the last, 1872, edition of the *Origin*) was being acknowledged from British Association platforms by 1866.

THE PATRIARCH IN HIS HOME LABORATORY

In the 1860s Down House continued to serve as Darwin's laboratory, where he experimented and revamped the *Origin* through six editions. Although quietly believing in natural selection, he answered critics by reemphasizing other causes of change—for example, the effects of continued use of an organ—and he bolstered the Lamarckian belief that such alterations through excessive use might be passed on. In *Variation of Animals and Plants under Domestication* (1868) he marshaled the facts and explored the causes of variation in domestic breeds.

In 1867 the engineer Fleeming Jenkin argued that any single favourable variation would be swamped and lost by back-breeding within the general population. No mechanism was known for inheritance, and so in the *Variation* Darwin devised his hypothesis of "pangenesis" to explain the discrete inheritance of traits. He imagined that each tissue of an organism threw out tiny "gemmules," which passed to the sex organs and permitted copies of themselves to be made in the next generation. But Darwin's cousin Francis Galton failed to find these gemmules in rabbit blood, and the theory was dismissed.

Darwin was adept at flanking movements in order to get around his critics. He would take seemingly intractable subjects—like orchid flowers—and make them test cases for "natural selection." Hence the book that appeared after the *Origin* was, to everyone's surprise, *The Various Contrivances by which British and Foreign Orchids are Fertilised by Insects* (1862). He showed that the orchid's beauty was not a piece of floral whimsy "designed" by God to please humans but honed by selection to attract insect cross-pollinators. The petals guided the bees to the nectaries, and pollen sacs were deposited exactly where they could be removed by a stigma of another flower.

But why the importance of cross-pollination? Darwin's botanical work was always subtly related to his evolutionary mechanism. He believed that cross-pollinated plants would produce fitter offspring than self-pollinators, and he used considerable ingenuity in conducting thousands of crossings to prove the point. The results appeared in *The Effects of Cross and Self Fertilization in the Vegetable Kingdom* (1876). His next book, *The Different Forms of Flowers on Plants of the Same Species* (1877), was again the result of long-standing work into the way evolution in some species favoured different male and female forms of flowers to facilitate outbreeding.

THE PRIVATE MAN AND THE PUBLIC DEBATE

Through the 1860s natural selection was already being applied to the growth of society. The trend to explain the evolution of human races, morality, and civilization was capped by Darwin in his two-volume *The Descent of Man, and Selection in Relation to Sex* (1871). The book was authoritative, annotated, and heavily anecdotal in places. The two volumes were discrete, the first discussing civilization and human origins among the Old World monkeys. (Darwin's depiction of a hairy human ancestor with pointed ears led to a spate of caricatures.) The second volume responded to critics who doubted that the iridescent hummingbird's plumage had any function—or any Darwinian explanation. Darwin argued that female birds were choosing mates for their gaudy plumage. Darwin as usual tapped his huge correspondence network of breeders, naturalists, and travelers worldwide to produce evidence for this. Such "sexual selection" happened among humans too. With primitive societies accepting diverse notions of beauty, aesthetic preferences, he believed, could account for the origin of the human races.

Darwin finished another long-standing line of work. Since studying the moody orangutans at London Zoo in 1838, Darwin had been fascinated by facial expression. As a student he had heard the attacks on the idea that people's facial muscles were designed by God to express their unique thoughts. Now his photographically illustrated *The Expression of the Emotions in Man and Animals* (1872) expanded the subject to include the rages and grimaces of asylum inmates, all to show the continuity of emotions and expressions between humans and animals.

The treadmill of experiment and writing gave much meaning to Darwin's life. But as he wrapped up his final, long-term interest, publishing *The Formation of Vegetable Mould, Through the Action of Worms* (1881), the future looked bleak. Such an earthy subject was typical Darwin: just as he had shown that today's ecosystems were built by infinitesimal degrees and the mighty Andes by tiny uplifts, so he ended on the monumental transformation of landscapes by the Earth's humblest denizens.

SIR FRANCIS GALTON

(b. Feb. 16, 1822, near Sparkbrook, Birmingham, Warwickshire, Eng.—d. Jan. 17, 1911, Grayshott House, Haslemere, Surrey)

English explorer, anthropologist, and eugenicist Sir Francis Galton was known for his pioneering studies of human intelligence. He was knighted in 1909.

TRAVELS AND EXPLORATION

When Galton was a young man, he traveled in southeastern Europe. From Vienna he made his way through Constanza, Constantinople, Smyrna, and Athens, and he brought back from the caves of Adelsberg (present-day Postojina, Slovenia) specimens of a blind amphibian named *Proteus*—the first to reach England. On his return Galton went to Trinity College, Cambridge, where he was a medical student and where, as a result of overwork, he broke down in his third year. But he recovered quickly on changing his mode of life, as he did from similar attacks later.

After leaving Cambridge without taking a degree, Galton continued his medical studies in London. But before they were completed, his father died, leaving him "a sufficient fortune to make me independent of the medical profession." Galton was then free to indulge his craving for travel. Leisurely expeditions in 1845–46 up the Nile with friends and into the Holy Land alone were preliminaries to a carefully organized penetration into unexplored parts of southwestern Africa. After consulting the Royal Geographical Society, Galton decided to investigate a possible opening from the south and west to Lake Ngami, which lies north of the Kalahari desert some 550 miles east of Walvis Bay.

The expedition, which included two journeys, one northward, the other eastward, from the same base, proved to be difficult and not without danger. Though the explorers did not reach Lake Ngami, they gained valuable information. As a result, at the age of only 31, Galton was in 1853 elected a fellow of the Royal Geographical Society and, three years later, of the Royal Society. In 1853, too, Galton married. There were no children of the marriage. Galton wrote 9 books and some 200 papers. They deal with many diverse subjects, including the use of fingerprints for personal identification, the correlational calculus (a branch of applied statistics)—in both of which Galton was a pioneer—twins, blood transfusions, criminality, the art of travel in undeveloped countries, and meteorology. Most of Galton's publications disclose his predilection for quantifying; an early paper, for example, dealt with a statistical test of the efficacy of prayer. Moreover, over a period of 34 years, he concerned himself with improving standards of measurement.

ADVOCACY OF EUGENICS

Although he made contributions to many fields of knowledge, eugenics remained Galton's fundamental interest, and he devoted the latter part of his life chiefly to propagating the idea of improving the physical and mental makeup of the human species by selective parenthood. Galton, a cousin of Charles Darwin, was among the first to recognize the implications for mankind of Darwin's theory of evolution. He saw that it invalidated much of contemporary theology and that it also opened possibilities for planned human betterment. Galton coined the word eugenics to denote scientific endeavours to increase the proportion of persons with better than average genetic endowment through selective mating of marriage partners. In his *Hereditary Genius* (1869), in which he used the word genius to denote "an ability that was exceptionally high and at the same time inborn," his main argument was that mental and physical features are equally inherited—a proposition that was not accepted at the time.

It is surprising that when Darwin first read this book, he wrote to the author: "You have made a convert of an opponent in one sense for I have always maintained that, excepting fools, men did not differ much in intellect, only in zeal and hard work." This book doubtless helped Darwin to extend his evolution theory to man. Galton, unmentioned in *Origin of Species* (1859), is several times quoted in Darwin's *Descent of Man* (1871). Galton's conviction that mental traits are no less inherited than are physical characteristics was strong enough to shape his personal religious philosophy. "We cannot doubt," he wrote, "the existence of a great power ready to hand and capable of being directed with vast benefit as soon as we have learned to understand and apply it."

Galton's *Inquiries into Human Faculty* (1883) consists of some 40 articles varying in length from 2 to 30 pages, which are mostly based on scientific papers written between 1869 and 1883. The book can in a sense be regarded as a summary of the author's views on the faculties of man. On all his topics, Galton has something original and interesting to say, and he says it with clarity, brevity, distinction, and modesty. Under the terms of his will, a eugenics chair was established at the University of London.

REPUTATION

In the 20th century Galton's name has been mainly associated with eugenics. Insofar as eugenics takes primary account of *inborn* differences between human beings, it has come under the suspicion of those who hold that cultural (social and educational) factors heavily outweigh inborn, or biological, factors in their contribution to human differences. Eugenics is accordingly often treated as an expression of class prejudice, and Galton as a reactionary. Yet to some extent this view misrepresents his thought, for his aim was not the creation of an aristocratic elite but of a population consisting entirely of superior men and women. His ideas, like those of Darwin, were limited by a lack of an adequate theory of inheritance; the rediscovery of the work of Mendel came too late to affect Galton's contribution in any significant way.

GREGOR MENDEL

(b. July 22, 1822, Heinzendorf, Austria [now Hynčice, Czech Rep.]— d. Jan. 6, 1884, Brünn, Austria-Hungary [now Brno, Czech Rep.])

Austrian botanist, teacher, and Augustinian prelate Gregor Mendel was the first to lay the mathematical foundation of the science of genetics, in what came to be called Mendelism.

EARLY CAREER

As his father's only son, Mendel was expected to take over the small family farm, but he chose instead to enter the Altbrünn monastery as a novitiate of the Augustinian order, where he was given the name Gregor (his birth name was Johann).

The move to the monastery took him to Brünn, the capital of Moravia, where Mendal was introduced to a diverse and intellectual community. Abbot Cyril Napp found him a substitute-teaching position at Znaim (Znojmo, Czech Rep.), where he proved very successful. However, in 1850, Mendel failed an exam—introduced through new legislation for teacher certification—and was sent to the University of Vienna for two years to benefit from a new program of scientific instruction. Mendel devoted his time at Vienna to physics and mathematics, working under Austrian physicist Christian Doppler and mathematical physicist Andreas von Ettinghausen. He also studied the anatomy and physiology of plants and the use of the microscope under botanist Franz Unger, an enthusiast for the cell theory and a supporter of the developmentalist (pre-Darwinian) view of the evolution of life.

In the summer of 1853, Mendel returned to the monastery in Brünn, and in the following year he was again given a teaching position, this time at the Brünn *Realschule* (secondary school), where he remained until elected abbot 14 years later. These years were his greatest in terms of success both as teacher and as consummate experimentalist.

EXPERIMENTAL PERIOD

In 1854, Abbot Cyril Napp permitted Mendel to plan a major experimental program in hybridization at the monastery. The aim of this program was to trace the transmission of hereditary characters in successive generations of hybrid progeny. Previous authorities had observed that progeny of fertile hybrids tended to revert to the originating species, and they had therefore concluded that hybridization could not be a mechanism used by nature to multiply species—though in exceptional cases some fertile hybrids did appear not to revert (the so-called "constant hybrids"). On the other hand, plant and animal breeders had long shown that crossbreeding could indeed produce a multitude of new forms. The latter point was of particular interest to landowners, including the abbot of the monastery, who was concerned about the monastery's future profits from the wool of its Merino sheep, owing to competing wool being supplied from Australia.

Mendel chose to conduct his studies with the edible pea (*Pisum sativum*) because of the numerous distinct varieties, the ease of culture and control of pollination, and the high proportion of successful seed germinations. From 1854 to 1856 he tested 34 varieties for constancy of their traits. In order to trace the transmission of characters, he chose seven traits that were expressed in a distinctive manner, such as plant height (short or tall) and seed colour (green or yellow). He referred to these alternatives as contrasted characters, or character-pairs. He crossed varieties that differed in one trait—for instance, tall crossed with short. The first generation of hybrids (F_1) displayed the character of one variety but not that of the other. In Mendel's terms, one character was dominant and the other recessive.

In the numerous progeny that he raised from these hybrids (the second generation, F_2), however, the recessive character reappeared, and the proportion of offspring bearing the dominant to offspring bearing the recessive was very close to a 3 to 1 ratio. Study of the descendants (F_3) of the dominant group showed that one-third of them were true-breeding and two-thirds were of hybrid constitution. The 3:1 ratio could hence be rewritten as 1:2:1, meaning that 50 percent of the F_2 generation were true-breeding and 50 percent were still hybrid. This was Mendel's major discovery, and it was unlikely to have been made by his predecessors, since they did not grow statistically significant populations, nor did they follow the individual characters separately to establish their statistical relations.

Mendel's approach to experimentation came from his training in physics and mathematics, especially combinatorial mathematics. The latter served him ideally to represent his result. If A represents the dominant characteristic and a the recessive, then the 1:2:1 ratio recalls the terms in the expansion of the binomial equation:

$$(A + a)^2 = A^2 + 2Aa + a^2$$

Mendel realized further that he could test his expectation that the seven traits are transmitted independently of one another. Crosses involving first two and then three of his seven traits yielded categories of offspring in proportions following the terms produced from combining two binomial equations, indicating that their transmission was independent of one another. Mendel's successors have called this conclusion the law of independent assortment.

THEORETICAL INTERPRETATION

Mendel went on to relate his results to the cell theory of fertilization, according to which a new organism is generated from the fusion of two cells. In order for pure breeding forms of both the dominant and the recessive type to be brought into the hybrid, there had to be some temporary accommodation of the two differing characters in the hybrid as well as a separation process in the formation of the pollen cells and the egg cells. In other words, the hybrid must form germ cells bearing the potential to yield either the one characteristic or the other. This has since been described as the law of segregation, or the doctrine of the purity of the germ cells. Since one pollen cell fuses with one egg cell, all possible combinations of the differing pollen and egg cells would yield just the results suggested by Mendel's combinatorial theory.

Mendel first presented his results in two separate lectures in 1865 to the Natural Science Society in Brünn. His paper "Experiments on Plant Hybrids" was published in the society's journal, *Verhandlungen des naturforschenden Vereines in Brünn*, the following year. It attracted little attention, although many libraries received it and reprints were sent out. The tendency of those who read it was to conclude that Mendel had simply demonstrated more accurately what was already widely assumed—namely, that hybrid progeny revert to their originating forms. They overlooked the potential for variability and the evolutionary implications that his demonstration of the recombination of traits made possible. Mendel appears to have made no effort to publicize his work, and it is not known how many reprints of his paper he distributed.

REDISCOVERY

In 1900, Dutch botanist and geneticist Hugo de Vries, German botanist and geneticist Carl Erich Correns, and Austrian botanist Erich Tschermak von Seysenegg independently reported results of hybridization experiments similar to Mendel's, though each later claimed not to have known of Mendel's work while doing their own experiments. However, both de Vries and Correns had read Mendel earlier—Correns even made detailed notes on the subject—but had forgotten. De Vries had a diversity of results in 1899, but it was not until he reread Mendel in 1900 that he was able to select and organize his data into a rational system. Tschermak had not read Mendel before obtaining his results, and his first account of his data offers an interpretation in terms of hereditary potency. He described the 3:1 ratio as an "unequal valancy" (*Wertigkeit*). In subsequent papers he incorporated the Mendelian theory of segregation and the purity of the germ cells into his text.

In Great Britain, biologist William Bateson became the leading proponent of Mendel's theory. Around him gathered an enthusiastic band of followers. However, Darwinian evolution was assumed to be based chiefly on the selection of small, blending variations, whereas Mendel worked with clearly nonblending variations. Bateson soon found that championing Mendel aroused opposition from Darwinians. He and his supporters were called Mendelians, and their work was considered irrelevant to evolution. It took some three decades before the Mendelian theory was sufficiently developed to find its rightful place in evolutionary theory.

The distinction between a characteristic and its determinant was not consistently made by Mendel or by his successors, the early Mendelians. In 1909, Danish botanist and geneticist Wilhelm Johannsen clarified this point and named the determinants genes. Four years later, American zoologist and geneticist Thomas Hunt Morgan located the genes on the chromosomes, and the popular picture of them as beads on a string emerged. This discovery had implications for Mendel's claim of an independent transmission of traits, for genes close together on the same chromosome are not transmitted independently. Today the gene is defined in several ways, depending upon the nature of the investigation. Genetic material can be synthesized, manipulated, and hybridized with genetic material from other species, but to fully understand its functions in the whole organism, an understanding of Mendelian inheritance is necessary. As the architect of genetic experimental and statistical analysis, Mendel remains the acknowledged father of genetics.

LOUIS PASTEUR

(b. Dec. 27, 1822, Dole, France—d. Sept. 28, 1895, Saint-Cloud, near Paris)

French chemist and microbiologist Louis Pasteur made some of the most varied and valuable discoveries in the history of science and industry. It was he who proved that microorganisms cause fermentation and disease; he who pioneered the use of vaccines for rabies, anthrax, and chicken cholera; he who saved the beer, wine, and silk industries of France and other countries; he who performed important pioneer work in stereochemistry; and he who originated the process known as pasteurization.

EARLY CAREER

Pasteur made his first important contribution to science on May 22, 1848, when he presented before the Paris Academy of Sciences a paper reporting a remarkable discovery—that certain chemical compounds were capable of splitting into a "right" component and a "left" component, one component being the mirror image of the other. His discoveries arose out of a crystallographic investigation of tartaric acid, an acid formed in grape fermentation that is widely used commercially, and racemic acid—a new, hitherto unknown acid that had been discovered in certain industrial processes in the Alsace region. Both acids not only had identical chemical compositions but also had the same structure; yet they showed marked differences in properties. Pasteur found that, when separated, the two types of crystals rotated plane polarized light to the same degree but in opposite directions (one to the right, or clockwise, and the other to the left, or counterclockwise). One of the two crystal forms of racemic acid proved to be identical with the tartaric acid of fermentation.

As Pasteur showed further, one component of the racemic acid (that identical with the tartaric acid from fermentation) could be utilized for nutrition by microorganisms, whereas the other, which is now termed its optical antipode, was not assimilable by living organisms. On the basis of these experiments, Pasteur elaborated his theory of molecular asymmetry, showing that the biological properties of chemical substances depend not only on the nature of the atoms constituting their molecules but also on the manner in which these atoms are arranged in space.

Research on Fermentation

In 1854 Pasteur became dean of the new science faculty at the University of Lille, where he initiated a highly modern educational concept: by instituting evening classes for the many young workmen of the industrial city, conducting his regular students around large factories in the area, and organizing supervised practical courses, he demonstrated the relationship that he believed should exist between theory and practice, between university and industry. At Lille, after receiving a query from an industrialist on the production of alcohol from grain and beet sugar, Pasteur began his studies on fermentation.

From studying the fermentation of alcohol he went on to the problem of lactic fermentation, showing yeast to be an organism capable of reproducing itself, even in artificial media, without free oxygen—a concept that became known as the Pasteur effect. He later announced that fermentation was the result of the activity of minute organisms and that when fermentation failed, either the necessary organism was absent or was unable to grow properly. Pasteur showed that milk could be soured by injecting a number of organisms from buttermilk or beer but could be kept unchanged if such organisms were excluded.

Spontaneous Generation and Pasteurization

As a logical sequel to Pasteur's work on fermentation, he began research on spontaneous generation (the concept that bacterial life arose spontaneously), a question which at that time divided scientists into two opposing camps. Pasteur's recognition of the fact that both lactic and alcohol fermentations were hastened by exposure to air led him to wonder whether his invisible organisms were always present in the atmosphere or whether they were

French scientist Louis Pasteur studies chemicals in his laboratory around 1870.
Hulton Archive/Getty Images

spontaneously generated. By means of simple and precise experiments, including the filtration of air and the exposure of unfermented liquids to the air of the high Alps, he proved that food decomposes when placed in contact with germs present in the air, which cause its putrefaction, and that it does not undergo transformation or putrefy in such a way as to spontaneously generate new organisms within itself.

After laying the theoretical groundwork, Pasteur proceeded to apply his findings to the study of vinegar and wine, two commodities of great importance in the economy of France; his pasteurization process, the destruction of harmful germs by heat, made it possible to produce, preserve, and transport these products without their undergoing deterioration.

RESEARCH ON SILKWORMS AND BREWING

In 1865 Pasteur undertook a government mission to investigate the diseases of the silkworm, which were about to put an end to the production of silk at a time when it comprised a major section of France's economy. To carry out the investigation, he moved to the south of France, the centre of silkworm breeding. Three years later he announced that he had isolated the bacilli of two distinct diseases and had found methods of preventing contagion and of detecting diseased stock.

In 1870 he devoted himself to the problem of beer. Following an investigation conducted both in France and among the brewers in London, he devised, as he had done for vinegar and wine, a procedure for manufacturing beer that would prevent its deterioration with time. British exporters, whose ships had to sail entirely around the African continent, were thus able to send British beer as far as India without fear of its deteriorating.

RESEARCH ON VACCINES

By 1881 Pasteur had perfected a technique for reducing the virulence of various disease-producing microorganisms, and he had succeeded in vaccinating a herd of sheep against the disease known as anthrax. Likewise, he was able to protect fowl from chicken cholera, for he had observed that once animals stricken with certain diseases had recovered they were later immune to a fresh attack. Thus, by isolating the germ of the disease and by cultivating an attenuated, or weakened, form of the germ and inoculating fowl with the culture, he could immunize the animals against the malady. In this he was following the example of the English physician Edward Jenner, who used cowpox to vaccinate against the closely related but more virulent disease smallpox.

On April 27, 1882, Pasteur was elected a member of the Académie Française, at which point he undertook research that proved to be the most spectacular of all—the preventive treatment of rabies. After experimenting with inoculations of saliva from infected animals, he came to the conclusion that the virus was also present in the nerve centres, and he demonstrated that a portion of the medulla oblongata of a rabid dog, when injected into the body of a healthy animal, produced symptoms of rabies. By further work on the dried tissues of infected animals and the effect of time and temperature on these tissues, he was able to obtain a weakened form of the virus that could be used for inoculation.

Having detected the rabies virus by its effects on the nervous system and attenuated its virulence, he applied his procedure to man; on July 6, 1885, he saved the life of a nine-year-old boy, Joseph Meister, who had been bitten by a rabid dog. The experiment was an outstanding success, opening the road to protection from a terrible disease.

ALFRED RUSSEL WALLACE

(b. Jan. 8, 1823, Usk, Monmouthshire, Wales—d. Nov. 7, 1913, Broadstone, Dorset, Eng.)

A lfred Russel Wallace was a British humanist, naturalist, geographer, and social critic. He became a public figure in England during the second half of the 19th century, known for his courageous views on scientific, social, and spiritualist subjects. His formulation of the theory of evolution by natural selection, which predated Charles Darwin's published contributions, is his most outstanding legacy, but it was just one of many controversial issues he studied and wrote about during his lifetime. Wallace's wide-ranging interests—from socialism to spiritualism, from island biogeography to life on Mars, from evolution to land nationalization—stemmed from his profound concern with the moral, social, and political values of human life.

EARLY TRAVELS

Wallace was an enthusiastic amateur naturalist with an intellectual bent, and he read widely in natural history, history, and political economy. Inspired by reading about organic evolution in Robert Chambers's controversial *Vestiges of the Natural History of Creation* (1844), unemployed, and ardent in his love of nature, Wallace and his naturalist friend Henry Walter Bates, who had introduced Wallace to entomology four years earlier, traveled to Brazil in 1848 as self-employed specimen collectors. Wallace and Bates participated in the culture of natural history collecting, honing practical skills to identify, collect, and send back to England biological objects that were highly valued in the flourishing trade in natural specimens.

Wallace spent a total of four years traveling, collecting, mapping, drawing, and writing in unexplored regions of the Amazon River basin. He studied the languages and habits of the peoples he encountered; he collected butterflies, other insects, and birds; and he searched for clues to solve the mystery of the origin of plant and animal species. Except for one shipment of specimens sent to his agent in London, however, most of Wallace's collections were lost on his voyage home when his ship went up in flames and sank. Nevertheless, he managed to save some of his notes before his rescue, and from these he published several scientific articles, two books (*Palm Trees of the Amazon and Their Uses* and *Narrative of Travels on the Amazon and Rio Negro*, both 1853), and a map depicting the course of the Negro River. These won him acclaim from the Royal Geographical Society, which helped to fund his next collecting venture, in the Malay Archipelago.

EVOLUTIONARY THEORY

Wallace spent eight years in the Malay Archipelago, from 1854 to 1862, traveling among the islands, collecting biological specimens for his own research and for sale, and writing scores of scientific articles on mostly zoological subjects. Among these were two extraordinary articles dealing with the origin of new species. The first of these, published in 1855, concluded with the assertion that "every species has come into existence coincident both in space and time with a pre-existing closely allied species." Wallace then proposed that new species arise by the progression and continued divergence of varieties that outlive the parent species in the struggle for existence.

In early 1858 he sent a paper outlining these ideas to Darwin, who saw such a striking coincidence to his own theory that he consulted his closest colleagues, the geologist

Charles Lyell and the botanist Joseph Dalton Hooker. The three men decided to present two extracts of Darwin's previous writings, along with Wallace's paper, to the Linnean Society. The resulting set of papers, with both Darwin's and Wallace's names, was published as a single article entitled "On the Tendency of Species to Form Varieties; and on the Perpetuation of Varieties and Species by Natural Means of Selection" in the *Proceedings of the Linnean Society* in 1858. This compromise sought to avoid a conflict of priority interests and was reached without Wallace's knowledge. Wallace's research on the geographic distribution of animals among the islands of the Malay Archipelago provided crucial evidence for his evolutionary theories and led him to devise what soon became known as Wallace's Line, the boundary that separates the fauna of Australia from that of Asia.

Wallace returned to England in 1862 an established natural scientist and geographer. He published a highly successful narrative of his journey, *The Malay Archipelago: The Land of the Orang-Utan, and the Bird of Paradise* (1869), and wrote *Contributions to the Theory of Natural Selection* (1870). In the latter volume and in several articles from this period on human evolution and spiritualism, Wallace parted from the scientific naturalism of many of his friends and colleagues in claiming that natural selection could not account for the higher faculties of human beings.

Wallace's two-volume *Geographical Distribution of Animals* (1876) and *Island Life* (1880) became the standard authorities in zoogeography and island biogeography, synthesizing knowledge about the distribution and dispersal of living and extinct animals in an evolutionary framework. In addition to his major scientific works, Wallace actively pursued a variety of social and political interests. In writings and public appearances he opposed vaccination, eugenics, and vivisection while strongly supporting women's rights and land nationalization.

WILLIAM THOMSON

(b. June 26, 1824, Belfast, County Antrim, Ire. [now in Northern
Ireland]—d. Dec. 17, 1907, Netherhall, near Largs, Ayrshire, Scot.)

Scottish engineer, mathematician, and physicist William
Thomson, also known as Baron Kelvin, profoundly
influenced the scientific thought of his generation.
Thomson, who was knighted and raised to the peerage in
recognition of his work in engineering and physics, was
foremost among the small group of British scientists who
helped to lay the foundations of modern physics. His contributions to science included a major role in the
development of the second law of thermodynamics; the
absolute temperature scale (measured in kelvins); the
dynamical theory of heat; the mathematical analysis of
electricity and magnetism, including the basic ideas for
the electromagnetic theory of light; the geophysical determination of the age of the Earth; and fundamental work in
hydrodynamics. His theoretical work on submarine teleg-
raphy and his inventions for use on submarine cables aided
Britain in capturing a preeminent place in world commu-
nication during the 19th century.

Thomson's worldview was based in part on the belief
that all phenomena that caused force—such as electricity, magnetism, and heat—were the result of invisible
material in motion. This belief placed him in the fore-
front of those scientists who opposed the view that
forces were produced by imponderable fluids. However,
it also placed him in opposition to the positivistic outlook that proved to be a prelude to 20th-century quantum
mechanics and relativity.

But Thomson's consistency in his worldview enabled
him to apply a few basic ideas to a number of areas of study.
He brought together disparate areas of physics—heat,
thermodynamics, mechanics, hydrodynamics, magnetism,

and electricity—and thus played a principal role in the great and final synthesis of 19th-century science, which viewed all physical change as energy-related phenomena. Thomson was also the first to suggest that there were mathematical analogies between kinds of energy.

UNIFIED THEORY

Thomson's scientific work was guided by the conviction that the various theories dealing with matter and energy were converging toward one great, unified theory. He pursued the goal of a unified theory even though he doubted that it was attainable in his lifetime or ever. By the middle of the 19th century it had been shown that magnetism and electricity, electromagnetism, and light were related, and Thomson had shown by mathematical analogy that there was a relationship between hydrodynamic phenomena and an electric current flowing through wires. James Prescott Joule also claimed that there was a relationship between mechanical motion and heat, and his idea became the basis for the science of thermodynamics.

By 1851 Thomson was able to give public recognition to Joule's theory, along with a cautious endorsement in a major mathematical treatise, "On the Dynamical Theory of Heat." Thomson's essay contained his version of the second law of thermodynamics, which was a major step toward the unification of scientific theories.

TRANSATLANTIC CABLE

Thomson's involvement in a controversy over the feasibility of laying a transatlantic cable changed the course of his professional work. His work on the project began in 1854 when he was asked for a theoretical explanation of the apparent delay in an electric current passing through a long cable. In his reply, Thomson referred to his early paper "On the Uniform Motion of Heat in Homogeneous Solid Bodies, and its Connexion with the Mathematical Theory of Electricity" (1842). Thomson's idea about the mathematical analogy between heat flow and electric current worked well in his analysis of the problem of sending telegraph messages through the planned 3,000-mile (4,800-kilometre) cable. His equations describing the flow of heat through a solid wire proved applicable to questions about the velocity of a current in a cable.

The Atlantic Telegraph Company's chief electrician E.O.W. Whitehouse claimed that practical experience refuted Thomson's theoretical findings, and for a time Whitehouse's view prevailed with the directors of the company. Despite their disagreement, Thomson participated, as chief consultant, in the hazardous early cable-laying expeditions. In 1858 Thomson patented his telegraph receiver, called a mirror galvanometer, for use on the Atlantic cable.

LATER CAREER

Thomson's interests in science included not only electricity, magnetism, thermodynamics, and hydrodynamics but also geophysical questions about tides, the shape of the Earth, atmospheric electricity, thermal studies of the ground, the Earth's rotation, and geomagnetism. He also entered the controversy over Charles Darwin's theory of evolution. Thomson opposed Darwin, remaining "on the side of the angels."

Thomson challenged the views on geologic and biological change of the early uniformitarians, including Darwin, who claimed that the Earth and its life had evolved over an incalculable number of years, during which the forces of nature always operated as at present. On the basis of thermodynamic theory and Fourier's studies, Thomson estimated in 1862 that more than one million years ago the Sun's heat and the temperature of the Earth must have been considerably greater and that these conditions had produced violent storms and floods and an entirely different type of vegetation. Thomson's speculations as to the age of the Earth and the Sun were inaccurate, but he did succeed in pressing his contention that biological and geologic theory had to conform to the well-established theories of physics.

Thomson's interest in the sea, roused aboard his yacht, the *Lalla Rookh*, resulted in a number of patents: a compass that was adopted by the British Admiralty; a form of analog computer for measuring tides in a harbour and for calculating tide tables for any hour, past or future; and sounding equipment. He established a company to manufacture these items and a number of electrical measuring devices. He also published a textbook, *Treatise on Natural Philosophy* (1867), a work on physics coauthored with Scottish mathematician and physicist Peter Guthrie Tait that helped shape the thinking of a generation of physicists.

JOSEPH LISTER

(b. April 5, 1827, Upton, Essex, Eng.—d. Feb. 10, 1912, Walmer, Kent)

British surgeon and medical scientist Joseph Lister was the founder of antiseptic medicine and a pioneer in preventive medicine. While his method, based on the use of antiseptics, is no longer employed, his principle—that bacteria must never gain entry to an operation wound—remains the basis of surgery to this day. He was made a baronet in 1883 and raised to the peerage in 1897.

EDUCATION

Lister was the second son of Joseph Jackson Lister and his wife, Isabella Harris, members of the Society of Friends, or Quakers. J.J. Lister, a wine merchant and amateur physicist and microscopist, was elected a fellow of the Royal Society for his discovery that led to the modern achromatic (non-colour-distorting) microscope. While both parents took an active part in Lister's education, his father instructing him in natural history and the use of the microscope, Lister received his formal schooling in two Quaker institutions, which laid far more emphasis upon natural history and science than did other schools. He became interested in comparative anatomy, and, before his 16th birthday, he had decided upon a surgical career.

After taking an arts course at University College, London, he enrolled in the faculty of medical science in October 1848. A brilliant student, he was graduated a bachelor of medicine with honours in 1852; in the same year he became a fellow of the Royal College of Surgeons and house surgeon at University College Hospital. A visit to Edinburgh in the fall of 1853 led to Lister's appointment as assistant to James Syme, the greatest surgical teacher of his day, and in October 1856 he was appointed surgeon to the Edinburgh Royal Infirmary. In April he had married Syme's eldest daughter. Lister, a deeply religious man, joined the Scottish Episcopal Church. The marriage, although childless, was a happy one, his wife entering fully into Lister's professional life.

When three years later the Regius Professorship of Surgery at Glasgow University fell vacant, Lister was elected from seven applicants. In August 1861 he was appointed surgeon to the Glasgow Royal Infirmary, where he was in charge of wards in the new surgical block. The managers hoped that hospital disease (now known as operative sepsis—infection of the blood by disease-producing microorganisms) would be greatly decreased in their new building. The hope proved vain, however. Lister reported that, in his Male Accident Ward, between 45 and 50 percent of his amputation cases died from sepsis between 1861 and 1865.

WORK IN ANTISEPSIS

In this ward Lister began his experiments with antisepsis. Much of his earlier published work had dealt with the mechanism of coagulation of the blood and role of the blood vessels in the first stages of inflammation. Both researches depended upon the microscope and were directly connected with the healing of wounds. Lister had already tried out methods to encourage clean healing and had formed theories to account for the prevalence of sepsis. Discarding the popular concept of miasma—direct infection by bad air—he postulated that sepsis might be caused by a pollen-like dust. There is no evidence that he believed this dust to be living matter, but he had come close to the truth. It is therefore all the more surprising that he became acquainted with the work of the bacteriologist Louis Pasteur only in 1865.

Pasteur had arrived at his theory that microorganisms cause fermentation and disease by experiments on fermentation and putrefaction. Lister's education and his familiarity with the microscope, the process of fermentation, and the natural phenomena of inflammation and coagulation of the blood impelled him to accept Pasteur's theory as the full revelation of a half-suspected truth. At the start he believed the germs were carried solely by the air. This incorrect opinion proved useful, for it obliged him to adopt the only feasible method of surgically clean treatment. In his attempt to interpose an antiseptic barrier between the wound and the air, he protected the site of operation from infection by the surgeon's hands and instruments. He found an effective antiseptic in carbolic acid, which had already been used as a means of cleansing foul-smelling sewers and had been empirically advised as a wound dressing in 1863. Lister first successfully used his new method on Aug. 12, 1865; in March 1867 he published a series of cases. The results were dramatic. Between 1865 and 1869, surgical mortality fell from 45 to 15 percent in his Male Accident Ward.

In 1869, Lister succeeded Syme in the chair of Clinical Surgery at Edinburgh. There followed the seven happiest years of his life when, largely as the result of German experiments with antisepsis during the Franco-German War, his clinics were crowded with visitors and eager students. In 1875 Lister made a triumphal tour of the leading surgical centres in Germany. The next year he visited America but was received with little enthusiasm except in Boston and New York City.

Lister's work had been largely misunderstood in England and the United States. Opposition was directed against his germ theory rather than against his "carbolic treatment." The majority of practicing surgeons were unconvinced; while not antagonistic, they awaited clear proof that antisepsis constituted a major advance. Lister was not a spectacular operative surgeon and refused to publish statistics. Edinburgh, despite the ancient fame of its medical school, was regarded as a provincial centre. Lister understood that he must convince London before the usefulness of his work would be generally accepted.

His chance came in 1877, when he was offered the chair of Clinical Surgery at King's College. On Oct. 26, 1877, Lister, at King's College Hospital, for the first time performed the then-revolutionary operation of wiring a fractured patella, or kneecap. It entailed the deliberate conversion of a simple fracture, carrying no risk to life, into a compound fracture, which often resulted in generalized infection and death. Lister's proposal was widely publicized and aroused much opposition. Thus, the entire success of his operation carried out under antiseptic conditions forced surgical opinion throughout the world to accept that his method had added greatly to the safety of operative surgery.

JAMES CLERK MAXWELL

(b. June 13, 1831, Edinburgh, Scot.—d. Nov. 5, 1879, Cambridge, Cambridgeshire, Eng.)

Scottish physicist James Clerk Maxwell was best known for his formulation of electromagnetic theory. He is regarded by most modern physicists as the scientist of the 19th century who had the greatest influence on 20th-century physics, and he is ranked with Sir Isaac Newton and Albert Einstein for the fundamental nature of his contributions. In 1931, on the 100th anniversary of Maxwell's birth, Einstein described the change in the conception of reality in physics that resulted from Maxwell's work as "the most profound and the most fruitful that physics has experienced since the time of Newton."

The concept of electromagnetic radiation originated with Maxwell, and his field equations, based on Michael Faraday's observations of the electric and magnetic lines of force, paved the way for Einstein's special theory of relativity, which established the equivalence of mass and energy. Maxwell's ideas also ushered in the other major innovation of 20th-century physics, the quantum theory. His description of electromagnetic radiation led to the development (according to classical theory) of the ultimately unsatisfactory law of heat radiation, which prompted Max Planck's formulation of the quantum hypothesis—i.e., the theory that radiant-heat energy is emitted only in finite amounts, or quanta. The interaction between electromagnetic radiation and matter, integral to Planck's hypothesis, in turn has played a central role in the development of the theory of the structure of atoms and molecules.

EARLY CAREER

Between 1860 and 1865 Maxwell experienced the most productive years of his career. During this period his two classic papers on the electromagnetic field were published, and his demonstration of colour photography took place. He was elected to the Royal Society in 1861. His theoretical and experimental work on the viscosity of gases also was undertaken during these years and culminated in a lecture to the Royal Society in 1866. He supervised the experimental determination of electrical units for the British Association for the Advancement of Science, and this work in measurement and standardization led to the establishment of the National Physical Laboratory. He also measured the ratio of electromagnetic and electrostatic units of electricity and confirmed that it was in satisfactory agreement with the velocity of light as predicted by his theory.

RESEARCH ON ELECTROMAGNETISM

In 1865 Maxwell retired to the family estate in Glenlair. He continued to visit London every spring and served as external examiner for the Mathematical Tripos (exams) at Cambridge. In the spring and early summer of 1867 he toured Italy. But most of his energy during this period was devoted to writing his famous treatise on electricity and magnetism.

It was Maxwell's research on electromagnetism that established him among the great scientists of history. In the preface to his *Treatise on Electricity and Magnetism* (1873), the best exposition of his theory, Maxwell stated that his major task was to convert British physicist and chemist Michael Faraday's physical ideas into mathematical form. In attempting to illustrate Faraday's law of induction (that a changing magnetic field gives rise to an induced electromagnetic field), Maxwell constructed a mechanical model. He found that the model gave rise to a corresponding "displacement current" in the dielectric medium, which could then be the seat of transverse waves. On calculating the velocity of these waves, he found that they were very close to the velocity of light. Maxwell concluded that he could "scarcely avoid the inference that light consists in the transverse undulations of the same medium which is the cause of electric and magnetic phenomena."

Other Contributions to Physics

In addition to his electromagnetic theory, Maxwell made major contributions to other areas of physics. While still in his 20s, he demonstrated his mastery of classical physics by writing a prizewinning essay on Saturn's rings, in which he concluded that the rings must consist of masses of matter not mutually coherent—a conclusion that was corroborated more than 100 years later by the first Voyager space probe to reach Saturn.

The Maxwell relations of equality between different partial derivatives of thermodynamic functions are included in every standard textbook on thermodynamics. Though Maxwell did not originate the modern kinetic theory of gases, he was the first to apply the methods of probability and statistics in describing the properties of an assembly of molecules. Thus he was able to demonstrate that the velocities of molecules in a gas, previously assumed to be equal, must follow a statistical distribution (known subsequently as the Maxwell-Boltzmann distribution law). In later papers Maxwell investigated the transport properties of gases—i.e., the effect of changes in temperature and pressure on viscosity, thermal conductivity, and diffusion.

Maxwell was far from being an abstruse theoretician. He was skillful in the design of experimental apparatus, as was shown early in his career during his investigations of colour vision. He devised a colour top with adjustable sectors of tinted paper to test the three-colour hypothesis of Thomas Young and later invented a colour box that made it possible to conduct experiments with spectral colours rather than pigments. His investigations of the colour theory led him to conclude that a colour photograph could be produced by photographing through filters of the three primary colours and then recombining the images. He demonstrated his supposition in a lecture to the Royal Institution of Great Britain in 1861 by projecting through filters a colour photograph of a tartan ribbon that had been taken by this method.

DMITRY IVANOVICH MENDELEYEV

(b. Jan. 27 [Feb. 8, New Style], 1834, Tobolsk, Siberia, Russian Empire—d. Jan. 20 [Feb. 2], 1907, St. Petersburg, Russia)

Russian chemist Dmitry Ivanovich Mendeleyev developed the periodic classification of the elements. Mendeleyev found that, when all the known chemical elements were arranged in order of increasing atomic weight, the resulting table displayed a recurring pattern, or periodicity, of properties within groups of elements. In his version of the periodic table of 1871, he left gaps in places where he believed unknown elements would find their place. He even predicted the likely properties of three of the potential elements. The subsequent proof of many of his predictions within his lifetime brought fame to Mendeleyev as the founder of the periodic law.

Formulation of the Periodic Law

Mendeleyev published a textbook on organic chemistry in 1861 that had been awarded the prestigious Demidov Prize. He then set out to write another one. The result was *Osnovy Khimii* (1868–71; *The Principles of Chemistry*), which became a classic, running through many editions and many translations. When Mendeleyev began to compose the chapter on the halogen elements (chlorine and its analogs) at the end of the first volume, he compared the properties of this group of elements to those of the group of alkali metals such as sodium. Within these two groups of dissimilar elements, he discovered similarities in the progression of atomic weights, and he wondered if other groups of elements exhibited similar properties.

After studying the alkaline earths, Mendeleyev established that the order of atomic weights could be used not only to arrange the elements within each group but also to arrange the groups themselves. Thus, in his effort to make sense of the extensive knowledge that already existed of the chemical and physical properties of the chemical elements and their compounds, Mendeleyev discovered the periodic law.

His newly formulated law was announced before the Russian Chemical Society in March 1869 with the statement "elements arranged according to the value of their atomic weights present a clear periodicity of properties." Mendeleyev's law allowed him to build up a systematic table of all the 70 elements then known. He had such faith in the validity of the periodic law that he proposed changes to the generally accepted values for the atomic weight of a few elements and predicted the locations within the table of unknown elements together with their properties. At first the periodic system did not raise interest among chemists. However, with the discovery of the predicted elements, notably gallium in 1875, scandium in 1879, and germanium in 1886, it began to win wide acceptance. Gradually the periodic law and table became the framework for a great part of chemical theory. By the time Mendeleyev died in 1907, he enjoyed international recognition and had received distinctions and awards from many countries.

OTHER SCIENTIFIC ACHIEVEMENTS

Since Mendeleyev is best known today as the discoverer of the periodic law, his chemical career is often viewed as a long process of maturation of his main discovery. Indeed, in the three decades following his discovery, Mendeleyev himself offered many recollections suggesting that there had been a remarkable continuity in his career, from his early dissertations on isomorphism and specific volumes, which involved the study of the relations between various properties of chemical substances, to the periodic law itself. In this account, Mendeleyev mentioned the Karlsruhe congress as the major event that led him to the discovery of the relations between atomic weights and chemical properties.

In the field of chemical science, Mendeleyev made various contributions; for example, in the field of physical chemistry, he conducted a broad research program throughout his career that focused on gases and liquids. In 1860, while working in Heidelberg, he defined the "absolute point of ebullition" (the point at which a gas in a container will condense to a liquid solely by the application of pressure). In 1864 he formulated a theory (subsequently discredited) that solutions are chemical combinations in fixed proportions. In 1871, as he published the final volume of the first edition of his *Principles of Chemistry*, he was investigating the elasticity of gases and gave a formula for their deviation from Boyle's law (now also known as the Boyle-Mariotte law, the principle that the volume of a gas varies inversely with its pressure). In the 1880s he studied the thermal expansion of liquids.

A second major feature of Mendeleyev's scientific work is his theoretical inclinations. From the beginning of his career, he continually sought to shape a broad theoretical scheme in the tradition of natural philosophy. This effort can be seen in his early adoption of the type theory of the French chemist Charles Gerhardt and in his rejection of electrochemical dualism as suggested by the great Swedish chemist Jöns Jacob Berzelius. Before and during Mendeleyev's time, many attempts at classifying the elements were based on the hypothesis of the English chemist William Prout that all elements derived from a unique primary matter. Mendeleyev insisted that elements were true individuals, and he fought against those who, like the British scientist William Crookes, used his periodic system in support of Prout's hypothesis.

With the discovery of electrons and radioactivity in the 1890s, Mendeleyev perceived a threat to his theory of the individuality of elements. In *Popytka khimicheskogo ponimania mirovogo efira* (1902; *An Attempt Towards a Chemical Conception of the Ether*), he explained these phenomena as movements of ether around heavy atoms, and he tried to classify ether as a chemical element above the group of inert gases (or noble gases). This bold (and ultimately discredited) hypothesis was part of Mendeleyev's project of extending Newton's mechanics to chemistry in an attempt to unify the natural sciences.

IVAN PETROVICH PAVLOV

(b. Sept. 14 [Sept. 26, New Style], 1849, Ryazan, Russia—d. Feb. 27, 1936, Leningrad [now St. Petersburg])

Russian physiologist Ivan Petrovich Pavlov was known chiefly for his development of the concept of the conditioned reflex. In a now-classic experiment, he trained a hungry dog to salivate at the sound of a bell, which was previously associated with the sight of food. He developed a similar conceptual approach, emphasizing the importance of conditioning, in his pioneering studies relating human behaviour to the nervous system. He was awarded the Nobel Prize for Physiology or Medicine in 1904 for his work on digestive secretions.

LAWS OF CONDITIONED REFLEX

During the years 1890–1900 especially, and to a lesser extent until about 1930, Pavlov studied the secretory activity of digestion. He devised an operation to prepare a miniature stomach, or pouch; he isolated the stomach from ingested foods, while preserving its vagal nerve supply. The surgical procedure enabled him to study the gastrointestinal secretions in a normal animal over its life span. This work culminated in his book *Lectures on the Work of the Digestive Glands* in 1897.

By observing irregularities of secretions in normal unanesthetized animals, Pavlov was led to formulate the laws of the conditioned reflex, a subject that occupied his attention from about 1898 until 1930. He used the salivary secretion as a quantitative measure of the psychical, or subjective, activity of the animal, in order to emphasize the advantage of objective, physiological measures of mental phenomena and higher nervous activity. He sought analogies between the conditional (commonly though incorrectly translated as "conditioned") reflex and the spinal reflex.

According to the physiologist Sir Charles Sherrington, the spinal reflex is composed of integrated actions of the nervous system involving such complex components as the excitation and inhibition of many nerves, induction (*i.e.*, the increase or decrease of inhibition brought on by previous excitation), and the irradiation of nerve impulses to many nerve centres. To these components, Pavlov added cortical and subcortical influences, the mosaic action of the brain, the effect of sleep on the spread of inhibition, and the origin of neurotic disturbances principally through a collision, or conflict, between cortical excitation and inhibition.

Beginning about 1930, Pavlov tried to apply his laws to the explanation of human psychoses. He assumed that the excessive inhibition characteristic of a psychotic person was a protective mechanism—shutting out the external world—in that it excluded injurious stimuli that had previously caused extreme excitation. In Russia this idea became the basis for treating psychiatric patients in quiet and nonstimulating external surroundings. During this period Pavlov announced the important principle of the language function in the human as based on long chains of conditioned reflexes involving words. The function of language involves not only words, he held, but an elaboration of generalizations not possible in animals lower than the human.

ASSESSMENT

Pavlov was able to formulate the idea of the conditioned reflex because of his ability to reduce a complex situation to the simple terms of an experiment. Recognizing that in so doing he omitted the subjective component, he insisted that it was not possible to deal with mental phenomena scientifically except by reducing them to measurable physiological quantities.

Although Pavlov's work laid the basis for the scientific analysis of behaviour, and notwithstanding his stature as a scientist and physiologist, his work was subject to certain limitations. Philosophically, while recognizing the preeminence of the subjective and its independence of scientific methods, he did not, in his enthusiasm for science, clarify or define this separation. Clinically, he accepted uncritically psychiatric views concerning schizophrenia and paranoia, and he adopted such neural concepts as induction and irradiation as valid for higher mental activity. Many psychiatrists now consider his explanations too limited.

A.A. MICHELSON

(b. Dec. 19, 1852, Strelno, Prussia [now Strzelno, Pol.]—d. May 9, 1931, Pasadena, Calif., U.S.)

German-born American physicist Albert Abraham Michelson established the speed of light as a fundamental constant and pursued other spectroscopic and metrological investigations. He received the 1907 Nobel Prize for Physics.

Michelson came to the United States with his parents when he was two years old. From New York City, the family made its way to Virginia City, Nev., and San Francisco, where the elder Michelson prospered as a merchant. At 17, Michelson entered the United States Naval Academy at Annapolis, Md., where he did well in science but was rather below average in seamanship. He graduated in 1873, then served as science instructor at the academy from 1875 until 1879.

In 1878 Michelson began work on what was to be the passion of his life, the accurate measurement of the speed of light. He was able to obtain useful values with homemade apparatuses. Feeling the need to study optics before he could be qualified to make real progress, he traveled to Europe in 1880 and spent two years in Berlin, Heidelberg, and Paris, resigning from the U.S. Navy in 1881. Upon his return to the United States, he determined the velocity of light to be 299,853 kilometres (186,329 miles) per second, a value that remained the best for a generation, until Michelson bettered it.

While in Europe, Michelson began constructing an interferometer, a device designed to split a beam of light in two, send the parts along perpendicular paths, then bring them back together. If the light waves had, in the interim, fallen out of step, interference fringes of alternating light and dark bands would be obtained. From the width and number of those fringes, unprecedentedly delicate measurements could be made, comparing the velocity of light rays traveling at right angles to each other.

It was Michelson's intention to use the interferometer to measure the Earth's velocity against the "ether" that was then thought to make up the basic substratum of the universe. If the Earth were traveling through the light-conducting ether, then the speed of the light traveling in the same direction would be expected to be equal to the velocity of light plus the velocity of the Earth, whereas the speed of light traveling at right angles to the Earth's path would be expected to travel only at the velocity of light. His earliest experiments in Berlin showed no interference fringes, however, which seemed to signify that there was no difference in the speed of the light rays and, therefore, no Earth motion relative to the ether.

In 1883 he accepted a position as professor of physics at the Case School of Applied Science in Cleveland and there concentrated his efforts on improving the delicacy of his interferometer experiment. By 1887, with the help of his colleague, American chemist Edward Williams Morley, he was ready to announce the results of what has since come to be called the Michelson-Morley experiment. Those results were still negative; there were no interference fringes and apparently no motion of the Earth relative to the ether.

It was perhaps the most significant negative experiment in the history of science. In terms of classical Newtonian physics, the results were paradoxical. Evidently, the speed of light plus any other added velocity was still equal only to the speed of light. To explain the result of the Michelson-Morley experiment, physics had to be recast on a new and more refined foundation, something that resulted, eventually, in Albert Einstein's formulation of the theory of relativity in 1905.

In 1892 Michelson, after serving as professor of physics at Clark University at Worcester, Mass., from 1889, was appointed professor and the first head of the department of physics at the newly organized University of Chicago, a position he held until his retirement in 1929. From 1923 to 1927 he served as president of the National Academy of Sciences. In 1907 he became the first American ever to receive a Nobel Prize in the sciences, for his spectroscopic and metrological investigations, the first of many honours he was to receive.

Michelson advocated using some particular wavelength of light as a standard of distance (a suggestion generally accepted in 1960) and, in 1893, measured the standard metre in terms of the red light emitted by heated cadmium. His interferometer made it possible for him to determine the width of heavenly objects by matching the light rays from the two sides and noting the interference fringes that resulted. In 1920, using a 6-metre (20-foot) interferometer attached to a 254-centimetre (100-inch) telescope, he succeeded in measuring the diameter of the star Betelgeuse (Alpha Orionis) as 386,160,000 km (300 times the diameter of the Sun). This was the first substantially accurate determination of the size of a star.

In 1923 Michelson returned to the problem of the accurate measurement of the velocity of light. In the California mountains he surveyed a 35-kilometre pathway between two mountain peaks, determining the distance to an accuracy of less than 2.5 cm. He made use of a special eight-sided revolving mirror and obtained a value of 299,798 km/sec for the velocity of light. To refine matters further, he made use of a long, evacuated tube through which a light beam was reflected back and forth until it had traveled 16 km through a vacuum. Michelson died before the results of his final tests could be evaluated, but in 1933 the final figure was announced as 299,774 km/sec, a value less than 2 km/sec higher than the value accepted in the 1970s.

ROBERT KOCH

(b. Dec. 11, 1843, Clausthal, Hannover [now Clausthal-Zellerfeld, Ger.] — d. May 27, 1910, Baden-Baden, Ger.)

German physician Robert Heinrich Hermann Koch was one of the founders of bacteriology. He discovered the anthrax disease cycle (1876) and the bacteria responsible for tuberculosis (1882) and cholera (1883). For his discoveries in regard to tuberculosis, he received the Nobel Prize for Physiology or Medicine in 1905.

ANTHRAX RESEARCH

Koch's career began with his research on anthrax. He cultivated anthrax organisms in suitable media on microscope slides, demonstrated their growth into long filaments, and discovered the formation within them of oval, translucent bodies — dormant spores. Koch found that the dried spores could remain viable for years, even under exposed conditions. The finding explained the recurrence of the disease in pastures long unused for grazing, for the dormant spores could, under the right conditions, develop into the rod-shaped bacteria (bacilli) that cause anthrax. The anthrax life cycle, which Koch had discovered, was announced and illustrated at Breslau in 1876, on the invitation of Ferdinand Cohn, an eminent botanist. Julius Cohnheim, a famous pathologist, was deeply impressed by Koch's presentation. "It leaves nothing more to be proved," he said.

Koch worked out the details of his pure-culture techniques a few years later. That a disease organism might be cultured outside the body was a concept introduced by Louis Pasteur, but the pure-culture techniques for doing so were perfected by Koch, whose precise and ingenious experiments demonstrated the complete life cycle of an important organism. The anthrax work afforded for the first time convincing proof of the definite causal relation of a particular microorganism to a particular disease.

CONTRIBUTIONS TO GENERAL BACTERIOLOGY AND PATHOLOGY

In 1877 Koch published an important paper on the investigation, preservation, and photographing of bacteria. His work was illustrated by superb photomicrographs. In his paper he described his method of preparing thin layers of bacteria on glass slides and fixing them by gentle heat. Koch also invented the apparatus and the procedure for the very useful hanging-drop technique, whereby microorganisms could be cultured in a drop of nutrient solution on the underside of a glass slide.

In 1878 Koch summarized his experiments on the etiology of wound infection. By inoculating animals with material from various sources, he produced six types of infection, each caused by a specific microorganism. He then transferred these infections by inoculation through several kinds of animals, reproducing the original six types. In that study, he observed differences in pathogenicity for different species of hosts and demonstrated that the animal body is an excellent apparatus for the cultivation of bacteria.

Koch, now recognized as a scientific investigator of the first rank, obtained a position in Berlin in the Imperial Health Office, where he set up a laboratory in bacteriology. With his collaborators, he devised new research methods to isolate pathogenic bacteria. Koch determined guidelines to prove that a disease is caused by a specific organism. These four basic criteria, called Koch's postulates, are:

- A specific microorganism is always associated with a given disease.
- The microorganism can be isolated from the diseased animal and grown in pure culture in the laboratory.
- The cultured microbe will cause disease when transferred to a healthy animal.
- The same type of microorganism can be isolated from the newly infected animal.

STUDIES OF TUBERCULOSIS AND CHOLERA

Koch concentrated his efforts on the study of tuberculosis, with the aim of isolating its cause. Although it was suspected that tuberculosis was caused by an infectious agent, the organism had not yet been isolated and identified. By modifying the method of staining, Koch discovered the tubercle bacillus and established its presence in the tissues of animals and humans suffering from the disease. A fresh difficulty arose when for some time it proved impossible to grow the organism in pure culture. But eventually Koch succeeded in isolating the organism in a succession of media and induced tuberculosis in animals by inoculating them with it. Its etiologic role was thereby established. On March 24, 1882, Koch announced before the Physiological Society of Berlin that he had isolated and grown the tubercle bacillus, which he believed to be the cause of all forms of tuberculosis.

Meanwhile, Koch's work was interrupted by an outbreak of cholera in Egypt and the danger of its transmission to Europe. As a member of a German government commission, Koch went to Egypt to investigate the disease. Although he soon had reason to suspect a particular comma-shaped bacterium (vibrio) as the cause of cholera, the epidemic ended before he was able to confirm his hypothesis. Nevertheless, he raised awareness of amebic dysentery and differentiated two varieties of Egyptian conjunctivitis. Proceeding to India, where cholera is endemic, he completed his task, identifying both the organism responsible for the disease and its transmission via drinking water, food, and clothing.

Resuming his studies of tuberculosis, Koch investigated the effect an injection of dead bacilli had on a person who subsequently received a dose of living bacteria and concluded that he may have discovered a cure for the disease. In his studies he used as the active agent a sterile liquid produced from cultures of the bacillus. However, the liquid, which he named tuberculin (1890), proved disappointing, and sometimes dangerous, as a curative agent. Consequently, its importance as a means of detecting a present or past tubercular state was not immediately recognized. Additional work on tuberculosis came later, but, after the seeming debacle of tuberculin, Koch was also occupied with a great variety of investigations into diseases of humans and animals—studies of leprosy, bubonic plague, livestock diseases, and malaria.

In 1901 Koch reported work done on the pathogenicity of the human tubercle bacillus in domestic animals. He believed that infection of human beings by bovine tuberculosis is so rare that it is not necessary to take any measures against it. That conclusion was rejected by commissions of inquiry in Europe and America but extensive and important work was stimulated by Koch. As a result, successful measures of prophylaxis were devised.

SIGMUND FREUD

(b. May 6, 1856, Freiberg, Moravia, Austrian Empire [now Příbor, Czech Republic] — d. Sept. 23, 1939, London, Eng.)

Austrian neurologist Sigmund Freud was the founder of psychoanalysis. Freud may justly be called the most influential intellectual legislator of his age. His creation of psychoanalysis was at once a theory of the human psyche, a therapy for the relief of its ills, and an optic for the interpretation of culture and society. Despite repeated criticisms, attempted refutations, and qualifications of Freud's work, its spell remained powerful well after his death and in fields far removed from psychology as it is narrowly defined. If, as the American sociologist Philip Rieff once contended, "psychological man" replaced such earlier notions as political, religious, or economic man as the 20th century's dominant self-image, it is in no small measure due to the power of Freud's vision and the seeming inexhaustibility of the intellectual legacy he left behind.

EARLY TRAINING

In Freud's writing "Entwurf einer Psychologie" ("Project for a Scientific Psychology"), written in 1895 and published in 1950, he affirmed his intention to find a physiological and materialist basis for his theories of the psyche. In late 1885 Freud went to the Salpêtrière clinic in Paris, where he worked under the guidance of Jean-Martin Charcot. His 19 weeks in the French capital proved a turning point in his career, for Charcot's work with patients classified as "hysterics" introduced Freud to the possibility that psychological disorders might have their source in the mind rather than the brain.

Freud later developed a partnership with the physician Josef Breuer after his return to Vienna from Paris. Freud turned to a clinical practice in neuropsychology, and the office he established at Berggasse 19 was to remain his consulting room for almost half a century. Before their collaboration began, during the early 1880s, Breuer had treated a patient named Bertha Pappenheim— or "Anna O.," as she became known in the literature—who was suffering from a variety of hysterical symptoms. Rather than using hypnotic suggestion, as had Charcot, Breuer allowed her to lapse into a state resembling auto-hypnosis, in which she would talk about the initial manifestations of her symptoms. To Breuer's surprise, the very act of verbalization seemed to provide some relief from their hold over her (although later scholarship has cast doubt on its permanence). "The talking cure" or "chimney sweeping," as Breuer and Anna O., respectively, called it, seemed to act cathartically to produce an abreaction, or discharge, of the pent-up emotional blockage at the root of the pathological behaviour.

Psychoanalyst Sigmund Freud, known for his interpretations of the human psyche. Hulton Archive/ Getty Images

Psychoanalytic Theory

Freud, still beholden to Charcot's hypnotic method, did not grasp the full implications of Breuer's experience until a decade later, when he developed the technique of free association. In part an extrapolation of the automatic writing promoted by the German Jewish writer Ludwig Börne a century before, in part a result of his own clinical experience with other hysterics, this revolutionary method was announced in the work Freud published jointly with Breuer in 1895, *Studien über Hysterie* (*Studies in Hysteria*).

By encouraging the patient to express any random thoughts that came associatively to mind, the technique aimed at uncovering hitherto unarticulated material from the realm of the psyche that Freud, following a long tradition, called the unconscious. Difficulty in freely associating—sudden silences, stuttering, or the like—suggested to Freud the importance of the material struggling to be expressed, as well as the power of what he called the patient's defenses against that expression. Such blockages Freud dubbed resistance, which had to be broken down in order to reveal hidden conflicts. Unlike Charcot and Breuer, Freud came to the conclusion, based on his clinical experience with female hysterics, that the most insistent source of resisted material was sexual in nature. And even more momentously, he linked the etiology of neurotic symptoms to the same struggle between a sexual feeling or urge and the psychic defenses against it.

Screen Memories

At first, however, Freud was uncertain about the precise status of the sexual component in this dynamic conception of the psyche. In a now famous letter to Fliess of Sept. 2, 1897, he concluded that, rather than being memories of actual events, these shocking recollections were the residues of infantile impulses and desires to be seduced by an adult. What was recalled was not a genuine memory but what he would later call a screen memory, or fantasy, hiding a primitive wish. That is, rather than stressing the corrupting initiative of adults in the etiology of neuroses, Freud concluded that the fantasies and yearnings of the child were at the root of later conflict.

THE INTERPRETATION OF DREAMS

In what many commentators consider Freud's master work, *Die Traumdeutung* (*The Interpretation of Dreams*), published in 1899, but given the date of the dawning century to emphasize its epochal character, Freud interspersed evidence from his own dreams with evidence from those recounted in his clinical practice. Freud contended that dreams played a fundamental role in the psychic economy. The mind's energy—which Freud called libido and identified principally, but not exclusively, with the sexual drive—was a fluid and malleable force capable of excessive and disturbing power. Needing to be discharged to ensure pleasure and prevent pain, it sought whatever outlet it might find. If denied the gratification provided by direct motor action, libidinal energy could seek its release through mental channels.

The Interpretation of Dreams provides a hermeneutic for the unmasking of the dream's disguise, or dreamwork, as Freud called it. The manifest content of the dream, that which is remembered and reported, must be understood as veiling a latent meaning. Dreams defy logical entailment and narrative coherence, for they intermingle the residues of immediate daily experience with the deepest, often most infantile wishes. Yet they can be ultimately decoded, and their mystifying effects can be reversed.

FURTHER THEORETICAL DEVELOPMENT

In 1904 Freud published *Zur Psychopathologie des Alltagslebens* (*The Psychopathology of Everyday Life*), in which he explored such seemingly insignificant errors as slips of the tongue or pen (later colloquially called Freudian slips), misreadings, or forgetting of names. These errors Freud understood to have symptomatic and thus interpretable importance. But unlike dreams they need not betray a repressed infantile wish yet can arise from more immediate hostile, jealous, or egoistic causes.

In 1905 Freud extended the scope of this analysis by examining *Der Witz und seine Beziehung zum Unbewussten* (*Jokes and Their Relation to the Unconscious*). Invoking the idea of "joke-work" as a process comparable to dreamwork, he also acknowledged the double-sided quality of jokes, at once consciously contrived and unconsciously revealing. Insofar as jokes are more deliberate than dreams or slips, they draw on the rational dimension of the psyche that Freud was to call the ego as much as on what he was to call the id. Also in that year, Freud published the work that first thrust him into the limelight as the alleged champion of a pansexualist understanding of the mind. *Drei Abhandlungen zur Sexualtheorie* (*Three Contributions to the Sexual Theory*, later translated as *Three Essays on the Theory of Sexuality*) outlined in greater detail than before his reasons for emphasizing the sexual component in the development of both normal and pathological behaviour.

According to Freud, an originally polymorphous sexuality first seeks gratification orally through sucking at the mother's breast. Initially unable to distinguish between self and breast, the infant soon comes to appreciate its mother as the first external love object. After the oral phase, during the second year, the child's focus shifts to its anus, stimulated by the struggle over toilet training.

During the anal phase the child's pleasure in defecation is confronted with the demands of self-control. The third phase, lasting from about the fourth to the sixth year, he called the phallic.

PSYCHONEUROSES AND ANALYSIS

In addition to the neurosis of hysteria, with its conversion of affective conflicts into bodily symptoms, Freud developed complicated etiological explanations for other typical neurotic behaviour, such as obsessive-compulsions, paranoia, and narcissism. These he called psychoneuroses, because of their rootedness in childhood conflicts, as opposed to the actual neuroses such as hypochondria, neurasthenia, and anxiety neurosis, which are due to problems in the present (the last, for example, being caused by the physical suppression of sexual release).

Freud developed the celebrated technique of having the patient lie on a couch, not looking directly at the analyst, and free to fantasize with as little intrusion of the analyst's real personality as possible. Restrained and neutral, the analyst functions as a screen for the displacement of early emotions, both erotic and aggressive. This transference onto the analyst is itself a kind of neurosis, but one in the service of an ultimate working through of the conflicting feelings it expresses. Only certain illnesses, however, are open to this treatment, for it demands the ability to redirect libidinal energy outward. The psychoses, Freud sadly concluded, are based on the redirection of libido back onto the patient's ego and cannot therefore be relieved by transference in the analytic situation. How successful psychoanalytic therapy has been in the treatment of psychoneuroses remains, however, a matter of considerable dispute.

Id, Ego, and Superego

Freud later attempted to clarify the relationship between his earlier topographical division of the psyche into the unconscious, preconscious, and conscious and his subsequent structural categorization into id, ego, and superego. The id was defined in terms of the most primitive urges for gratification in the infant, urges dominated by the desire for pleasure through the release of tension and the cathexis of energy. The id is ruled by what Freud called the primary process directly expressing somatically generated instincts. The secondary process that results leads to the growth of the ego, which follows what Freud called the reality principle in contradistinction to the pleasure principle dominating the id.

The last component in Freud's trichotomy, the superego, develops from the internalization of society's moral commands through identification with parental dictates. Only partly conscious, the superego gains some of its punishing force by borrowing certain aggressive elements in the id, which are turned inward against the ego and produce feelings of guilt. But it is largely through the internalization of social norms that the superego is constituted, an acknowledgement that prevents psychoanalysis from conceptualizing the psyche in purely biologistic or individualistic terms.

Freud's understanding of the primary process underwent a crucial shift in the course of his career. Initially he counterposed a libidinal drive that seeks sexual pleasure to a self-preservation drive whose telos is survival. But in 1914, while examining the phenomenon of narcissism, he came to consider the latter instinct as merely a variant of the former. Unable to accept so monistic a drive theory, Freud sought a new dualistic alternative. He arrived at the speculative assertion that there exists in the psyche an innate, regressive drive for stasis that aims to end life's inevitable tension. This striving for rest he christened the Nirvana principle and the drive underlying it the death instinct, or Thanatos, which he could substitute for self-preservation as the contrary of the life instinct, or Eros.

MAX PLANCK

(b. April 23, 1858, Kiel, Schleswig [Germany]—d. Oct. 4, 1947, Göttingen, W. Ger.)

German theoretical physicist Max Planck originated quantum theory, which won him the Nobel Prize for Physics in 1918. Planck made many contributions to theoretical physics, but his fame rests primarily on his role as originator of the quantum theory. This theory revolutionized modern understanding of atomic and subatomic processes, just as Albert Einstein's theory of relativity revolutionized the understanding of space and time. Together they constitute the fundamental theories of 20th-century physics. Both have forced humans to revise some of their most cherished philosophical beliefs, and both have led to industrial and military applications that affect every aspect of modern life.

ENERGY AND THERMODYNAMICS

Planck's intellectual capacities were brought to a focus as the result of his independent study, especially of Rudolf Clausius's writings on thermodynamics.

Planck recalled that his "original decision to devote myself to science was a direct result of the discovery . . . that the laws of human reasoning coincide with the laws governing the sequences of the impressions we receive from the world about us; that, therefore, pure reasoning can enable man to gain an insight into the mechanism of the [world]. . . ." In other words, he deliberately decided to become a theoretical physicist at a time when theoretical physics was not yet recognized as a discipline in its own right. But he went further: he concluded that the existence of physical laws presupposes that the "outside world is something independent from man, something absolute, and the quest for the laws which apply to this absolute appeared . . . as the most sublime scientific pursuit in life."

The first instance of an absolute in nature that impressed Planck deeply was the law of the conservation of energy, the first law of thermodynamics. Later, during his university years, he became equally convinced that the entropy law, the second law of thermodynamics, was also an absolute law of nature. The second law lay at the core of the researches that led him to discover the quantum of action, now known as Planck's constant h, in 1900.

PLANCK'S RADIATION LAW

One of the first problems that Planck attempted to solve concerned blackbody radiation. By the 1890s various experimental and theoretical attempts had been made to determine the spectral energy distribution—the curve displaying how much radiant energy is emitted at different frequencies for a given temperature of the blackbody. Planck was particularly attracted to the formula found in 1896 by his colleague Wilhelm Wien, and he subsequently made a series of attempts to derive "Wien's law" on the basis of the second law of thermodynamics. By October 1900, however, others had found definite indications that Wien's law, while valid at high frequencies, broke down completely at low frequencies.

Planck learned of these results just before a meeting of the German Physical Society on Oct. 19, 1900. He knew how the entropy of the radiation had to depend mathematically upon its energy in the high-frequency region if Wien's law held there. He also saw what this dependence had to be in the low-frequency region in order to reproduce the experimental results there. Planck guessed, therefore, that he should try to combine these two expressions in the simplest way possible, and to transform the result into a formula relating the energy of the radiation to its frequency.

The result, which is known as Planck's radiation law, was hailed as indisputably correct. To Planck, however, it was simply a guess, a "lucky intuition." If it was to be taken seriously, it had to be derived somehow from first principles. That was the task to which Planck immediately directed his energies, and by Dec. 14, 1900, he had succeeded—but at great cost. To achieve his goal, Planck found that he had to relinquish one of his own most cherished beliefs, that the second law of thermodynamics was an absolute law of nature.

In addition, Planck had to assume that the oscillators comprising the blackbody and re-emitting the radiant energy incident upon them could not absorb this energy continuously but only in discrete amounts, in quanta of energy; only by statistically distributing these quanta, each containing an amount of energy hv proportional to its frequency, over all of the oscillators present in the blackbody could Planck derive the formula he had hit upon two months earlier. He adduced additional evidence for the importance of his formula by using it to evaluate the constant h (his value was 6.55×10^{-27} erg-second, close to the modern value), as well as the so-called Boltzmann constant (the fundamental constant in kinetic theory and statistical mechanics), Avogadro's number, and the charge of the electron.

As time went on physicists recognized ever more clearly that—because Planck's constant was not zero but had a small but finite value—the microphysical world, the world of atomic dimensions, could not in principle be described by ordinary classical mechanics.

In 1905, independently of Planck's work, Albert Einstein argued that under certain circumstances radiant energy itself seemed to consist of quanta (light quanta, later called photons), and in 1907 he showed the generality of the quantum hypothesis by using it to interpret the temperature dependence of the specific heats of solids. In October 1911 he was among the group of prominent physicists who attended the first Solvay conference in Brussels. The discussions there stimulated Henri Poincaré to provide a mathematical proof that Planck's radiation law necessarily required the introduction of quanta.

LATER CAREER

Planck was 42 years old in 1900 when he made the famous discovery that in 1918 won him the Nobel Prize for Physics and that brought him many other honours. It is not surprising that he subsequently made no discoveries of comparable importance. Nevertheless, he continued to contribute at a high level to various branches of optics, thermodynamics and statistical mechanics, physical chemistry, and other fields. He was also the first prominent physicist to champion Einstein's special theory of relativity (1905). "The velocity of light is to the Theory of Relativity," Planck remarked, "as the elementary quantum of action is to the Quantum Theory; it is its absolute core."

In his later years, Planck devoted more and more of his writings to philosophical, aesthetic, and religious questions. Planck believed that the physical universe is an objective entity existing independently of humans; the observer and the observed are not intimately coupled.

NETTIE MARIA STEVENS

(b. July 7, 1861, Cavendish, Vt., U.S. — d. May 4, 1912, Baltimore, Md.)

American biologist and geneticist Nettie Maria Stevens was one of the first scientists to find that sex is determined by a particular configuration of chromosomes.

Stevens's early life is somewhat obscure, although it is known that she taught school and attended the State Normal School (now Westfield State College) in Westfield, Massachusetts, in 1881–83. In 1896 she entered Stanford University, earning a B.A. in 1899 and an M.A. in 1900. She began doctoral studies in biology at Bryn Mawr College, which included a year of study (1901–02) at the Zoological Station in Naples, Italy, and at the Zoological Institute of the University of Würzburg, Germany. She received a Ph.D. from Bryn Mawr in 1903 and remained at the college as a research fellow in biology for a year, as reader in experimental morphology for another year, and as associate in experimental morphology from 1905 until her death.

Stevens's earliest field of research was the morphology and taxonomy of the ciliate protozoa; her first published paper, in 1901, had dealt with such a protozoan. She soon turned to cytology and the regenerative process. One of her major papers in that field was written in 1904 with zoologist and geneticist Thomas Hunt Morgan, who in 1933 would win the Nobel Prize for his work. Her investigations into regeneration led her to a study of differentiation in embryos and then to a study of chromosomes. In 1905, after experiments with the yellow mealworm (*Tenebrio molitor*), she published a paper in which she announced her finding that a particular combination of the chromosomes known as X and Y was responsible for the determination of the sex of an individual.

This discovery, also announced independently that year by Edmund Beecher Wilson of Columbia University, not only ended the long-standing debate over whether sex was a matter of heredity or embryonic environmental influence but also was the first firm link between a heritable characteristic and a particular chromosome. Stevens continued her research on the chromosome makeup of various insects, discovering supernumerary chromosomes in certain insects and the paired state of chromosomes in flies and mosquitoes.

WILLIAM BATESON

(b. Aug. 8, 1861, Whitby, Yorkshire, Eng.—d. Feb. 8, 1926, London)

British biologist William Bateson founded and named the science of genetics. His experiments provided evidence basic to the modern understanding of heredity. A dedicated evolutionist, he cited embryo studies to support his contention in 1885 that chordates evolved from primitive echinoderms, a view now widely accepted. In 1894 he published his conclusion (*Materials for the Study of Variation*) that evolution could not occur through a continuous variation of species, since distinct features often appeared or disappeared suddenly in plants and animals. Realizing that discontinuous variation could be understood only after something was known about the inheritance of traits, Bateson began work on the experimental breeding of plants and animals.

In 1900, he discovered an article, "Experiments with Plant Hybrids," written by Gregor Mendel, an Austrian monk, 34 years earlier. The paper, found in the same year by Hugo de Vries, Carl Correns, and Erich Tschermak von Seysenegg, dealt with the appearance of certain features in successive generations of garden peas. Bateson noted that his breeding results were explained perfectly by Mendel's paper and that the monk had succinctly described the transmission of elements governing heritable traits in his plants.

Bateson translated Mendel's paper into English and during the next 10 years became Mendel's champion in England, corroborating his principles experimentally. He published, with Reginald Punnett, the results of a series of breeding experiments (1905–08) that not only extended Mendel's principles to animals (poultry) but showed also that certain features were consistently inherited together, apparently counter to Mendel's findings. This phenomenon, which came to be termed linkage, is now known to be the result of the occurrence of genes located in close proximity on the same chromosome. Bateson's experiments also demonstrated a dependence of certain characters on two or more genes. Unfortunately, he misinterpreted his results, refusing to accept the interpretation of linkage advanced by the geneticist Thomas Hunt Morgan. In fact, he opposed Morgan's entire chromosome theory, advocating his own vibratory theory of inheritance, founded on laws of force and motion, a concept that found little acceptance among other scientists.

Bateson later became the first British professor of genetics at the University of Cambridge (1908). He left this chair in 1910 to spend the rest of his life directing the John Innes Horticultural Institution at Merton, South London (later moved to Norwich), transforming it into a centre for genetic research. His books include *Mendel's Principles of Heredity* (1902, 2nd edition published in 1909) and *Problems of Genetics* (1913).

PIERRE CURIE

(b. May 15, 1859, Paris, France—d. April 19, 1906, Paris)

Pierre Curie was a French physical chemist and cowinner of the Nobel Prize for Physics in 1903. He and his wife, Marie Curie, discovered radium and polonium in

their investigation of radioactivity. An exceptional physicist, he was one of the main founders of modern physics.

Educated by his father, a doctor, Pierre Curie developed a passion for mathematics at the age of 14 and showed
a particular aptitude for spatial geometry, which later
helped him in his work on crystallography. Matriculating
at the age of 16 and obtaining his *licence ès sciences* at 18, he
was taken on as laboratory assistant at the Sorbonne in
1878. There Curie carried out his first work on the calculation of the wavelength of heat waves. This was followed by
very important studies on crystals, in which he was helped
by his elder brother Jacques. The problem of the distribution of crystalline matter according to the laws of symmetry
was to become one of his major preoccupations.

The Curie brothers associated the phenomenon of
pyroelectricity with a change in the volume of the crystal
in which it appears, and thus they arrived at the discovery
of piezoelectricity. Later, Pierre was able to formulate the
principle of symmetry, which states the impossibility of
bringing about a specific physical process in an environment lacking a certain minimal dissymmetry characteristic
of the process. Further, this dissymmetry cannot be found
in the effect if it is not preexistent in the cause. He went on
to define the symmetry of different physical phenomena.

Appointed supervisor (1882) at the School of Physics
and Industrial Chemistry at Paris, Curie resumed his own
research and, after a long study of buffered movements,
managed to perfect the analytical balance by creating an
aperiodic balance with direct reading of the last weights.
Then he began his celebrated studies on magnetism. He
undertook to write a doctoral thesis with the aim of discovering if there exist any transitions between the three
types of magnetism: ferromagnetism, paramagnetism,
and diamagnetism. In order to measure the magnetic

coefficients, he constructed a torsion balance that measured 0.01 mg, which, in a simplified version, is still used and called the magnetic balance of Curie and Chèneveau. He discovered that the magnetic coefficients of attraction of paramagnetic bodies vary in inverse proportion to the absolute temperature—Curie's Law. He then established an analogy between paramagnetic bodies and perfect gases and, as a result of this, between ferromagnetic bodies and condensed fluids. The totally different character of paramagnetism and diamagnetism demonstrated by Curie was later explained theoretically by Paul Langevin. In 1895 Curie defended his thesis on magnetism and obtained a doctorate of science.

In the spring of 1894, Curie met Marie Skłodowska. Their marriage (July 25, 1895) marked the beginning of a world-famous scientific achievement, beginning with the discovery (1898) of polonium and then of radium. The phenomenon of radioactivity, discovered in 1896 by Henri Becquerel, had attracted Marie Curie's attention. She and Pierre determined to study a mineral, pitchblende, the specific activity of which is superior to that of pure uranium. While working with Marie to extract pure substances from ores, an undertaking that really required industrial resources but that they achieved in relatively primitive conditions, Pierre himself concentrated on the physical study (including luminous and chemical effects) of the new radiations. Through the action of magnetic fields on the rays given out by the radium, he proved the existence of particles electrically positive, negative, and neutral; these Ernest Rutherford was afterward to call alpha, beta, and gamma rays. Pierre then studied these radiations by calorimetry and also observed the physiological effects of radium, thus opening the way to radium therapy.

Refusing a chair at the University of Geneva in order to continue his joint work with Marie, Pierre Curie was appointed lecturer (1900) and professor (1904) at the Sorbonne. He was elected to the Academy of Sciences (1905), having received the Royal Society's Davy Medal jointly with Marie in 1903 and, jointly with her and Becquerel, the Nobel Prize for Physics. He was run over by a dray, which is a heavy cart used for hauling material, in the rue Dauphine in Paris in 1906 and died instantly. His complete works were published posthumously in 1908.

MARIE CURIE

(b. Nov. 7, 1867, Warsaw, Poland, Russian Empire—d. July 4, 1934, near Sallanches, France)

Polish-born French physicist Marie Curie (née Maria Skłodowska) was famous for her work on radioactivity. Curie was the first woman to win a Nobel Prize, and she is the only woman to win the award in two different fields. With Henri Becquerel and her husband, Pierre Curie, she was awarded the 1903 Nobel Prize for Physics. She was the sole winner of the 1911 Nobel Prize for Chemistry.

In 1891 Curie went to Paris and began to follow the lectures of Paul Appel, Gabriel Lippmann, and Edmond Bouty at the Sorbonne. There she met physicists who were already well known—Jean Perrin, Charles Maurain, and Aimé Cotton. She worked far into the night in her student-quarters garret and virtually lived on bread and butter and tea. She came first in the *licence* of physical sciences in 1893 and began to work in Lippmann's research laboratory. In 1894 she was placed second in the *licence* of mathematical sciences. It was in the spring of that year that she met Pierre Curie. They married the following year.

Following Henri Becquerel's discovery (1896) of a new phenomenon (which later was called "radioactivity"), Marie Curie, looking for a subject for a thesis, decided to find out if the property discovered in uranium was to be found in other matter. She discovered that this was true for thorium at the same time as G.C. Schmidt. Turning her attention to minerals, she found her interest drawn to pitchblende, a mineral whose activity, superior to that of pure uranium, could be explained only by the presence in the ore of small quantities of an unknown substance of very high activity.

Pierre Curie then joined her in the work that she had undertaken to resolve this problem and that led to the discovery of the new elements, polonium and radium. While Pierre Curie devoted himself chiefly to the physical study of the new radiations, Marie Curie struggled to obtain pure radium in the metallic state—achieved with the help of the

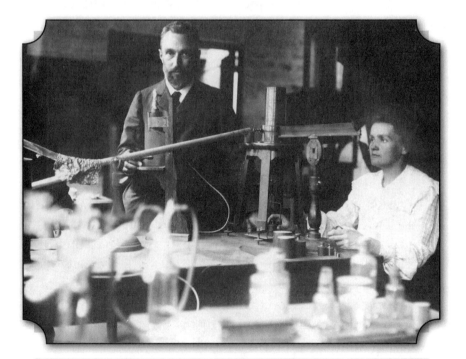

Marie Curie, who received the Nobel Prize in chemistry in 1911, working in a lab with her husband Pierre Curie. Fox Photos/Hulton Archive/ Getty Images

chemist André-Louis Debierne, one of Pierre Curie's pupils. On the results of this research, Marie Curie received her doctorate of science in June 1903 and, with Pierre, was awarded the Davy Medal of the Royal Society. That was also the year in which they shared with Becquerel the Nobel Prize for Physics for the discovery of radioactivity.

The birth of her two daughters, Irène and Ève, in 1897 and 1904 did not interrupt Marie's intensive scientific work. She was appointed lecturer in physics at the École Normale Supérieure for girls in Sèvres (1900) and introduced there a method of teaching based on experimental demonstrations. In December 1904 she was appointed chief assistant in the laboratory directed by Pierre Curie.

The sudden death of Pierre Curie (April 19, 1906) was a bitter blow to Marie Curie, but it was also a decisive turning point in her career. Henceforth she was to devote all her energy to completing alone the scientific work that they had undertaken. On May 13, 1906, she was appointed to the professorship that had been left vacant on her husband's death; she was the first woman to teach in the Sorbonne. In 1908 she became titular professor, and in 1910 her fundamental treatise on radioactivity was published. After being awarded a second Nobel Prize, for the isolation of pure radium, she saw the completion of the building of the laboratories of the Radium Institute (Institut du Radium) at the University of Paris.

Throughout World War I, Marie Curie, with the help of her daughter Irène, devoted herself to the development of the use of X-radiography. In 1918 the Radium Institute, the staff of which Irène had joined, began to operate in earnest, and it was to become a universal centre for nuclear physics and chemistry. Now at the highest point of her fame, Marie Curie devoted her researches to the study of the chemistry of radioactive substances and the medical applications of these substances.

In 1921, accompanied by her two daughters, Marie Curie made a triumphant journey to the United States, where President Warren G. Harding presented her with a gram of radium bought as the result of a collection among American women. She gave lectures, especially in Belgium, Brazil, Spain, and Czechoslovakia. She was made a member of the Academy of Medicine in 1922, and also was a member of the International Commission on Intellectual Co-operation by the Council of the League of Nations. In addition, she had the satisfaction of seeing the development of the Curie Foundation in Paris and the inauguration in 1932 in Warsaw of the Radium Institute, of which her sister Bronisława became director.

One of Marie Curie's outstanding achievements was to have understood the need to accumulate intense radioactive sources, not only to treat illness but also to maintain an abundant supply for research in nuclear physics. The resultant stockpile was an unrivaled instrument until the appearance after 1930 of particle accelerators. The existence of a stock of 1.5 grams of radium in Paris at the Radium Institute—in which, over a period of several years, radium D and polonium had accumulated—made a decisive contribution to the success of the experiments undertaken in the years around 1930, in particular those performed by Irène Curie in conjunction with Frédéric Joliot, whom she had married in 1926. This work prepared the way for the discovery of the neutron by Sir James Chadwick and, above all, for the discovery in 1934 by Irène and Frédéric Joliot-Curie of artificial radioactivity.

A few months after this discovery, Marie Curie died as a result of leukemia caused by the action of radiation. Her contribution to physics had been immense, not only in her own work, the importance of which had been demonstrated by the award to her of two Nobel Prizes, but because of her influence on subsequent generations of nuclear physicists and chemists.

HENRIETTA SWAN LEAVITT
(b. July 4, 1868, Lancaster, Mass., U.S.—d. Dec. 12, 1921, Cambridge, Mass.)

American astronomer Henrietta Swan Leavitt was known for her discovery of the relationship between period and luminosity in Cepheid variables, pulsating stars that vary regularly in brightness in periods ranging from a few days to several months.

Leavitt attended Oberlin College for two years (1886–88) and then transferred to the Society for the Collegiate Instruction of Women (later Radcliffe College), from which she graduated in 1892. Following an interest aroused in her senior year, she became a volunteer assistant in the Harvard Observatory in 1895. In 1902 she received a permanent staff appointment. From the outset she was employed in the observatory's great project, begun by Edward C. Pickering, of determining the brightnesses of all measurable stars. In this work she was associated with the older Williamina Fleming and the more nearly contemporary Annie Jump Cannon.

Leavitt soon advanced from routine work to a position as head of the photographic stellar photometry department. A new phase of the work began in 1907 with Pickering's ambitious plan to ascertain photographically standardized values for stellar magnitudes. The vastly increased accuracy permitted by photographic techniques, which unlike the subjective eye were not misled by the different colours of the stars, depended upon the establishment of a basic sequence of standard magnitudes for comparison. The problem was given to Leavitt, who began with a sequence of 46 stars in the vicinity of the north celestial pole. Devising new methods of analysis, she determined their magnitudes and then those of a much larger sample in the same region, extending the scale of standard brightnesses down to the 21st magnitude. These standards were published in 1912 and 1917.

She then established secondary standard sequences of from 15 to 22 reference stars in each of 48 selected "Harvard Standard Regions" of the sky, using photographs supplied by observatories around the world. Her North Polar Sequence was adopted for the Astrographic Map of the Sky, an international project undertaken in 1913, and by the time of her death she had completely determined magnitudes for stars in 108 areas of the sky. Her system remained in general use until improved technology made possible photoelectrical measurements of far greater accuracy. One result of her work on stellar magnitudes was her discovery of 4 novas and some 2,400 variable stars, the latter figure comprising more than half of all those known even by 1930. Leavitt continued her work at the Harvard Observatory until her death.

Leavitt's outstanding achievement was her discovery in 1912 that in a certain class of variable stars, the Cepheid variables, the period of the cycle of fluctuation in brightness is highly regular and is determined by the actual luminosity of the star. The subsequent calibration of the period-luminosity curve allowed American astronomers Edwin Hubble, Harlow Shapley, and others to determine the distances of many Cepheid stars and consequently of the star clusters and galaxies in which they were observed. The most dramatic application was Hubble's use in 1924 of a Cepheid variable to determine the distance to the great nebula in Andromeda, which was the first distance measurement for a galaxy outside the Milky Way. Although it was later discovered that there are actually two different types of Cepheid variable, the same method can still be applied separately to each type.

ERNEST RUTHERFORD

(b. Aug. 30, 1871, Spring Grove, N.Z.—d. Oct. 19, 1937, Cambridge, Cambridgeshire, Eng.)

New Zealand-born British physicist Ernest Rutherford was considered the greatest experimentalist since Michael Faraday (1791–1867). Rutherford was the central figure in the study of radioactivity, and with his concept of the nuclear atom he led the exploration of nuclear physics. He won the Nobel Prize for Chemistry in 1908, was president of the Royal Society (1925–30) and the British Association for the Advancement of Science (1923), was conferred the Order of Merit in 1925, and was raised to the peerage as Lord Rutherford of Nelson in 1931.

UNIVERSITY OF CAMBRIDGE

In 1895 Rutherford won a scholarship that had been created with profits from the famous Great Exhibition of 1851 in London. He chose to continue his study at the Cavendish Laboratory of the University of Cambridge, which J.J. Thomson, Europe's leading expert on electromagnetic radiation, had taken over in 1884. At Cambridge, Rutherford determined that a magnetized needle lost some of its magnetization in a magnetic field produced by an alternating current. This made the needle a detector of electromagnetic waves, a phenomenon that had only recently been discovered. Rutherford's apparatus for detecting electromagnetic waves, or radio waves, was simple and had commercial potential. He spent the next year in the Cavendish Laboratory increasing the range and sensitivity of his device, which could receive signals from half a mile away.

Rutherford accepted Thomson's invitation to collaborate on an investigation of the way in which X-rays changed the conductivity of gases. This yielded a classic paper on ionization—the breaking of atoms or molecules into positive and negative parts (ions)—and the charged particles' attraction to electrodes of the opposite polarity. He then pursued other radiations that produced ions, looking first at ultraviolet radiation and then at radiation emitted by uranium. Placement of uranium near thin foils revealed to Rutherford that the radiation was more complex than previously thought: one type was easily absorbed or blocked by a very thin foil, but another type often penetrated the same thin foils. He named these radiation types alpha and beta, respectively, for simplicity.

McGill University

Rutherford's research ability won him a professorship at McGill University, Montreal, which had an exceptionally well-equipped laboratory. Turning his attention to another of the few elements then known to be radioactive, he and a colleague found that thorium emitted a gaseous radioactive product, which he called "emanation." This in turn left a solid active deposit, which soon was resolved into thorium A, B, C, and so on. Curiously, after chemical treatment, some radioelements lost their radioactivity but eventually regained it, while other materials, initially strong, gradually lost activity. This led to the concept of half-life—in modern terms, the interval of time required for one-half of the atomic nuclei of a radioactive sample to decay—which ranges from seconds to billions of years and is unique for each radioelement and thus an excellent identifying tag.

Rutherford recognized his need for expert chemical help with the growing number of radioelements. Sequentially, he attracted the skills of Frederick Soddy, a demonstrator at McGill; Bertram Borden Boltwood, a professor at Yale University; and Otto Hahn, a postdoctoral researcher from Germany. With Soddy, Rutherford in 1902–03 developed the transformation theory, or disintegration theory, as an explanation for radioactivity—his greatest accomplishment at McGill. Rutherford and Soddy claimed that the energy of radioactivity came from within the atom, and the spontaneous emission of an alpha or beta particle signified a chemical change from one element into another.

Before long it was recognized that the radioelements fell into three families, or decay series, headed by uranium, thorium, and actinium and all ending in inactive lead. Rutherford determined that the alpha particle carried a positive charge, but he could not distinguish whether it was a hydrogen or helium ion.

UNIVERSITY OF MANCHESTER

In 1907 Rutherford accepted a chair at the University of Manchester, whose physics laboratory was excelled in England only by Thomson's Cavendish Laboratory.

With the German physicist Hans Geiger, Rutherford developed an electrical counter for ionized particles; when perfected by

Ernest Rutherford. Library of Congress, Washington, D.C. (neg. no. 36570u)

Geiger, the Geiger counter became the universal tool for measuring radioactivity. Rutherford and his student Thomas Royds were able to isolate some alpha particles and perform a spectrochemical analysis, proving that the particles were helium ions. Boltwood then visited Rutherford's laboratory, and together they redetermined the rate of production of helium by radium, from which they calculated a precise value of Avogadro's number.

THE RUTHERFORD GOLD-FOIL EXPERIMENT

In 1911, Rutherford disproved William Thomson's model of the atom as a uniformly distributed substance. Because a few of the alpha particles in his beam were scattered by large angles after striking the gold foil, Rutherford knew that the gold atom's mass must be concentrated in a tiny, dense nucleus. Continuing his long-standing interest in the alpha particle, Rutherford studied its slight scattering when it hit a foil. Geiger joined him, and they obtained ever more quantitative data. In 1909 when an undergraduate, Ernest Marsden, needed a research project, Rutherford suggested that he look for large-angle scattering. Marsden found that a small number of alphas were turned more than 90 degrees from their original direction.

THE RUTHERFORD ATOMIC MODEL

Pondering how such a heavy, charged particle as the alpha could be turned by electrostatic attraction or repulsion through such a large angle, Rutherford conceived in 1911 that the atom could not be a uniform solid but rather consisted mostly of empty space, with its mass concentrated in a tiny nucleus. This insight, combined with his supporting experimental evidence, was Rutherford's greatest scientific contribution, but it received little attention beyond Manchester.

In 1913, however, the Danish physicist Niels Bohr showed its importance. Bohr had visited Rutherford's laboratory the year before, and he returned as a faculty member for the period 1914–16. Radioactivity, he explained, lies in the nucleus, while chemical properties are due to orbital electrons. His theory wove the new concept of quanta (or specific discrete energy values) into the electrodynamics of orbits, and he explained spectral lines as the release or absorption of energy by electrons as they jump from orbit to orbit. Henry Moseley, another of Rutherford's many pupils, similarly explained the sequence of the X-ray spectrum of elements as due to the charge on the nucleus. Thus, a coherent new picture of atomic physics, as well as the field of nuclear physics, was developed.

Rutherford later examined the collision of alpha particles with gases. With hydrogen, as expected, nuclei (individual protons) were propelled to the detector. But, surprisingly, protons also appeared when alphas crashed into nitrogen. In 1919 Rutherford explained his third great discovery: he had artificially provoked a nuclear reaction in a stable element.

RETURN TO CAMBRIDGE

Such nuclear reactions occupied Rutherford for the remainder of his career, which was spent back at the University of Cambridge, where he succeeded Thomson in 1919 as director of the Cavendish Laboratory.

The Cavendish was home to exciting work. The neutron's existence had been predicted in a speech by Rutherford in 1920. After a long search, Rutherford's colleague, physicist James Chadwick, discovered this neutral particle in 1932, indicating that the nucleus was composed of neutrons and protons. With a gift of some of the newly discovered heavy water from the United States, in 1934 Rutherford, Australian physicist Mark Oliphant, and German physical chemist Paul Harteck bombarded deuterium with deuterons, producing tritium in the first fusion reaction.

CARL JUNG

(b. July 26, 1875, Kesswil, Switz.—d. June 6, 1961, Küsnacht)

Swiss psychologist and psychiatrist Carl Jung founded analytic psychology, in some aspects a response to Sigmund Freud's psychoanalysis. Jung proposed and developed the concepts of the extraverted and the introverted personality, archetypes, and the collective unconscious. His work has been influential in psychiatry and in the study of religion, literature, and related fields.

ASSOCIATION WITH FREUD

Jung's early researches led him to understand Freud's investigations; his findings confirmed many of Freud's ideas, and, for a period of five years (between 1907 and 1912), he was Freud's close collaborator. He held important positions in the psychoanalytic movement and was widely thought of as the most likely successor to the founder of psychoanalysis. However, Jung differed with Freud largely over the latter's insistence on the sexual bases of neurosis. A serious disagreement came in 1912, with the publication of Jung's *Wandlungen und Symbole der Libido* (*Psychology of the Unconscious*, 1916), which ran counter to many of Freud's ideas.

Jung's first achievement was to differentiate two classes of people according to attitude types: extraverted (outward-looking) and introverted (inward-looking). Later he differentiated four functions of the mind—thinking, feeling, sensation, and intuition—one or more of which predominate in any given person. Results of this study were embodied in *Psychologische Typen* (1921; *Psychological Types*, 1923).

Jung later developed the theory that powerful fantasies and natural free expression came from an area of the mind that he called the collective unconscious, which he held was shared by everyone. This much-contested conception was combined with a theory of archetypes that Jung held as fundamental to the study of the psychology of religion. In Jung's terms, archetypes are instinctive patterns, have a universal character, and are expressed in behaviour and images.

CHARACTER OF HIS PSYCHOTHERAPY

Jung devoted the rest of his life to developing his ideas, especially those on the relation between psychology and religion. In his view, obscure and often neglected texts of writers in the past shed unexpected light not only on Jung's own dreams and fantasies but also on those of his patients; he thought it necessary for the successful practice of their art that psychotherapists become familiar with writings of the old masters.

Besides the development of new psychotherapeutic methods that derived from his own experience and the theories developed from them, Jung gave fresh importance to the so-called Hermetic tradition. He conceived that the Christian religion was part of a historic process necessary for the development of consciousness, and he also thought that the heretical movements, starting with Gnosticism and ending in alchemy, were manifestations of unconscious archetypal elements not adequately expressed in the mainstream forms of Christianity. He was particularly impressed with his finding that alchemical-like symbols could be found frequently in modern dreams and fantasies, and he thought that alchemists had constructed a kind of textbook of the collective unconscious. He expounded on this in 4 out of the 18 volumes that make up his *Collected Works*.

His historical studies aided him in pioneering the psychotherapy of the middle-aged and elderly, especially those who felt their lives had lost meaning. He helped them to appreciate the place of their lives in the sequence of history. Most of these patients had lost their religious belief; Jung found that if they could discover their own myth as expressed in dream and imagination they would become more complete personalities. He called this process individuation.

ALBERT EINSTEIN

(b. March 14, 1879, Ulm, Württemberg, Ger. — d. April 18, 1955, Princeton, N.J., U.S.)

German-born physicist Albert Einstein developed the special and general theories of relativity. He won the Nobel Prize for Physics in 1921 for his explanation of the photoelectric effect. Einstein is generally considered the most influential physicist of the 20th century.

SPECIAL RELATIVITY

In 1902 Einstein reached perhaps the lowest point in his life. He could not marry Meliva Maric, whom he loved, and support a family without a job. Desperate and unemployed, Einstein took lowly jobs. The turning point came later that year, when the father of his lifelong friend, Marcel Grossman, was able to recommend him for a position as a clerk in the Swiss patent office in Bern.

Einstein married Maric on Jan. 6, 1903. Their children, Hans Albert and Eduard, were born in Bern in 1904 and 1910, respectively. In hindsight, Einstein's job at the patent office was a blessing. He would quickly finish analyzing patent applications, leaving him time to daydream about the vision that had obsessed him since he was 16: What will happen if you race alongside a light beam?

Einstein had studied Maxwell's equations, which describe the nature of light, and discovered that the speed of light remained the same no matter how fast one moved. This violated Newton's laws of motion, however, because there is no absolute velocity in Isaac Newton's theory. This insight led Einstein to formulate the principle of relativity: "the speed of light is a constant in any inertial frame (constantly moving frame)."

During 1905, often called Einstein's "miracle year," he published four papers in the *Annalen der Physik*, each of which would alter the course of modern physics:

1. "Über einen die Erzeugung und Verwandlung des Lichtes betreffenden heuristischen Gesichtspunkt" ("On a Heuristic Viewpoint Concerning the Production and Transformation of Light"), in which Einstein applied the quantum theory to light in order to explain the photoelectric effect. If light occurs in tiny packets (later called photons), then it should knock out electrons in a metal in a precise way.

2. "Über die von der molekularkinetischen Theorie der Wärme geforderte Bewegung von in ruhenden Flüssigkeiten suspendierten Teilchen" ("On the Movement of Small Particles Suspended in Stationary Liquids Required by the Molecular-Kinetic Theory of Heat"), in which Einstein offered the first

experimental proof of the existence of atoms. By analyzing the motion of tiny particles suspended in still water, called Brownian motion, he could calculate the size of the jostling atoms and Avogadro's number.

3. "Zur Elektrodynamik bewegter Körper" ("On the Electrodynamics of Moving Bodies"), in which Einstein laid out the mathematical theory of special relativity.

4. "Ist die Trägheit eines Körpers von seinem Energieinhalt abhängig?" ("Does the Inertia of a Body Depend Upon Its Energy Content?"), submitted almost as an afterthought, which showed that relativity theory led to the equation $E = mc^2$. This provided the first mechanism to explain the energy source of the Sun and other stars.

Einstein was the first to assemble the whole theory together and to realize that it was a universal law of nature, not a curious figment of motion in the ether.

GENERAL RELATIVITY

At first Einstein's 1905 papers were ignored by the physics community. This began to change after he received the attention of just one physicist, perhaps the most influential physicist of his generation, Max Planck, the founder of the quantum theory. Soon, owing to Planck's laudatory comments and to experiments that gradually confirmed his theories, Einstein rose rapidly in the academic world.

One of the deep thoughts that consumed Einstein from 1905 to 1915 was a crucial flaw in his own theory: it made no mention of gravitation or acceleration. For the next 10 years, Einstein would be absorbed with

German physicist and mathematician Albert Einstein, known for his theory of relativity, relaxes at his home in Princeton, New Jersey. Lucien Aigner/ Hulton Archive/Getty Images

formulating a theory of gravity in terms of the curvature of space-time. To Einstein, Newton's gravitational force was actually a by-product of a deeper reality: the bending of the fabric of space and time. In November 1915 Einstein finally completed the general theory of relativity, which he considered to be his masterpiece.

Einstein was convinced that general relativity was correct because of its mathematical beauty and because it accurately predicted the perihelion of Mercury's orbit around the Sun. His theory also predicted a measurable deflection of light around the Sun. As a consequence, he even offered to help fund an expedition to measure the deflection of starlight during an eclipse of the Sun.

DELAYED CONFIRMATION

After World War I, two expeditions were sent to test Einstein's prediction of deflected starlight near the Sun. One set sail for the island of Principe, off the coast of West Africa, and the other to Sobral in northern Brazil in order to observe the solar eclipse of May 29, 1919. On Nov. 6, 1919, the results were announced in London at a joint meeting of the Royal Society and the Royal Astronomical Society.

The headline of *The Times* of London read, "Revolution in Science—New Theory of the Universe—Newton's Ideas Overthrown—Momentous Pronouncement—Space 'Warped.'" Almost immediately, Einstein became a world-renowned physicist, the successor to Isaac Newton.

In 1921 Einstein received the Nobel Prize for Physics, but for the photoelectric effect rather than for his relativity theories. During his acceptance speech, Einstein startled the audience by speaking about relativity instead of the photoelectric effect.

Einstein also launched the new science of cosmology. His equations predicted that the universe is dynamic—expanding or contracting. This contradicted the prevailing view that the universe was static, so he reluctantly introduced a "cosmological term" to stabilize his model of the universe. In 1929 astronomer Edwin Hubble found that the universe was indeed expanding, thereby confirming Einstein's earlier work. In 1930, in a visit to the Mount Wilson Observatory near Los Angeles, Einstein met with Hubble and declared the cosmological constant to be his "greatest blunder." Recent satellite data, however, have shown that the cosmological constant is probably not zero but actually dominates the matter-energy content of the entire universe. Einstein's "blunder" apparently determines the ultimate fate of the universe.

Coming to America

Inevitably, Einstein's fame and the great success of his theories created a backlash. The rising Nazi movement found a convenient target in relativity, branding it "Jewish physics" and sponsoring conferences and book burnings to denounce Einstein and his theories.

In December 1932 Einstein decided to leave Germany forever (he would never go back). It became obvious to Einstein that his life was in danger. Einstein settled at the newly formed Institute for Advanced Study at Princeton, N.J., which soon became a mecca for physicists from around the world.

Personal Sorrow

The 1930s were hard years for Einstein. His son Eduard was diagnosed with schizophrenia and suffered a mental breakdown in 1930. His beloved wife, Elsa Löwenthal, whom he married after having divorced Mileva in 1919, died in 1936. To his horror, during the late 1930s, physicists began seriously to consider whether his equation $E = mc^2$ might make an atomic bomb possible. Then, in 1938–39, a group of physicists showed that vast amounts of energy could be unleashed by the splitting of the uranium atom.

Einstein was granted permanent residency in the United States in 1935 and became an American citizen in 1940, although he chose to retain his Swiss citizenship. During the war, Einstein's colleagues were asked to journey to the desert town of Los Alamos, N.M., to develop the first atomic bomb for the Manhattan Project. Einstein, the man whose equation had set the whole effort into motion, was never asked to participate because the U.S. government feared Einstein's lifelong association with peace and socialist organizations. Instead, during the war Einstein was asked to help the U.S. Navy evaluate designs for future weapons systems. Einstein also helped the war effort by auctioning off priceless personal manuscripts. In particular, a handwritten copy of his 1905 paper on special relativity was sold for $6.5 million. It is now located in the Library of Congress.

Einstein was on vacation when he heard the news that an atomic bomb had been dropped on Japan. Almost immediately he was part of an international effort to try to bring the atomic bomb under control, forming the Emergency Committee of Atomic Scientists.

Professional Isolation

Although Einstein continued to pioneer many key developments in the theory of general relativity—such as wormholes, higher dimensions, the possibility of time travel, the existence of black holes, and the creation of the universe—he was increasingly isolated from the rest of the physics community. Because of the huge strides made by quantum theory in unraveling the secrets of atoms and molecules, the majority of physicists were working on the quantum theory, not relativity. Einstein tried to find logical inconsistencies in the quantum theory, particularly its lack of a deterministic mechanism. Einstein would often say that "God does not play dice with the universe."

In 1935 Einstein's most celebrated attack on the quantum theory led to the EPR (Einstein-Podolsky-Rosen) thought experiment. According to quantum theory, under certain circumstances two electrons separated by huge distances would have their properties linked, as if by an umbilical cord. Under these circumstances, if the properties of the first electron were measured, the state of the second electron would be known instantly—faster than the speed of light. This conclusion, Einstein claimed, clearly violated relativity. (Experiments conducted since then have confirmed that the quantum theory, rather than Einstein, was correct about the EPR experiment. In essence, what Einstein had actually shown was that quantum mechanics is nonlocal; i.e., random information can travel faster than light. This does not violate relativity, because the information is random and therefore useless.)

The other reason for Einstein's increasing detachment from his colleagues was his obsession, beginning in 1925, with discovering a unified field theory—an all-embracing theory that would unify the forces of the universe, and thereby the laws of physics, into one framework. In his later years he stopped opposing the quantum theory and tried to incorporate it, along with light and gravity, into a larger unified field theory.

ASSESSMENT

In some sense, Einstein, instead of being a relic, may have been too far ahead of his time. The strong force, a major piece of any unified field theory, was still a total mystery in

Einstein's lifetime. Only in the 1970s and '80s did physicists begin to unravel the secret of the strong force with the quark model.

ALFRED LOTHAR WEGENER

(b. Nov. 1, 1880, Berlin, Ger.—d. Nov. 1930, Greenland)

German meteorologist and geophysicist Alfred Lothar Wegener formulated the first complete statement of the continental drift hypothesis. The son of an orphanage director, Wegener earned a Ph.D. degree in astronomy from the University of Berlin in 1905. He had meanwhile become interested in paleoclimatology, and in 1906–08 he took part in an expedition to Greenland to study polar air circulation. He made three more expeditions to Greenland, in 1912–13, 1929, and 1930. He taught meteorology at Marburg and Hamburg and was a professor of meteorology and geophysics at the University of Graz from 1924 to 1930. He died during his last expedition to Greenland in 1930.

Like certain other scientists before him, Wegener became impressed with the similarity in the coastlines of eastern South America and western Africa and speculated that those lands had once been joined together. In about 1910 he began toying with the idea that in the Late Paleozoic era (about 250 million years ago) all the present-day continents had formed a single large mass, or supercontinent, which had subsequently broken apart. Wegener called this ancient continent Pangaea. Other scientists had proposed such a continent but had explained the separation of the modern world's continents as having resulted from the subsidence, or sinking, of large portions of the supercontinent to form the Atlantic and Indian oceans. Wegener, by contrast, proposed that Pangaea's constituent portions had slowly moved thousands of miles apart over long periods of geologic time. His term for this movement was *die*

Verschiebung der Kontinente ("continental displacement"), which gave rise to the term continental drift.

Wegener first presented his theory in lectures in 1912 and published it in full in 1915 in his most important work, *Die Entstehung der Kontinente und Ozeane (The Origin of Continents and Oceans)*. He searched the scientific literature for geological and paleontological evidence that would buttress his theory, and he was able to point to many closely related fossil organisms and similar rock strata that occurred on widely separated continents, particularly those found in both the Americas and in Africa. Wegener's theory of continental drift won some adherents in the ensuing decade, but his postulations of the driving forces behind the continents' movement seemed implausible. By 1930 his theory had been rejected by most geologists, and it sank into obscurity for the next few decades, only to be resurrected as part of the theory of plate tectonics during the 1960s.

SIR ALEXANDER FLEMING

(b. Aug. 6, 1881, Lochfield Farm, Darvel, Ayrshire, Scot.—d. March 11, 1955, London, Eng.)

Scottish bacteriologist Sir Alexander Fleming was best known for his discovery of penicillin. Fleming had a genius for technical ingenuity and original observation. His work on wound infection and lysozyme, an antibacterial enzyme found in tears and saliva, guaranteed him a place in the history of bacteriology. But it was his discovery of penicillin in 1928, which started the antibiotic revolution, that sealed his lasting reputation. Fleming was recognized for this achievement in 1945, when he received the Nobel Prize for Physiology or Medicine, along with Australian pathologist Howard Walter Florey and British biochemist Ernst Boris Chain, both of whom isolated and purified penicillin.

EARLY CAREER

After working as a London shipping clerk, Fleming began his medical studies at St. Mary's Hospital Medical School in 1901. At first he planned to become a surgeon, but a temporary position in the laboratories of the Inoculation Department at St. Mary's Hospital persuaded him that his future lay in the new field of bacteriology.

In November 1921 Fleming discovered lysozyme, an enzyme present in body fluids such as saliva and tears that has a mild antiseptic effect. This was the first of his major discoveries. It came about when he had a cold and a drop of his nasal mucus fell onto a culture plate of bacteria. Realizing that his mucus might have an effect on bacterial growth, he mixed the mucus into the culture and a few weeks later saw signs of the bacteria having been dissolved. Fleming's study of lysozyme, which he considered his best work as a scientist, was a significant contribution to the understanding of how the body fights infection. Unfortunately, lysozyme had no effect on the most pathogenic bacteria.

DISCOVERY OF PENICILLIN

On Sept. 3, 1928, Fleming noticed that a culture plate of *Staphylococcus aureus* he had been working on had become contaminated by a fungus. A mold, later identified as *Penicillium notatum* (also called *P. chrysogenum*), had inhibited the growth of the bacteria. He at first called the substance "mould juice" and then "penicillin," after the mold that produced it. Fleming decided to investigate further, because he thought that he had found an enzyme more potent than lysozyme. In fact, it was not an enzyme but an antibiotic—one of the first to be discovered. By the time Fleming had established this, he was interested in penicillin for itself.

Very much the lone researcher with an eye for the unusual, Fleming had the freedom to pursue anything that interested him. While this approach was ideal for taking advantage of a chance observation, the therapeutic development of penicillin required multidisciplinary teamwork. Fleming, working with two young researchers, failed to stabilize and purify penicillin. However, he did point out that penicillin had clinical potential, both as a topical antiseptic and as an injectable antibiotic, if it could be isolated and purified.

Penicillin eventually came into use during World War II as the result of the work of a team of scientists led by Howard Florey at the University of Oxford. Though Florey, his coworker Ernst Chain, and Fleming shared the

Penicillium notatum, the source of penicillin. Carlo Bevilacqua — SCALA/Art Resource, New York

1945 Nobel Prize, their relationship was clouded due to the issue of who should gain the most credit for penicillin. Fleming's role was emphasized by the press because of the romance of his chance discovery and his greater willingness to speak to journalists.

NIELS BOHR

(b. Oct. 7, 1885, Copenhagen, Den.—d. Nov. 18, 1962, Copenhagen)

Danish physicist Niels Bohr is generally regarded as one of the foremost physicists of the 20th century. He was the first to apply the quantum concept, which restricts the energy of a system to certain discrete values, to the problem of atomic and molecular structure. For this work he received the Nobel Prize for Physics in 1922. His manifold roles in the origins and development of quantum physics may be his most important contribution, but through his long career his involvements were substantially broader, both inside and outside the world of physics.

BOHR ATOMIC MODEL

Bohr's first contribution to the emerging new idea of quantum physics started in 1912. Only the year before, Ernest Rutherford and his collaborators at the University of Manchester had established experimentally that the atom consists of a heavy positively charged nucleus with substantially lighter negatively charged electrons circling around it at considerable distance. According to classical physics, such a system would be unstable, and Bohr felt compelled to postulate, in a substantive trilogy of articles published in *The Philosophical Magazine* in 1913, that electrons could only occupy particular orbits determined by the quantum of action and that electromagnetic radiation from an atom occurred only when an electron jumped to a lower-energy orbit. Although radical and unacceptable to most physicists at the time, the Bohr atomic model was able to account for an ever-increasing number of experimental data, famously starting with the spectral line series emitted by hydrogen.

Already in his 1913 trilogy, Bohr had sought to apply his theory to the understanding of the periodic table of elements. At the University of Copenhagen, where Bohr had established an Institute for Theoretical Physics, he improved upon this aspect of his work, developing an elaborate scheme building up the periodic table by adding electrons one after another to the atom according to his atomic model. When Bohr was awarded the Nobel Prize for his work in 1922, the Hungarian physical chemist Georg Hevesy, together with the physicist Dirk Coster from Holland, were working at Bohr's institute to establish experimentally that the as-yet-undiscovered atomic element 72 would behave as predicted by Bohr's theory. They succeeded in 1923, thus proving both the strength of Bohr's theory and the truth in practice of Bohr's words at the institute's inauguration about the important role of experiment. The element was named hafnium (Latin for Copenhagen).

COPENHAGEN INTERPRETATION OF QUANTUM MECHANICS

During the academic year 1926–27, Werner Heisenberg served as Bohr's assistant in Copenhagen, where he formulated the fundamental uncertainty principle as a consequence of quantum mechanics. Bohr, Heisenberg, and a few others then went on to develop what came to be known as the Copenhagen interpretation of quantum mechanics, which still provides a conceptual basis for the theory. A central element of the Copenhagen interpretation is Bohr's complementarity principle, presented for the first time in 1927 at a conference in Como, Italy.

According to complementarity, on the atomic level a physical phenomenon expresses itself differently depending on the experimental setup used to observe it. Thus, light appears sometimes as waves and sometimes as particles. For a complete explanation, both aspects, which according to classical physics are contradictory, need to be taken into account. The other towering figure of physics in the 20th century, Albert Einstein, never accepted the Copenhagen interpretation, famously declaring against its probabilistic implications that "God does not play dice." The discussions between Bohr and Einstein, especially at two of the renowned series of Solvay Conferences in physics, in 1927 and 1930, constitute one of the most fundamental and inspired discussions between physicists in the 20th century. For the rest of his life, Bohr worked to generalize complementarity as a guiding idea applying far beyond physics.

NUCLEAR PHYSICS

In the early 1930s Bohr, together with Hevesy and the Danish physiologist August Krogh, applied for support from the Rockefeller Foundation to build a cyclotron—a kind of particle accelerator recently invented by Ernest O. Lawrence in the United States—as a means to pursue biological studies. Although Bohr intended to use the cyclotron primarily for investigations in nuclear physics, it could also produce isotopes of elements involved in organic processes, making it possible in particular to extend the radioactive indicator method, invented and promoted by Hevesy, to biological purposes.

SPLITTING THE ATOM

After the German physicists Otto Hahn and Fritz Strassmann in late 1938 had made the unexpected and unexplained experimental discovery that a uranium atom can be split in two approximately equal halves when bombarded with neutrons, a theoretical explanation based on Bohr's recently proposed theory of the compound nucleus was suggested by two Austrian physicists close to Bohr—Lise Meitner and her nephew Otto Robert Frisch; the explanation was soon confirmed in experiments by Meitner and Frisch at the institute. By this time, at the beginning of 1939, Bohr was in the United States, where a fierce race to confirm experimentally the so-called fission of the nucleus began after the news of the German experiments and their explanation had become known. In the United States, Bohr did path-breaking work with his younger American colleague John Archibald Wheeler at Princeton University to explain fission theoretically.

The Atomic Bomb

After the discovery of fission, Bohr was acutely aware of the theoretical possibility of making an atomic bomb. In early 1943 Bohr received a secret message from his British colleague James Chadwick, inviting Bohr to join him in England to do important scientific work. Although Chadwick's letter was vaguely formulated, Bohr understood immediately that the work had to do with developing an atomic bomb. Convinced of the infeasibility of such a project, Bohr answered that there was greater need for him in occupied Denmark.

In the fall of 1943, the political situation in Denmark changed dramatically after the Danish government's collaboration with the German occupiers broke down. After being warned about his imminent arrest, Bohr escaped by boat with his family across the narrow sound to Sweden. In Stockholm the invitation to England was repeated, and

Bohr was brought by a military airplane to Scotland and then on to London.

Upon being briefed about the state of the Allied atomic bomb project on his arrival in London, Bohr changed his mind immediately about its feasibility. Concerned about a corresponding project being pursued in Germany, Bohr willingly joined the Allied project. Taking part for several weeks at a time in the work in Los Alamos, N.M., to develop the atomic bomb, he made significant technical contributions, notably to the design of the so-called initiator for the plutonium bomb. His most important role, however, was to serve, in J. Robert Oppenheimer's words, "as a scientific father confessor to the younger men."

Bohr was allowed to return home only after the atomic bomb had been dropped on Japan in August 1945. He later took part in the establishment of CERN, the European experimental particle physics facility near Geneva, Switz., as well as of the Nordic Institute for Atomic Physics (Nordita) adjacent to his institute.

ERWIN SCHRÖDINGER
(b. Aug. 12, 1887, Vienna, Austria—d. Jan. 4, 1961, Vienna)

Austrian theoretical physicist Erwin Schrödinger contributed to the wave theory of matter and to other fundamentals of quantum mechanics. He shared the 1933 Nobel Prize for Physics with the British physicist P.A.M. Dirac.

Schrödinger entered the University of Vienna in 1906 and obtained his doctorate in 1910, upon which he accepted a research post at the university's Second Physics Institute. He saw military service in World War I and then went to the University of Zürich in 1921, where he remained for the next six years. There, in a six-month period in 1926, at the age of 39, a remarkably late age for original work by theoretical physicists, he produced the papers that gave the foundations of quantum wave mechanics. In those papers he described his partial differential equation that is the basic equation of quantum mechanics and bears the same relation to the mechanics of the atom as Newton's equations of motion bear to planetary astronomy.

Adopting a proposal made by Louis de Broglie in 1924 that particles of matter have a dual nature and in some situations act like waves, Schrödinger introduced a theory describing the behaviour of such a system by a wave equation that is now known as the Schrödinger equation. The solutions to Schrödinger's equation, unlike the solutions to Newton's equations, are wave functions that can only be related to the probable occurrence of physical events. The definite and readily visualized sequence of events of the planetary orbits of Newton is, in quantum mechanics, replaced by the more abstract notion of probability. (This aspect of the quantum theory made Schrödinger and several other physicists profoundly unhappy, and he devoted much of his later life to formulating philosophical objections to the generally accepted interpretation of the theory that he had done so much to create.)

In 1927 Schrödinger accepted an invitation to succeed Max Planck, the inventor of the quantum hypothesis, at the University of Berlin, and he joined an extremely distinguished faculty that included Albert Einstein. He remained at the university until 1933, at which time he reached the decision that he could no longer live in a country in which the persecution of Jews had become a national policy. He then began a seven-year odyssey that took him to Austria, Great Britain, Belgium, the Pontifical Academy of Science in Rome, and—finally in 1940—the Dublin Institute for Advanced Studies, founded under the influence of Premier Eamon de Valera, who had been a mathematician before turning to politics. Schrödinger remained in Ireland for the next 15 years, doing research both in physics and in the philosophy and history of science. During this period he wrote *What Is Life?* (1944), an attempt to show how quantum physics can be used to explain the stability of genetic structure. Although much of what Schrödinger had to say in this book has been modified and amplified by later developments in molecular biology, his book remains one of the most useful and profound introductions to the subject. In 1956 Schrödinger retired and returned to Vienna as professor emeritus at the university.

Of all of the physicists of his generation, Schrödinger stands out because of his extraordinary intellectual versatility. He was at home in the philosophy and literature of all of the Western languages, and his popular scientific writing in English, which he had learned as a child, is among the best of its kind. His study of ancient Greek science and philosophy, summarized in his *Nature and the Greeks* (1954), gave him both an admiration for the Greek invention of the scientific view of the world and a skepticism toward the relevance of science as a unique tool with which to unravel the ultimate mysteries of human existence. Schrödinger's own metaphysical outlook, as expressed in his last book, *Meine Weltansicht* (1961; *My View of the World*), closely paralleled the mysticism of the Vedānta.

Because of his exceptional gifts, Schrödinger was able in the course of his life to make significant contributions to nearly all branches of science and philosophy, an almost unique accomplishment at a time when the trend was toward increasing technical specialization in these disciplines.

SELMAN ABRAHAM WAKSMAN

(b. July 22, 1888, Priluka, Ukraine, Russian Empire [now Pryluky, Ukraine]—d. Aug. 16, 1973, Hyannis, Mass., U.S.)

Ukrainian-born American biochemist Selman Abraham Waksman was one of the world's foremost authorities on soil microbiology. After the discovery of penicillin, he played a major role in initiating a calculated, systematic search for antibiotics among microbes. His consequent codiscovery of the antibiotic streptomycin, the first specific agent effective in the treatment of tuberculosis, brought him the 1952 Nobel Prize for Physiology or Medicine.

A naturalized U.S. citizen (1916), Waksman spent most of his career at Rutgers University, New Brunswick, New Jersey, where he served as professor of soil microbiology (1930–40), professor of microbiology and chairman of the department (1940–58), and director of the Rutgers Institute of Microbiology (1949–58). During his extensive study of the actinomycetes (filamentous, bacteria-like microorganisms found in the soil), he extracted from them antibiotics (a term he coined in 1941) valuable for their killing effect not only on gram-positive bacteria, against which penicillin is effective, but also on gram-negative bacteria, of which the tubercle bacillus (*Mycobacterium tuberculosis*) is one.

In 1940 Waksman, along with Albert Schatz and Elizabeth Bugie, isolated actinomycin from soil bacteria but found it to be extremely toxic when given to test animals. Three years later they extracted the relatively nontoxic streptomycin from the actinomycete *Streptomyces griseus* and found that it exercised repressive influence on tuberculosis. In combination with other chemotherapeutic agents, streptomycin has become a major factor in controlling the disease. Waksman also isolated and developed several other antibiotics, including neomycin, that have been used in treating many infectious diseases of humans, domestic animals, and plants.

Among Waksman's books are *Principles of Soil Microbiology* (1927), regarded as one of the most exhaustive works on the subject, and *My Life with the Microbes* (1954), an autobiography.

EDWIN POWELL HUBBLE

(b. Nov. 20, 1889, Marshfield, Mo., U.S.—d. Sept. 28, 1953, San Marino, Calif.)

American astronomer Edwin Powell Hubble is considered the founder of extragalactic astronomy. He provided the first evidence of the expansion of the universe.

Hubble's interest in astronomy flowered at the University of Chicago, where he was inspired by the astronomer George E. Hale. At Chicago, Hubble earned both an undergraduate degree in mathematics and astronomy (1910) and a reputation as a fine boxer. Upon graduation, however, Hubble turned away from both astronomy and athletics, preferring to study law as a Rhodes Scholar at the University of Oxford (B.A., 1912). He joined the Kentucky bar in 1913 but dissolved his practice soon after, finding himself bored with law. A man of many talents, he finally chose to focus them on astronomy, returning to the University of Chicago and its Yerkes Observatory in Wisconsin. After earning a Ph.D. in astronomy (1917) and serving in World War I, Hubble settled down to work at the Mount Wilson Observatory near Pasadena, Calif., and began to make discoveries concerning extragalactic phenomena.

While at Mount Wilson, Hubble discovered (1922–24) that not all nebulae in the sky are part of the Milky Way

The astronomer Edwin Hubble looks through the 100-inch (254 cm) telescope at the Mount Wilson Observatory in Los Angeles in 1937. Margaret Bourke-White/Time & Life Pictures/Getty Images

Galaxy, the vast star system to which the Sun belongs. He found that certain nebulae contain stars called Cepheid variables, for which a correlation was already known to exist between periodicity and absolute magnitude. Using the further relationship among distance, apparent magnitude, and absolute magnitude, Hubble determined that these Cepheids are several hundred thousand light-years away and thus outside the Milky Way system and that the nebulae in which they are located are actually galaxies distinct from the Milky Way. This discovery, announced in 1924, forced astronomers to revise their ideas about the cosmos.

Soon after discovering the existence of these external galaxies, Hubble undertook the task of classifying them according to their shapes (1926) and exploring their stellar contents and brightness patterns. In studying the galaxies, Hubble made his second remarkable discovery—namely, that these galaxies are apparently receding from the Milky Way and that the further away they are, the faster they are receding (1927). The implications of this discovery were immense. The universe, long considered static, was expanding; and, even more remarkably, as Hubble discovered in 1929, the universe was expanding in such a way that the ratio of the speed of the galaxies to their distance is a constant now called Hubble's constant.

Although Hubble was correct that the universe was expanding, his calculation of the value of the constant was incorrect, implying that the Milky Way system was larger than all other galaxies and that the entire universe was younger than the surmised age of the Earth. Subsequent astronomers, however, revised Hubble's result and rescued his theory, creating a picture of a cosmos that has been expanding at a constant rate for 10 billion to 20 billion years.

For his achievements in astronomy, Hubble received many honours and awards. Among his publications were

Red Shifts in the Spectra of Nebulae (1934) and *The Hubble Atlas of Galaxies* (published posthumously, 1961, and edited by Allan Sandage). Hubble remained an active observer of galaxies until his death.

LINUS PAULING

(b. Feb. 28, 1901, Portland, Ore., U.S.—d. Aug. 19, 1994, Big Sur, Calif.)

American theoretical physical chemist Linus Pauling became the only person to have won two unshared Nobel Prizes. His first prize (1954) was awarded for research into the nature of the chemical bond and its use in elucidating molecular structure; the second (1962) recognized his efforts to ban the testing of nuclear weapons.

ELUCIDATION OF MOLECULAR STRUCTURES

In 1927 Pauling began a long career of teaching and research at the California Institute of Technology (Caltech). Analyzing chemical structure became the central theme of his scientific work. By using the technique of X-ray diffraction, he determined the three-dimensional arrangement of atoms in several important silicate and sulfide minerals. In 1930, during a trip to Germany, Pauling learned about electron diffraction, and upon his return to California he used this technique of scattering electrons from the nuclei of molecules to determine the structures of some important substances. This structural knowledge assisted him in developing an electronegativity scale in which he assigned a number representing a particular atom's power of attracting electrons in a covalent bond.

To complement the experimental tool that X-ray analysis provided for exploring molecular structure, Pauling turned to quantum mechanics as a theoretical tool. He used quantum mechanics to determine the equivalent strength in each of the four bonds surrounding the carbon atom. He developed a valence bond theory in which he proposed that a molecule could be described by an intermediate structure that was a resonance combination (or hybrid) of other structures. His book *The Nature of the Chemical Bond, and the Structure of Molecules and Crystals* (1939) provided a unified summary of his vision of structural chemistry.

By the mid-1930s Pauling was performing successful magnetic studies on the protein hemoglobin. He developed further interests in protein and, together with biochemist Alfred Mirsky, Pauling published a paper in 1936 on general protein structure. In this work the authors explained that protein molecules naturally coiled into specific configurations but became "denatured" (uncoiled) and assumed some random form once certain weak bonds were broken.

On one of his trips to visit Mirsky in New York, Pauling met Karl Landsteiner, the discoverer of blood types, who became his guide into the field of immunochemistry. Pauling was fascinated by the specificity of antibody-antigen reactions, and he later developed a theory that accounted for this specificity through a unique folding of the antibody's polypeptide chain. World War II interrupted this theoretical work, and Pauling's focus shifted to more practical problems, including the preparation of an artificial substitute for blood serum useful to wounded soldiers and an oxygen detector useful in submarines and airplanes.

After the war Pauling became interested in the study of sickle-cell anemia. He perceived that the sickling of cells noted in this disease might be caused by a genetic mutation in the globin portion of the blood cell's hemoglobin. In 1949 he and his coworkers published a paper identifying the particular defect in hemoglobin's structure that was responsible for sickle-cell anemia, which thereby made this disorder the first "molecular disease" to be discovered.

While serving as a visiting professor at the University of Oxford in 1948, Pauling returned to a problem that had intrigued him in the late 1930s—the three-dimensional structure of proteins. By folding a paper on which he had drawn a chain of linked amino acids, he discovered a cylindrical coil-like configuration, later called the alpha helix. The most significant aspect of Pauling's structure was its determination of the number of amino acids per turn of the helix. During this same period he became interested in deoxyribonucleic acid (DNA), and early in 1953 he and protein crystallographer Robert Corey published their version of DNA's structure, three strands twisted around each other in ropelike fashion. Shortly thereafter James Watson and Francis Crick published DNA's correct structure, a double helix. Pauling was awarded the 1954 Nobel Prize for Chemistry "for his research into the nature of the chemical bond and its application to the elucidation of the structure of complex substances."

HUMANITARIAN ACTIVITIES

During the 1950s Pauling and his wife became well known to the public through their crusade to stop the atmospheric testing of nuclear weapons. Pauling's sentiments were also promulgated through his book *No More War!* (1958), a passionate analysis of the implications of nuclear war for humanity. In 1960 he was called upon to defend his actions regarding a test ban before a congressional subcommittee. His work on behalf of world peace was recognized with the 1962 Nobel Prize for Peace awarded on Oct. 10, 1963, the date that the Nuclear Test Ban Treaty went into effect. Pauling also later published a paper on orthomolecular psychiatry that explained how mental health could be achieved by manipulating substances normally present in the body.

LATER YEARS

In Pauling's later career, his scientific interests centred on a particular molecule—ascorbic acid (vitamin C). He examined the published reports about this vitamin and concluded that, when taken in large enough quantities (megadoses), it would help the body fight off colds and other diseases. The outcome of his research was the book *Vitamin C and the Common Cold* (1970), which became a best-seller. Pauling's interest in vitamin C in particular and orthomolecular medicine in general led, in 1973, to his founding an institute that eventually bore his name—the Linus Pauling Institute of Science and Medicine. During his tenure at this institute, he became embroiled in controversies about the relative benefits and risks of ingesting megadoses of various vitamins. The controversy intensified when he advocated vitamin C's usefulness in the treatment of cancer. Pauling and his collaborator, the Scottish physician Ewan Cameron, published their views in *Cancer and Vitamin C* (1979).

Although he continued to receive recognition for his earlier accomplishments, Pauling's later work provoked considerable skepticism and controversy. His cluster model of the atomic nucleus was rejected by physicists, his interpretation of the newly discovered quasicrystals received little support, and his ideas on vitamin C were rejected by the medical establishment. In an effort to raise money to support his increasingly troubled institute, Pauling published *How to Live Longer and Feel Better* (1986), but the book failed to become the success that he and his associates had anticipated. Despite their personal reliance upon megadoses of vitamin C, both Pauling and his wife developed cancer.

ENRICO FERMI

(b. Sept. 29, 1901, Rome, Italy—d. Nov. 28, 1954, Chicago, Ill., U.S.)

I talian-born American scientist Enrico Fermi was one of the chief architects of the nuclear age. He developed the mathematical statistics required to clarify a large class of subatomic phenomena, explored nuclear transformations caused by neutrons, and directed the first controlled chain reaction involving nuclear fission. He was awarded the 1938 Nobel Prize for Physics, and the Enrico Fermi Award of the U.S. Department of Energy is given in his honour. Fermilab, the National Accelerator Laboratory, in Illinois, is named for him, as is fermium, element number 100.

EUROPEAN CAREER

In 1924 Fermi took a position as a lecturer in mathematical physics at the University of Florence in Italy. His early research was in general relativity, statistical mechanics, and quantum mechanics. Examples of gas degeneracy (appearance of unexpected phenomena) had been known, and some cases were explained by Bose-Einstein statistics, which describes the behaviour of subatomic particles known as bosons. Between 1926 and 1927, Fermi and the English physicist P.A.M. Dirac independently developed new statistics, now known as Fermi-Dirac statistics, to handle the subatomic particles that obey the Pauli exclusion principle; these particles, which include electrons, protons, neutrons (not yet discovered), and other particles with half-integer spin, are now known as fermions.

In 1927 Fermi became a full professor at the University of Rome. In 1929 Fermi, as Italy's first professor of theoretical physics and a rising star in European science, was named by Italian Prime Minister Benito Mussolini to his new Accademia d'Italia, a position that included a

Italian-born physicist Enrico Fermi, explaining a problem in physics, c. *1950.*
National Archives, Washington, D.C.

substantial salary (much larger than that for any ordinary university position), a uniform, and a title ("Excellency").

During the late 1920s, Fermi changed his focus to the more primitively developed field of nuclear physics. He began to study the neutrino, an almost undetectable particle that had been postulated a few years earlier by the Austrian-born physicist Wolfgang Pauli. This led to Fermi's recognition that beta decay from radioactive particles was a manifestation of the weak force, one of the four known universal forces (the others being gravitation, electromagnetism, and the strong force).

In the 1930s Fermi reasoned that the neutral neutron would be an ideal projectile with which to bombard charged nuclei in order to initiate such reactions. With his colleagues, Fermi subjected more than 60 elements to neutron bombardment, using a Geiger-Müller counter to detect emissions and conducting chemical analyses to determine the new radioactive isotopes produced. Along the way, they found by chance that neutrons that had been slowed in their velocity often were more effective. When testing uranium they observed several activities, but they could not interpret what occurred. Some scientists thought that they had produced transuranium elements, namely elements higher than uranium at atomic number 92. The issue was not resolved until 1938, when it was revealed that the uranium had split and the several radioactivities detected were from fission fragments.

Fermi was little interested in politics, yet he grew increasingly uncomfortable with the fascist politics of his homeland. When Italy adopted the anti-Semitic policies of its ally, Nazi Germany, a crisis occurred, for Fermi's wife, Laura, was Jewish. The award of the 1938 Nobel Prize for Physics serendipitously provided the excuse for the family to travel abroad, and the prize money helped to establish them in the United States.

AMERICAN CAREER

Fermi began his new life at Columbia University, in New York City. Within weeks of his arrival, news that uranium could fission astounded the physics community. Scientists had known for many years that nuclei could disgorge small chunks, such as alpha particles, beta particles, protons, and neutrons, either in natural radioactivity or upon bombardment by a projectile. However, they had never seen a nucleus split almost in two. The implications were both exciting and ominous, and they were recognized widely.

When uranium fissioned, some mass was converted to energy, according to Albert Einstein's famous formula $E = mc^2$. Uranium also emitted a few neutrons in addition to the larger fragments. If these neutrons could be slowed to maximize their efficiency, they could participate in a controlled chain reaction to produce energy; that is, a nuclear reactor could be built. The same neutrons traveling at their initial high speed could also participate in an uncontrolled chain reaction, liberating an enormous amount of energy through many generations of fission events, all within a fraction of a second; that is, an atomic bomb could be built.

Working primarily with the Hungarian-born physicist Leo Szilard, Fermi constructed experimental arrangements of neutron sources and pieces of uranium. They sought to determine the necessary size of a structure, the best material to use as a moderator to slow neutrons, the necessary purity of all components (so neutrons would not be lost), and the best substance for forming control rods that could absorb neutrons to slow or stop the reaction.

When the United States entered World War II in December 1941, nuclear research was consolidated to some degree. Fermi had built a series of "piles," as he called them, at Columbia. Now he moved to the University of

Chicago, where he continued to construct piles in a space under the stands of the football field. The final structure, a flattened sphere about 7.5 metres (25 feet) in diameter, contained 380 tons of graphite blocks as the moderator and 6 tons of uranium metal and 40 tons of uranium oxide as the fuel, distributed in a careful pattern. The pile went "critical" on Dec. 2, 1942, proving that a nuclear reaction could be initiated, controlled, and stopped. Chicago Pile-1, as it was called, was the first prototype for several large nuclear reactors constructed at Hanford, Wash., where plutonium, a man-made element heavier than uranium, was produced. Plutonium also could fission and thus was another route to the atomic bomb.

In 1944 Fermi became an American citizen and moved to Los Alamos, N.M., where physicist J. Robert Oppenheimer led the Manhattan Project's laboratory, whose mission was to fashion weapons out of the rare uranium-235 isotope and plutonium. When the first plutonium bomb was tested on July 16, 1945, near Alamogordo, N.M., Fermi ingeniously made a rough calculation of its explosive energy by noting how far slips of paper were blown from the vertical.

After the war ended, Fermi accepted a permanent position at the University of Chicago, where he subsequently redirected his sights on reactions at higher energies, a field called elementary particle physics, or high-energy physics. However, Fermi went for a time back to Los Alamos to assist in the development of fusion weapons, however with the hope that they might prove impossible to construct.

Fermi primarily investigated subatomic particles, particularly pi mesons and muons, after returning to Chicago. He was also known as a superb teacher, and many of his lectures are still in print. During his later years he raised a question now known as the Fermi paradox: "Where is everybody?" He was asking why no extraterrestrial civilizations seemed to be around to be detected, despite the great size and age of the universe. He pessimistically thought that the answer might involve nuclear annihilation.

MARGARET MEAD

(b. Dec. 16, 1901, Philadelphia, Pa., U.S.—d. Nov. 15, 1978, New York, N.Y.)

American anthropologist Margaret Mead was noted for the force of her personality, her outspokenness, and the quality of her scientific work. Mead entered DePauw University in 1919 and transferred to Barnard College a year later. She graduated from Barnard in 1923 and entered the graduate school of Columbia University, where she studied with and was greatly influenced by anthropologists Franz Boas and Ruth Benedict (a lifelong friend). Mead received an M.A. in 1924 and a Ph.D. in 1929.

In 1925, during the first of her many field trips to the South Seas, she gathered material for the first of her 23 books, *Coming of Age in Samoa* (1928; new ed., 1968), a perennial best-seller and a characteristic example of her reliance on observation rather than statistics for data. The book clearly indicates her belief in cultural determinism, a position that caused some later 20th-century anthropologists to question both the accuracy of her observations and the soundness of her conclusions. Her other works include *Growing Up in New Guinea* (1930; new ed., 1975), *Sex and Temperament in Three Primitive Societies* (1935; reprinted, 1968), *Balinese Character: A Photographic Analysis* (1942, with Gregory Bateson, to whom she was married in 1936–51), *Continuities in Cultural Evolution* (1964), and *A Rap on Race* (1971, with James Baldwin).

During her many years with the American Museum of Natural History in New York City, she successively served as assistant curator (1926–42), associate curator (1942–64), curator of ethnology (1964–69), and curator emeritus (1969–78). Her contributions to science received special recognition when, at the age of 72, she was elected to the presidency of the American Association for the Advancement of Science. In 1979 she was posthumously awarded the Presidential Medal of Freedom, the United States's highest civilian honour.

As an anthropologist, Mead was best known for her studies of the nonliterate peoples of Oceania, especially with regard to various aspects of psychology and culture, the cultural conditioning of sexual behaviour, natural character, and culture change. As a celebrity, she was most notable for her forays into such far-ranging topics

Cultural anthropologist Margaret Mead conducts an interview on United Nations Radio about the Seminar on Mental Health and Infant Development. Hulton Archive/Getty Images

as women's rights, childrearing, sexual morality, nuclear proliferation, race relations, drug abuse, population control, environmental pollution, and world hunger.

Some of her other works are *Male and Female: A Study of the Sexes in a Changing World* (1949; new ed., 1975), *Anthropology: A Human Science* (1964), *Culture and Commitment* (1970), *Ruth Benedict* (1974), a biography of that anthropologist, and an autobiography of her own early years, *Blackberry Winter* (1972). *Letters from the Field* (1977) is a selection of Mead's correspondence written during the Samoa expedition.

BARBARA McCLINTOCK

(b. June 16, 1902, Hartford, Conn., U.S.—d. Sept. 2, 1992, Huntington, N.Y.)

American scientist Barbara McClintock discovered mobile genetic elements, or "jumping genes," which won her the Nobel Prize for Physiology or Medicine in 1983. McClintock, whose father was a physician, took great pleasure in science as a child and evidenced early the independence of mind and action that she would exhibit throughout her life. After attending high school, she enrolled as a biology major at Cornell University in 1919. She received a B.S. in 1923, a master's degree two years later, and, having specialized in cytology, genetics, and zoology, a Ph.D. in 1927. During graduate school she began the work that would occupy her entire life: the chromosomal analysis of corn (maize). She used a microscope and a staining technique that allowed her to examine, identify, and describe individual corn chromosomes.

In 1931 she and a colleague, Harriet Creighton, published "A Correlation of Cytological and Genetical Crossing-over in *Zea mays*," a paper that established that chromosomes formed the basis of genetics. Based on her experiments and publications during the 1930s, McClintock was elected vice president of the Genetics Society of America in 1939 and president of the Genetics Society in 1944. She received a Guggenheim Fellowship in 1933 to study in Germany, but she left early owing to the rise of Nazism. When she returned to Cornell, her alma mater, she found that the university would not hire a female professor. The Rockefeller Foundation funded her research at Cornell (1934–36) until she was hired by the University of Missouri (1936–41).

In 1941 McClintock moved to Long Island, New York, to work at the Cold Spring Harbor Laboratory, where she spent the rest of her professional life. In the 1940s, by observing and experimenting with variations in the coloration of kernels of corn, she discovered that genetic information is not stationary. By tracing pigmentation changes in corn and using a microscope to examine that plant's large chromosomes, she isolated two genes that she called "controlling elements." These genes controlled the genes that were actually responsible for pigmentation. McClintock found that the controlling elements could move along the chromosome to a different site, and that these changes affected the behaviour of neighbouring genes. She suggested that these transposable elements were responsible for new mutations in pigmentation or other characteristics.

McClintock's work was ahead of its time and was for many years considered too radical—or was simply ignored— by her fellow scientists. Deeply disappointed with her colleagues, she stopped publishing the results of her work and ceased giving lectures, though she continued doing research. Not until the late 1960s and '70s, after biologists had determined that the genetic material was DNA, did members of the scientific community begin to verify her early findings. When recognition finally came, McClintock was inundated with awards and honours, most notably the 1983 Nobel Prize for Physiology or Medicine. She was the first woman to be the sole winner of this award.

LEAKEY FAMILY

(Louis Leakey, b. Aug. 7, 1903, Kabete, Kenya—d. Oct. 1, 1972, London, Eng.); (Mary Douglas Leakey, b. Feb. 6, 1913, London, Eng.—d. Dec. 9, 1996, Nairobi, Kenya); (Richard Leakey, b. Dec. 19, 1944, Nairobi, Kenya)

Louis S.B. Leakey, Mary Douglas Leakey, and their son, Richard Leakey, respectively, heavily influenced modern archaeology and paleoanthropology. They are known for their discoveries of hominin and other fossil remains in eastern Africa. In addition to their discoveries, the family inspired several now well-known zoologists and ethologists, who have themselves made groundbreaking discoveries concerning humans and their ancestors.

Louis S. B. Leakey

Kenyan archaeologist and anthropologist Louis Seymour Bazett Leakey was known for his fossil discoveries in East Africa, which proved that humans were far older than had previously been believed and that human evolution was centred in Africa, rather than in Asia, as earlier discoveries had suggested. Leakey was also noted for his controversial interpretations of these archaeological finds.

Born of British missionary parents, Leakey spent his youth with the Kikuyu people of Kenya, about whom he later wrote. He was educated at the University of Cambridge and began his archaeological research in East Africa in 1924; he was later aided by his second wife, the archaeologist Mary Douglas Leakey (née Nicol), and their sons. He held various appointments at major British and

American universities and was curator of the Coryndon Memorial Museum in Nairobi from 1945 to 1961.

In 1931 Leakey began his research at Olduvai Gorge in Tanzania, which became the site of his most famous discoveries. The first finds were animal fossils and crude stone tools, but in 1959 Mary Leakey uncovered a fossil hominin (member of the human lineage) that was given the name *Zinjanthropus* (now generally regarded as a form of *Paranthropus*, similar to *Australopithecus*) and was believed to be about 1.7 million years old. Leakey later theorized that *Zinjanthropus* was not a direct ancestor of modern man. He claimed this distinction for other hominin fossil remains that his team discovered at Olduvai Gorge in 1960–63, which Leakey named *Homo habilis*.

Leakey held that *H. habilis* lived contemporaneously with *Australopithecus* in East Africa and represented a more advanced hominin on the direct evolutionary line to *H. sapiens*. Initially many scientists disputed Leakey's interpretations and classifications of the fossils he had found, although they accepted the significance of the finds themselves. They contended that *H. habilis* was not sufficiently different from *Australopithecus* to justify a separate classification. Subsequent finds by the Leakey family and others, however, established that *H. habilis* does indeed represent an evolutionary step between the australopiths (who eventually became extinct) and *H. erectus*, who may have been a direct ancestor of modern man.

Among the other important finds made by Leakey's team was the discovery in 1948 at Rusinga Island in Lake Victoria, Kenya, of the remains of *Proconsul africanus*, a common ancestor of both humans and apes that lived about 25 million years ago. At Fort Ternan (east of Lake Victoria) in 1962, Leakey's team discovered the remains of *Kenyapithecus*, another link between apes and early man that lived about 14 million years ago.

Leakey's discoveries formed the basis for the most important subsequent research into the earliest origins of human life. He was also instrumental in persuading Jane Goodall, Dian Fossey, and Biruté M.F. Galdikas to undertake their pioneering long-term studies of chimpanzees, gorillas, and orangutans in those animals' natural habitats. The Louis Leakey Memorial Institute for African Prehistory in Nairobi was founded by his son Richard Leakey as a fossil repository and postgraduate study centre and laboratory.

Leakey wrote *Adam's Ancestors* (1934; rev. ed., 1953), *Stone Age Africa* (1936), *White African* (1937), *Olduvai Gorge* (1951), *Mau Mau and the Kikuyu* (1952), *Olduvai Gorge, 1951–61* (1965), *Unveiling Man's Origins* (1969; with Vanne Morris Goodall), and *Animals of East Africa* (1969).

Mary Douglas Leakey

English-born archaeologist and paleoanthropologist Mary Douglas Leakey (née Mary Douglas Nicol) made several fossil finds of great importance in the understanding of human evolution. Her early finds were interpreted and publicized by her husband, the noted anthropologist Louis S.B. Leakey.

As a girl, Mary exhibited a natural talent for drawing and was interested in archaeology. After undergoing sporadic schooling, she participated in excavations of a Neolithic Period site at Hembury, Devon, England, by which time she had become skilled at making reproduction-quality drawings of stone tools. She met Louis Leakey in 1933, and they were married in 1936. Shortly thereafter they left for an expedition to East Africa, an area that became the central location of their work.

Working alongside Louis Leakey for the next 30 years, Mary Leakey oversaw the excavation of various prehistoric sites in Kenya. Her skill at the painstaking work of excavation surpassed her husband's, whose brilliance lay in interpreting and publicizing the fossils that they uncovered. In 1948, on Rusinga Island in Lake Victoria, she discovered the skull of *Proconsul africanus*, an ancestor of both apes and early humans that lived about 25 million years ago. In 1959 at Olduvai Gorge, Tanzania, she discovered the skull of an early hominin (member of the human lineage) that her husband named *Zinjanthropus*, or "eastern man," though it is now regarded as *Paranthropus*, a type of australopith, or "southern ape."

After her husband's death in 1972, Leakey continued her work in Africa. In 1978 she discovered at Laetoli, a site south of Olduvai Gorge, several sets of footprints made in volcanic ash by early hominins that lived about 3.5 million years ago. The footprints indicated that their makers walked upright; this discovery pushed back the advent of human bipedalism to a date earlier than the scientific community had previously suspected. Among Mary Leakey's books were *Olduvai Gorge: My Search for Early Man* (1979) and the autobiographical *Disclosing the Past* (1984).

RICHARD LEAKEY

Kenyan anthropologist, conservationist, and political figure Richard Leakey was responsible for extensive fossil finds related to human evolution and campaigned publicly for responsible management of the environment in East Africa. The son of noted anthropologists Louis S.B. Leakey and Mary Leakey, Richard was originally reluctant to follow his parents' career and instead became a safari guide. In 1967 he joined an expedition to the Omo River valley in Ethiopia. It was during this trip that he first noticed the site of Koobi Fora, along the shores of Lake Turkana (Lake Rudolf) in Kenya, where he led a preliminary search that uncovered several stone tools. From this site alone in the subsequent decade, Leakey and his fellow workers uncovered some 400 hominin fossils representing perhaps 230 individuals, making Koobi Fora the site of the richest and most varied assemblage of early human remains found to date anywhere in the world.

Leakey proposed controversial interpretations of his fossil finds. In two books written with science writer Roger Lewin, *Origins* (1977) and *People of the Lake* (1978), Leakey presented his view that, some 3 million years ago, three hominin forms coexisted: *Homo habilis*, *Australopithecus africanus*, and *Australopithecus boisei*. He argued that the two australopith forms eventually died out and that *H. habilis* evolved into *Homo erectus*, the direct ancestor of *Homo sapiens*, or modern human beings. He claimed to have found evidence at Koobi Fora to support this theory. Of particular importance is an almost completely reconstructed fossil skull found in more than 300 fragments in 1972 (coded as KNM-ER 1470). Leakey believed that the skull represented *H. habilis* and that this relatively large-brained, upright, bipedal form of *Homo* lived in eastern Africa as early as 2.5 million or even 3.5 million years ago. Further elaboration of Leakey's views was given in his work *The Making of Mankind* (1981).

From 1968 to 1989 Leakey was director of the National Museums of Kenya. In 1989 he was made director of the Wildlife Conservation and Management Department (the precursor to the Kenya Wildlife Service [KWS]). Devoted to the preservation of Kenya's wildlife and sanctuaries, he embarked on a campaign to reduce corruption within the KWS, crack down (often using force) on ivory poachers, and restore the security of Kenya's national parks. In doing so he made numerous enemies. In 1993 he survived a plane crash in which he lost both his legs below the knee. The following year he resigned his post at the KWS, citing interference by

Kenyan President Daniel arap Moi's government, and became a founding member of the opposition political party Safina (Swahili for "Noah's ark"). Pressure by foreign donors led to Leakey's brief return to the KWS (1998–99) and to a short stint as secretary to the cabinet (1999–2001). Thereafter he dedicated himself to lecturing and writing on the conservation of wildlife and the environment.

Another book with Roger Lewin was *The Sixth Extinction: Patterns of Life and the Future of Humankind* (1995), in which he argued that human beings have been responsible for a catastrophic reduction in the number of plant and animal species living on the Earth. Leakey later collaborated with Virginia Morell to write his second memoir, *Wildlife Wars: My Fight to Save Africa's Natural Treasures* (2001; his first memoir, *One Life*, was written in 1983). In 2004 Leakey founded WildlifeDirect, an Internet-based nonprofit conservation organization designed to disseminate information about endangered species and to connect donors to conservation efforts. He also served in 2007 as interim chair of the Kenya branch of Transparency International, a global coalition against corruption.

GEORGE GAMOW

(b. March 4, 1904, Odessa, Russian Empire [now in Ukraine]—d. Aug. 19, 1968, Boulder, Colo., U.S.)

R ussian-born American nuclear physicist and cosmologist George Gamow was one of the foremost advocates of the big-bang theory, according to which the universe was formed in a colossal explosion that took place billions of years ago. In addition, his work on deoxyribonucleic acid (DNA) made a basic contribution to modern genetic theory.

Gamow attended Leningrad (now St. Petersburg) University, where he studied briefly with A.A. Friedmann, a mathematician and cosmologist who suggested that the universe should be expanding. At that time Gamow did not pursue Friedmann's suggestion, preferring instead to delve into quantum theory. After graduating in 1928, he traveled to Göttingen, where he developed his quantum theory of radioactivity, the first successful explanation of the behaviour of radioactive elements, some of which decay in seconds while others decay over thousands of years.

His achievement earned him a fellowship at the Copenhagen Institute of Theoretical Physics (1928–29), where he continued his investigations in theoretical nuclear physics. There he proposed his "liquid drop" model of atomic nuclei, which served as the basis for the modern theories of nuclear fission and fusion. He also collaborated with F. Houtermans and R. Atkinson in developing a theory of the rates of thermonuclear reactions inside stars.

In 1934, after emigrating from the Soviet Union, Gamow was appointed professor of physics at George Washington University in Washington, D.C. There he collaborated with Edward Teller in developing a theory of beta decay (1936), a nuclear decay process in which an electron is emitted. Soon after, Gamow resumed his study of the relations between small-scale nuclear processes and cosmology. He used his knowledge of nuclear reactions to interpret stellar evolution, collaborating with Teller on a theory of the internal structures of red giant stars (1942). From his work on stellar evolution, Gamow postulated that the Sun's energy results from thermonuclear processes.

Gamow and Teller were both proponents of the expanding-universe theory that had been advanced by Friedmann, Edwin Hubble, and Georges LeMaître. Gamow, however, modified the theory, and he, Ralph Alpher, and Hans Bethe published this theory in a paper called "The Origin of Chemical Elements" (1948). This paper, attempting to explain the distribution of chemical elements throughout the universe, posits a primeval thermonuclear explosion, the big bang that began the universe. According to the theory, after the big bang, atomic nuclei were built up by the successive capture of neutrons by the initially formed pairs and triplets.

In 1954 Gamow's scientific interests grew to encompass biochemistry. He proposed the concept of a genetic code and maintained that the code was determined by the order of recurring triplets of nucleotides, the basic components of DNA. His proposal was vindicated during the rapid development of genetic theory that followed.

Gamow held the position of professor of physics at the University of Colorado, Boulder, from 1956 until his death. He is perhaps best known for his popular writings, designed to introduce to the nonspecialist such difficult subjects as relativity and cosmology. His first such work, *Mr. Tomkins in Wonderland* (1936), gave rise to the multivolume "Mr. Tomkins" series (1939–67). Among his other writings are *One, Two, Three . . . Infinity* (1947), *The Creation of the Universe* (1952; rev. ed., 1961), *A Planet Called Earth* (1963), and *A Star Called the Sun* (1964).

J. ROBERT OPPENHEIMER

(b. April 22, 1904, New York, N.Y., U.S.—d. Feb. 18, 1967, Princeton, N.J.)

American theoretical physicist and science administrator Julius Robert Oppenheimer was director of the Los Alamos laboratory during development of the atomic bomb (1943–45) and director of the Institute for Advanced Study, Princeton (1947–66). Accusations of disloyalty led to a government hearing that resulted in the loss of his security clearance and of his position as adviser to the highest echelons of the U.S. government. The case became a cause célèbre in the world of science because of its implications concerning political and moral issues relating to the role of scientists in government.

Oppenheimer was the son of a German immigrant who had made his fortune by importing textiles in New York City. During his undergraduate studies at Harvard University, Oppenheimer excelled in Latin, Greek, physics, and chemistry, published poetry, and studied Oriental philosophy. After graduating in 1925, he sailed for England to do research at the Cavendish Laboratory at the University of Cambridge, which, under the leadership of Lord Ernest Rutherford, had an international reputation for its pioneering studies on atomic structure. At the Cavendish, Oppenheimer had the opportunity to collaborate with the British scientific community in its efforts to advance the cause of atomic research.

Max Born invited Oppenheimer to Göttingen University, where he met other prominent physicists, such as Niels Bohr and P.A.M. Dirac, and where, in 1927, he received his doctorate. After short visits at science centres in Leiden and Zürich, he returned to the United States to teach physics at the University of California at Berkeley and the California Institute of Technology.

In the 1920s the new quantum and relativity theories were engaging the attention of science. That mass was equivalent to energy and that matter could be both wavelike and corpuscular carried implications seen only dimly at that time. Oppenheimer's early research was devoted in particular to energy processes of subatomic particles, including electrons, positrons, and cosmic rays. Since quantum theory had been proposed only a few years before, the university post provided him an excellent opportunity to devote his entire career to the exploration and development of its full significance. In addition, he trained a whole generation of U.S. physicists, who were greatly affected by his qualities of leadership and intellectual independence.

The rise of Adolf Hitler in Germany stirred his first interest in politics. In 1936 he sided with the republic during the Civil War in Spain, where he became acquainted with Communist students. Although his father's death in 1937 left Oppenheimer a fortune that allowed him to subsidize anti-Fascist organizations, the tragic suffering inflicted by Joseph Stalin on Russian scientists led him to withdraw his associations with the Communist Party—in fact, he never joined the party—and at the same time reinforced in him a liberal democratic philosophy.

After the invasion of Poland by Nazi Germany in 1939, the physicists Albert Einstein and Leo Szilard warned the U.S. government of the danger threatening all of humanity if the Nazis should be the first to make a nuclear bomb. Oppenheimer then began to seek a process for the separation of uranium-235 from natural uranium and to determine the critical mass of uranium required to make such a bomb. In August 1942 the U.S. Army was given the responsibility of organizing the efforts of British and U.S. physicists to seek a way to harness nuclear energy for military purposes, an effort that became known as the Manhattan Project. Oppenheimer was instructed to establish and administer a laboratory to carry out this assignment. In 1943 he chose the plateau of Los Alamos, near Santa Fe, New Mexico, where he had spent part of his childhood in a boarding school.

For reasons that have not been made clear, Oppenheimer in 1942 initiated discussions with military security agents that culminated with the implication that some of his friends and acquaintances were agents of the Soviet government. This led to the dismissal of a personal friend on the faculty at the University of California. In a 1954 security hearing he described his contribution to those discussions as "a tissue of lies."

The joint effort of outstanding scientists at Los Alamos culminated in the first nuclear explosion on July 16, 1945, at the Trinity Site near Alamogordo, New Mexico, after the surrender of Germany. In October of the same year, Oppenheimer resigned his post. In 1947 he became head of the Institute for Advanced Study and served from 1947 until 1952 as chairman of the General Advisory Committee of the Atomic Energy Commission, which in October 1949 opposed development of the hydrogen bomb.

On December 21, 1953, he was notified of a military security report unfavourable to him and was accused of having associated with Communists in the past, of delaying the naming of Soviet agents, and of opposing the building of the hydrogen bomb. A security hearing declared him not guilty of treason but ruled that he should not have access to military secrets. As a result, his contract as adviser to the Atomic Energy Commission was cancelled. The Federation of American Scientists immediately came to his defense with a protest against the trial. Oppenheimer was made the worldwide symbol of the scientist, who, while trying to resolve the moral problems that arise from scientific discovery, becomes the victim of a witch-hunt. He spent the last years of his life working out ideas on the relationship between science and society.

In 1963 President Lyndon B. Johnson presented Oppenheimer with the Enrico Fermi Award of the Atomic Energy Commission. Oppenheimer retired from the

Institute for Advanced Study in 1966 and died of throat cancer the following year.

HANS BETHE

(b. July 2, 1906, Strassburg, Ger. [now Strasbourg, France]—d. March 6, 2005, Ithaca, N.Y., U.S.)

German-born American theoretical physicist Hans Albrecht Bethe helped shape quantum physics and increased the understanding of the atomic processes responsible for the properties of matter and of the forces governing the structures of atomic nuclei. He received the Nobel Prize for Physics in 1967 for his work on the production of energy in stars. Moreover, he was a leader in emphasizing the social responsibility of science.

EARLY WORK

Bethe wrote two book-length reviews in the 1933 *Handbuch der Physik*—the first with German physicist Arnold Sommerfeld on solid-state physics and the second on the quantum theory of one- and two-electron systems—that exhibited his remarkable powers of synthesis. Along with a review on nuclear physics in *Reviews of Modern Physics* (1936–37), these works were instant classics. All of Bethe's reviews were syntheses of the fields under review, giving them coherence and unity while charting the paths to be taken in addressing new problems. They usually contained much new material that Bethe had worked out in their preparation.

In the fall of 1932, Bethe obtained an appointment at the University of Tübingen as an acting assistant professor of theoretical physics. In April 1933, after Adolf Hitler's accession to power, he was dismissed because his maternal grandparents were Jews. Sommerfeld was able to help him by awarding him a fellowship for the summer of 1933, and he got William Lawrence Bragg to invite him to the University of Manchester, Eng., for the following academic year. Bethe then went to the University of Bristol for the 1934 fall semester before accepting a position at Cornell University, Ithaca, N.Y. He arrived at Cornell in February 1935, and he stayed there for the rest of his life.

Bethe came to the United States at a time when the American physics community was undergoing enormous growth. The Washington Conferences on Theoretical Physics were paradigmatic of the meetings organized to assimilate the insights quantum mechanics was giving to many fields, especially atomic and molecular physics and the emerging field of nuclear physics. Bethe attended the 1935 and 1937 Washington Conferences, but he agreed to participate in the 1938 conference on stellar energy generation only after repeated urgings by Edward Teller. As a result of what he learned at the latter conference, Bethe was able to give definitive answers to the problem of energy generation in stars. By stipulating and analyzing the nuclear reactions responsible for the phenomenon, he explained how stars could continue to burn for billions of years. His 1939 *Physical Review* paper on energy generation in stars created the field of nuclear astrophysics and led to his being awarded the Nobel Prize.

From Atomic Warrior to "Political Physicist"

During World War II Bethe first worked on problems in radar, spending a year at the Radiation Laboratory at the Massachusetts Institute of Technology. In 1943 he joined the Los Alamos Laboratory (now the Los Alamos National Laboratory) in New Mexico as the head of its theoretical division. He and the division were part of the Manhattan Project, and they made crucial contributions to the feasibility and design of the uranium and the plutonium atomic bombs. The years at Los Alamos changed his life.

In the aftermath of the development of these fission weapons, Bethe became deeply involved with investigating the feasibility of developing fusion bombs, hoping to prove that no terrestrial mechanism could accomplish the task. He believed their development to be immoral. When the Teller-Ulam mechanism for igniting a fusion reaction was advanced in 1951 and the possibility of a hydrogen bomb, or H-bomb, became a reality, Bethe helped to design it. He believed that the Soviets would likewise be able to build one and that only a balance of terror would prevent their use.

As a result of these activities, Bethe became deeply occupied with what he called "political physics," the attempt to educate the public and politicians about the consequences of the existence of nuclear weapons. He became a relentless champion of nuclear arms control, writing many essays (collected in *The Road from Los Alamos* [1991]). He also became deeply committed to making peaceful applications of nuclear power economical and safe. Throughout his life, Bethe was a staunch advocate of nuclear power, defending it as an answer to the inevitable exhaustion of fossil fuels.

In 1972 Bethe's cogent and persuasive arguments helped prevent the deployment of antiballistic missile systems. He was influential in opposing President Ronald Reagan's Strategic Defense Initiative, arguing that a space-based laser defense system could be easily countered and that it would lead to further arms escalation. By virtue of these activities, and his general comportment, Bethe became the science community's conscience. It was indicative of Bethe's constant grappling with moral issues that in 1995 he urged fellow scientists to collectively take a "Hippocratic oath" not to work on designing new nuclear weapons.

Throughout the political activism that marked his later life, Bethe never abandoned his scientific researches. Until well into his 90s, he made important contributions at the frontiers of physics and astrophysics. He helped elucidate the properties of neutrinos and explained the observed rate of neutrino emission by the Sun. With the American physicist Gerald Brown, he worked to understand why massive old stars can suddenly become supernovas.

MARIA GOEPPERT MAYER

(b. June 28, 1906, Kattowitz, Ger. [now Katowice, Pol.]—d. Feb. 20, 1972, San Diego, Calif., U.S.)

German-born American physicist Maria Goeppert Mayer (née Maria Goeppert) shared one-half of the 1963 Nobel Prize for Physics with J. Hans D. Jensen of West Germany for their proposal of the shell nuclear model. (The other half of the prize was awarded to Eugene P. Wigner of the United States for unrelated work.)

Maria Goeppert studied physics at the University of Göttingen (Ph.D., 1930) under a committee of three Nobel Prize winners. In 1930 she married the American chemical physicist Joseph E. Mayer, and a short time later she accompanied him to Johns Hopkins University in Baltimore, Maryland. Over the next nine years she was associated with Johns Hopkins as a volunteer associate. During that time she collaborated with Karl Herzfeld and her husband in the study of organic molecules. She became a U.S. citizen in 1933. In 1939 she and her husband both received appointments in chemistry at Columbia University, where Maria Mayer worked on the separation of uranium isotopes for the atomic bomb project. The Mayers published *Statistical Mechanics* in 1940. Although they remained at Columbia throughout World War II, Maria Mayer also lectured at Sarah Lawrence College (1942–45).

After the war Mayer's interests centred increasingly on nuclear physics, and in 1945 she became a volunteer professor of physics in the Enrico Fermi Institute for Nuclear Studies at the University of Chicago. She received a regular appointment as full professor in 1959. From 1948 to 1949 Mayer published several papers concerning the stability and configuration of protons and neutrons that constitute the atomic nucleus. She developed a theory that the nucleus consists of several shells, or orbital levels, and that the distribution of protons and neutrons among these shells produces the characteristic degree of stability of each species of nucleus. A similar theory was developed at the same time in Germany by J. Hans D. Jensen, with whom she subsequently collaborated on *Elementary Theory of Nuclear Shell Structure* (1955). The work established her as a leading authority in the field. Also noted for her work in quantum electrodynamics and spectroscopy, Mayer accepted an appointment at the University of California at San Diego in 1960, as did her husband.

RACHEL CARSON

(b. May 27, 1907, Springdale, Pa., U.S.—d. April 14, 1964, Silver Spring, Md.)

American biologist Rachel Carson was well known for her writings on environmental pollution and the natural history of the sea. Carson early developed a deep interest in the natural world. She entered Pennsylvania College for Women with the intention of becoming a writer but soon changed her major field of study from English to biology. After taking her bachelor's degree in 1929, she did graduate work at Johns Hopkins University (M.A., 1932) and in 1931 joined the faculty of the University of Maryland, where she taught for five years. From 1929 to 1936 she also taught in the Johns Hopkins summer school and pursued postgraduate studies at the Marine Biological Laboratory in Woods Hole, Mass.

In 1936 Carson took a position as aquatic biologist with the U.S. Bureau of Fisheries (from 1940 the U.S. Fish and Wildlife Service), where she remained until 1952, the last three years as editor in chief of the service's publications. An article in *The Atlantic Monthly* in 1937 served as the basis for her first book, *Under the Sea-Wind*, published in 1941. It was widely praised, as were all her books, for its remarkable combination of scientific accuracy and thoroughness with an elegant and lyrical prose style. *The Sea Around Us* (1951) became a national

Rachel Carson, conducting research in Florida, 1952. Alfred Eisenstadt/Time & Life Pictures/Getty Images

best-seller, won a National Book Award, and was eventually translated into 30 languages. Her third book, *The Edge of the Sea*, was published in 1955.

Carson's prophetic *Silent Spring* (1962) was first serialized in *The New Yorker* and then became a best-seller, creating worldwide awareness of the dangers of environmental pollution. The vision of the environmental movement of the 1960s and early '70s was generally pessimistic, reflecting a pervasive sense of "civilization malaise" and a conviction that the Earth's long-term prospects were bleak. Carson's *Silent Spring* suggested that the planetary ecosystem was reaching the limits of what it could sustain. Carson stood behind her warnings of the consequences of indiscriminate pesticide use, despite the threat of lawsuits from the chemical industry and accusations that she engaged in "emotionalism" and "gross distortion." Some critics even claimed that she was a communist. Carson died before she could see any substantive results from her work on this issue, but she left behind some of the most influential environmental writing ever published.

JACQUES-YVES COUSTEAU

(b. June 11, 1910, Saint-André-de-Cubzac, France — d. June 25, 1997, Paris)

French naval officer and ocean explorer Jacques-Yves Cousteau was known for his extensive underseas investigations. Not formally trained as a scientist, Cousteau was drawn to undersea exploration by his love both of the ocean and of diving. After graduating from France's naval academy in 1933, he was commissioned a second lieutenant. His plans to become a navy pilot were undermined by an almost fatal automobile accident in which both of his arms were broken.

In 1943 Cousteau and the French engineer Émile Gagnan developed the first fully automatic compressed-air Aqua-Lung. Cousteau helped to invent many other tools useful to oceanographers, including the diving saucer, a small, easily maneuverable submarine for seafloor exploration, and a number of underwater cameras.

Cousteau served in World War II as a gunnery officer in France and was also a member of the French Resistance. He later was awarded the Legion of Honour for his espionage work. Cousteau's experiments with underwater filmmaking began during the war, and when the war ended, he continued this work by founding and heading the French navy's Undersea Research Group at Toulon.

This picture, taken in 1965, shows famed oceanographer Jacques Cousteau preparing to conduct research. AFP/Getty Images

To expand his work in marine exploration, he founded numerous marketing, manufacturing, engineering, and research organizations, which were incorporated (1973) as the Cousteau Group. In 1950 Cousteau converted a British minesweeper into the *Calypso*, an oceanographic research ship aboard which he and his crew carried out numerous expeditions. Cousteau eventually popularized oceanographic research and the sport of scuba diving in the book *Le Monde du silence* (1952; *The Silent World*), written with Frédéric Dumas. Two years later he adapted the book into a documentary film that won both the Palme d'Or at the 1956 Cannes International Film Festival and an Academy Award in 1957, one of three Oscars his films received.

Cousteau was the founder of the French Office of Underseas Research at Marseille, Fr. (renamed the Centre of Advanced Marine Studies in 1968), and he became director of the Oceanographic Museum of Monaco in 1957. He also led the Conshelf Saturation Dive Program, conducting experiments in which men live and work for extended periods of time at considerable depths along the continental shelves. The undersea laboratories were called Conshelf I, II, and III.

Cousteau produced and starred in many television programs, including the U.S. series "The Undersea World of Jacques Cousteau" (1968-76). In 1974 he formed the Cousteau Society, a nonprofit environmental group dedicated to marine conservation. In addition to *The Silent World*, Cousteau also wrote *Par 18 mètres de fond* (1946; "Through 18 Metres of Water"), *The Living Sea* (1963), *Three Adventures: Galápagos, Titicaca, the Blue Holes* (1973), *Dolphins* (1975), and *Jacques Cousteau: The Ocean World* (1985). His last book, *The Human, the Orchid, and the Octopus* (2007), was published posthumously.

LUIS W. ALVAREZ

(b. June 13, 1911, San Francisco, Calif., U.S.—d. Sept. 1, 1988, Berkeley, Calif.)

American experimental physicist Luis W. Alvarez was awarded the Nobel Prize for Physics in 1968 for work that included the discovery of many resonance particles (subatomic particles having extremely short lifetimes and occurring only in high-energy nuclear collisions).

Alvarez studied physics at the University of Chicago (B.S., 1932; M.S., 1934; Ph.D., 1936). He joined the faculty of the University of California, Berkeley, in 1936, becoming professor of physics in 1945 and professor emeritus in 1978. In 1938 Alvarez discovered that some radioactive elements decay by orbital-electron capture; i.e., an orbital electron merges with its nucleus, producing an element with an atomic number smaller by one. In 1939 he and Felix Bloch made the first measurement of the magnetic moment of the neutron, a characteristic of the strength and direction of its magnetic field.

Alvarez worked on microwave radar research at the Massachusetts Institute of Technology, Cambridge (1940–43), and participated in the development of the atomic bomb at the Los Alamos Scientific Laboratory, Los Alamos, N.M., in 1944–45. He suggested the technique for detonating the implosion type of atomic bomb. He also participated in the development of microwave beacons, linear radar antennas, the ground-controlled landing approach system, and a method for aerial bombing using radar to locate targets.

After World War II Alvarez helped construct the first proton linear accelerator. In this accelerator, electric fields are set up as standing waves within a cylindrical metal "resonant cavity," with drift tubes suspended along the central axis. The electric field is zero inside the drift tubes, and, if their lengths are properly chosen, the protons cross the gap between adjacent drift tubes when the direction of the field produces acceleration and are shielded by the drift tubes when the field in the tank would decelerate them. The lengths of the drift tubes are proportional to the speeds of the particles that pass through them. In addition to this work, Alvarez also developed the liquid hydrogen bubble chamber in which subatomic particles and their reactions are detected.

In about 1980 Alvarez helped his son, the geologist Walter Alvarez, publicize Walter's discovery of a worldwide layer of clay that has a high iridium content and which occupies rock strata at the geochronological boundary between the Mesozoic and Cenozoic eras; i.e., about 66.4 million years ago. They postulated that the iridium had been deposited following the impact on Earth of an asteroid or comet and that the catastrophic climatic effects of this massive impact caused the extinction of the dinosaurs. Though initially controversial, this widely publicized theory gradually gained

Luis Alvarez. Courtesy of the Lawrence Radiation Laboratory, the University of California, Berkeley

support as the most plausible explanation of the abrupt demise of the dinosaurs.

Alvarez's autobiography, *Alvarez: Adventures of a Physicist*, was published in 1987.

ALAN M. TURING

(b. June 23, 1912, London, Eng.—d. June 7, 1954, Wilmslow, Cheshire)

B ritish mathematician and logician Alan Mathison Turing made major contributions to mathematics, cryptanalysis, logic, philosophy, and biology and to the new areas later named computer science, cognitive science, artificial intelligence, and artificial life.

EARLY LIFE AND CAREER

The son of a British member of the Indian civil service, Turing entered King's College, University of Cambridge, to study mathematics in 1931. After graduating in 1934, Turing was elected to a fellowship at King's College in recognition of his research in probability theory. In 1936 Turing's seminal paper *On Computable Numbers, with an Application to the Entscheidungsproblem [Decision Problem]* was recommended for publication by the American mathematician-logician Alonzo Church, who had himself just published a paper that reached the same conclusion as Turing's. Later that year, Turing moved to Princeton University to study for a Ph.D. in mathematical logic under Church's direction (completed in 1938).

The *Entscheidungsproblem* seeks an effective method for deciding which mathematical statements are provable within a given formal mathematical system and which are not. In 1936 Turing and Church independently showed that in general this problem has no solution, proving that no consistent formal system of arithmetic is decidable.

This result and others—notably the mathematician-logician Kurt Gödel's incompleteness theorems—ended the dream of a system that could banish ignorance from mathematics forever. (In fact, Turing and Church showed that even some purely logical systems, considerably weaker than arithmetic, are undecidable.)

An important argument of Turing's and Church's was that the class of lambda-definable functions (functions on the positive integers whose values can be calculated by a process of repeated substitution) coincides with the class of all functions that are effectively calculable—or computable. This claim is now known as Church's thesis—or as the Church-Turing thesis when stated in the form that any effectively calculable function can be calculated by a universal Turing machine, a type of abstract computer that Turing had introduced in the course of his proof. (Turing showed in 1936 that the two formulations of the thesis are equivalent by proving that the lambda-definable functions and the functions that can be calculated by a universal Turing machine are identical.) In a review of Turing's work, Church acknowledged the superiority of Turing's formulation of the thesis over his own, saying that the concept of computability by a Turing machine "has the advantage of making the identification with effectiveness . . . evident immediately."

CODE BREAKER

In the summer of 1938 Turing returned from the United States to his fellowship at King's College. At the outbreak of hostilities with Germany in September 1939, he joined the wartime headquarters of the Government Code and Cypher School at Bletchley Park, Buckinghamshire. The British government had just been given the details of efforts by the Poles, assisted by the French, to break the

Enigma code, used by the German military for their radio communications. As early as 1932, a small team of Polish mathematician-cryptanalysts, led by Marian Rejewski, had succeeded in reconstructing the internal wiring of the type of Enigma machine used by the Germans, and by 1938 they had devised a code-breaking machine, code-named *Bomba* (the Polish word for a type of ice cream). The *Bomba* depended for its success on German operating procedures, and a change in procedures in May 1940 rendered the *Bomba* virtually useless.

During 1939 and the spring of 1940, Turing and others designed a radically different code-breaking machine known as the Bombe. Turing's ingenious Bombes kept the Allies supplied with intelligence for the remainder of the war. By early 1942 the Bletchley Park cryptanalysts were decoding about 39,000 intercepted messages each month, which rose subsequently to more than 84,000 per month. At the end of the war, Turing was made an officer of the Order of the British Empire for his code-breaking work.

COMPUTER DESIGNER

In 1945, the war being over, Turing was recruited to the National Physical Laboratory (NPL) in London to design and develop an electronic computer. His design for the Automatic Computing Engine (ACE) was the first relatively complete specification of an electronic stored-program general-purpose digital computer. Had Turing's ACE been built as planned, it would have had considerably more memory than any of the other early computers, as well as being faster. However, his colleagues at NPL thought the engineering too difficult to attempt, and a much simpler machine was built, the Pilot Model ACE.

In the end, NPL lost the race to build the world's first working electronic stored-program digital computer—an honour that went to the Royal Society Computing Machine Laboratory at the University of Manchester in June 1948. Discouraged by the delays at NPL, Turing took up the deputy directorship of the Computing Machine Laboratory in that year (there was no director). His earlier theoretical concept of a universal Turing machine had been a fundamental influence on the Manchester computer project from its inception. Turing's principal practical contribution after his arrival at Manchester was to design the programming system of the Ferranti Mark I, the world's first commercially available electronic digital computer.

ARTIFICIAL INTELLIGENCE PIONEER

Turing was a founding father of modern cognitive science and a leading early exponent of the hypothesis that the human brain is in large part a digital computing machine. He theorized that the cortex at birth is an "unorganised machine" that through "training" becomes organized "into a universal machine or something like it." A pioneer of artificial intelligence, Turing proposed (1950) what subsequently became known as the Turing test as a criterion for whether a machine thinks.

Though he was elected a fellow of the Royal Society in March 1951, Turing's life was about to suffer a major reversal. In March 1952 he was prosecuted for homosexuality, then a crime in Britain, and sentenced to 12 months of hormone "therapy"—a treatment that he seems to have borne with amused fortitude. Judged a security risk by the British government, Turing lost his security clearance and his access to ongoing government work with codes and computers. He spent the rest of his short career at the University of Manchester, where he was appointed to a specially created readership in the theory of computing in May 1953.

From 1951 Turing had been working on what is now known as artificial life. He wrote "The Chemical Basis of Morphogenesis," which described some of his research on the development of pattern and form in living organisms, and he used the Ferranti Mark I computer to model chemical mechanisms by which genes could control the development of anatomical structure in plants and animals. In the midst of this groundbreaking work, Turing was discovered dead in his bed, poisoned by cyanide. A homemade apparatus for silver-plating teaspoons, which included a tank of cyanide, was found in the room next to his bedroom. The official verdict was suicide, but no motive was ever discovered.

NORMAN ERNEST BORLAUG

(b. March 25, 1914, Cresco, Iowa, U.S.)

American agricultural scientist and plant pathologist Norman Ernest Borlaug helped to lay the groundwork of the so-called Green Revolution, the agricultural technological advance that promised to alleviate world hunger. For his achievements he was awarded the Nobel Prize for Peace in 1970.

Borlaug studied plant biology and forestry at the University of Minnesota and earned a Ph.D. in plant pathology there in 1941. From 1944 to 1960 he served as research scientist at the Rockefeller Foundation's Cooperative Mexican Agricultural Program in Mexico. Borlaug's work was founded on earlier discoveries of ways to induce genetic mutations in plants. These methods led to modern plant breeding, with momentous results that included the tailoring of crop varieties for regions of climatic extremes. At a research station at Campo Atizapan he developed strains of grain that dramatically increased crop yields. Borlaug ultimately developed short-stemmed ("dwarf") wheat, a key element in the Green Revolution in developing countries.

The Green Revolution resulted in increased production of food grains (especially wheat and rice) and was due in large part from the introduction into developing countries of new, high-yielding varieties, beginning in the mid-20th century with Borlaug's work. Its early dramatic successes were in Mexico and the Indian subcontinent. Wheat production in Mexico multiplied threefold in the time that Borlaug worked with the Mexican government. In addition, "dwarf" wheat imported in the mid-1960s was responsible for a 60 percent increase in harvests in Pakistan and India.

Borlaug also created a wheat–rye hybrid known as triticale. The increased yields resulting from Borlaug's new

Nobel Prize–winning biologist Dr. Norman Borlaug poses with some of the wheat he crossbred to be more disease resistant. Art Rickerby/Time & Life Pictures/Getty Images

strains enabled many developing countries to become agriculturally self-sufficient. However, since their introduction, these new varieties have been discovered to require large amounts of chemical fertilizers and pesticides to produce their high yields, raising concerns about cost and potentially harmful environmental effects. As a result, newer varieties of food grains, which are high-yielding and resistant to local pests and diseases, have been developed.

Borlaug served as director of the Inter-American Food Crop Program (1960–63) and as director of the International Maize and Wheat Improvement Center, Mexico City, from 1964 to 1979. In 1986 Borlaug created the World Food Prize as a way to honour individuals who have contributed to improving the availability and quality of food worldwide. In constant demand as a consultant, Borlaug has served on numerous committees and advisory panels on agriculture, population control, and renewable resources.

JONAS EDWARD SALK

(b. Oct. 28, 1914, New York, N.Y., U.S.—d. June 23, 1995, La Jolla, Calif.)

American physician and medical researcher Jonas Edward Salk developed the first safe and effective vaccine for polio. Salk received his M.D. in 1939 from New York University College of Medicine, where he worked with Thomas Francis, Jr., who was conducting killed-virus immunology studies. Salk joined Francis in 1942 at the University of Michigan School of Public Health and became part of a group that was working to develop an immunization against influenza.

In 1947 Salk became associate professor of bacteriology and head of the Virus Research Laboratory at the University of Pittsburgh School of Medicine. At Pittsburgh, he began research on polio, an acute viral infectious disease of the nervous system that usually begins with general symptoms such as fever and headache and is sometimes followed by a more serious and permanent paralysis of muscles in one or more limbs, the throat, or the chest. In the mid-20th century hundreds of thousands of children were struck by the disease every year. Working with scientists from other universities in a program to classify the various strains of poliovirus, Salk corroborated other studies in identifying three separate strains. He then demonstrated that killed virus of each of the three, although incapable of producing the disease, could induce antibody formation in monkeys. In 1952 he conducted field tests of his killed-virus vaccine, first on children who had recovered from polio and then on subjects who had not had the disease; both tests were successful in that the children's antibody levels rose significantly and no subjects contracted polio from the vaccine. His findings were published the following year.

In 1954 Francis conducted a mass field trial, and the vaccine, injected by needle, was found to safely reduce the incidence of polio. On April 12, 1955, the vaccine was released for use in the United States. In the following years, the incidence of polio in the United States fell from 18 cases per 100,000 people to fewer than 2 per 100,000. In the 1960s a second type of polio vaccine, known as oral poliovirus vaccine (OPV) or Sabin vaccine, named for its inventor American physician and microbiologist Albert Sabin, was developed. OPV contains live attenuated (weakened) virus and is given orally.

Salk served successively as professor of bacteriology, preventive medicine, and experimental medicine at Pittsburgh, and in 1963 he became fellow and director of the Institute for Biological Studies in San Diego, California, later called the Salk Institute. Among his many honours was the Presidential Medal of Freedom, awarded in 1977.

SIR FRED HOYLE

(b. June 24, 1915, Bingley, Yorkshire [now West Yorkshire], Eng.—d. Aug. 20, 2001, Bournemouth, Dorset)

B ritish mathematician and astronomer Sir Fred Hoyle was best known as the foremost proponent and defender of the steady-state theory of the universe. This theory holds both that the universe is expanding and that matter is being continuously created to keep the mean density of matter in space constant.

Hoyle was educated at Emmanuel College and St. John's College, Cambridge, and spent six years during World War II with the British Admiralty, working on radar development. In 1945 he returned to Cambridge as a lecturer in mathematics. Three years later, in collaboration with the astronomer Thomas Gold and the mathematician Hermann Bondi, he announced the steady-state theory. Within the framework of Albert Einstein's theory of relativity, Hoyle formulated a mathematical basis for the steady-state theory, making the expansion of the universe and the creation of matter interdependent. Einstein assumed that the universe as a whole is static—i.e., its large-scale properties do not vary with time. This assumption, made before American astronomer Edward Hubble's observational discovery of the expansion of the universe, was also natural; it was the simplest approach, as Aristotle had discovered, if one wishes to avoid a discussion of a creation event. The notion that the universe on average is not only homogeneous and isotropic in space but also constant in time was philosophically attractive. Hoyle, Bondi, and Gold called it the perfect cosmological principle.

In the late 1950s and early '60s, controversy about the steady-state theory grew. New observations of distant galaxies and other phenomena, supporting the big-bang theory (a phrase that Hoyle had coined in derision in the 1940s), weakened the steady-state theory, and it has since fallen out of favour with most cosmologists. Although Hoyle was forced to alter some of his conclusions, he tenaciously tried to make his theory consistent with new evidence.

Hoyle was elected to the Royal Society in 1957, a year after joining the staff of the Hale Observatories (now the Mount Wilson and Palomar observatories). In collaboration with William Fowler and others in the United States, he formulated theories about the origins of stars as well as about the origins of elements within stars. Hoyle was director of the Institute of Theoretical Astronomy at Cambridge (1967–73), an institution he was instrumental in founding. He received a knighthood in 1972.

Hoyle is known for his popular science works, including *The Nature of the Universe* (1951), *Astronomy and Cosmology* (1975), and *The Origin of the Universe and the Origin of Religion* (1993). He also wrote novels, plays, short stories, and an autobiography, *The Small World of Fred Hoyle* (1986).

FRANCIS HARRY COMPTON CRICK

(b. June 8, 1916, Northampton, Northamptonshire, Eng.—d. July 28, 2004, San Diego, Calif., U.S.)

British biophysicist Francis Crick received the 1962 Nobel Prize for Physiology or Medicine, along with James Watson and Maurice Wilkins, for determining the molecular structure of deoxyribonucleic acid (DNA), the chemical substance ultimately responsible for hereditary control of life functions. This accomplishment became a cornerstone of genetics and was widely regarded as one of the most important discoveries of 20th-century biology.

During World War II, Crick interrupted his education to work as a physicist in the development of magnetic mines for use in naval warfare, but afterward he turned to biology at the Strangeways Research Laboratory, University of Cambridge (1947). Interested in pioneering efforts to determine the three-dimensional structures of large molecules found in living organisms, he transferred to the university's Medical Research Council Unit at the Cavendish Laboratories in 1949.

In 1951, when the American biologist James Watson arrived at the laboratory, it was known that the mysterious nucleic acids, especially DNA, played a central role in the hereditary determination of the structure and function of each cell. Watson convinced Crick that knowledge of DNA's three-dimensional structure would make its hereditary role apparent. Using the X-ray diffraction studies of DNA done by Wilkins and X-ray diffraction pictures produced by Rosalind Franklin, Watson and Crick were able to construct a molecular model consistent with the known physical and chemical properties of DNA. The model consisted of two intertwined helical (spiral) strands of sugar-phosphate, bridged horizontally by flat organic bases. Watson and Crick theorized that if the strands were separated, each would serve as a template (pattern) for the formation, from small molecules in the cell, of a new sister strand identical to its former partner. This copying process explained replication of the gene and, eventually, the chromosome, known to occur in dividing cells. Their model also indicated that the sequence of bases along the DNA molecule spells some kind of code "read" by a cellular mechanism that translates it into the specific proteins responsible for a cell's particular structure and function.

By 1961 Crick had evidence to show that each group of three bases (a codon) on a single DNA strand designates the position of a specific amino acid on the backbone of a protein molecule. He also helped to determine which codons code for each of the 20 amino acids normally found in protein and thus helped clarify the way in which the cell eventually uses the DNA "message" to build proteins.

From 1977 until his death, Crick held the position of distinguished professor at the Salk Institute for Biological Studies in San Diego, California, where he conducted research on the neurological basis of consciousness. His book *Of Molecules and Men* (1966) discusses the implications of the revolution in molecular biology. *What Mad Pursuit: A Personal View of Scientific Discovery* was published in 1988. In 1991 Crick received the Order of Merit.

JAMES DEWEY WATSON
(b. April 6, 1928, Chicago, Ill., U.S.)

American geneticist and biophysicist James Dewey Watson played a crucial role in the discovery of the molecular structure of deoxyribonucleic acid (DNA), the substance that is the basis of heredity. For this accomplishment he was awarded the 1962 Nobel Prize for Physiology or Medicine with Francis Crick and Maurice Wilkins.

Watson enrolled at the University of Chicago when only 15 and graduated in 1947. From his virus research at Indiana University (Ph.D., 1950), and from the experiments of Canadian-born American bacteriologist Oswald Avery, which proved that DNA affects hereditary traits, Watson became convinced that the gene could be understood only after something was known about nucleic acid molecules. He learned that scientists working in the Cavendish Laboratories at the University of Cambridge were using photographic patterns made by X rays that had been shot through protein crystals to study the structure of protein molecules.

After working at the University of Copenhagen, where he first determined to investigate DNA, he did research at the Cavendish Laboratories (1951–53). There Watson learned X-ray diffraction techniques and worked with Crick on the problem of DNA structure. In 1952 he determined the structure of the protein coat surrounding the tobacco mosaic virus but made no dramatic progress with DNA. Suddenly, in the spring of 1953, Watson saw that the essential DNA components—four organic bases—must be linked in definite pairs.

This discovery was the key factor that enabled Watson and Crick to formulate a molecular model for DNA—a double helix, which can be likened to a spiraling staircase or a twisting ladder. The DNA double helix consists of two intertwined sugar-phosphate chains, with the flat base pairs forming the steps between them. Watson and Crick's model also showed how the DNA molecule could duplicate itself. Thus it became known how genes, and eventually chromosomes, duplicate themselves. Watson and Crick published their epochal discovery in two papers in the British journal *Nature* in April–May 1953. Their research answered one of the fundamental questions in genetics.

Watson subsequently taught at Harvard University (1955–76), where he served as professor of biology (1961–76). He conducted research on the role of nucleic acids in the synthesis of proteins. In 1965 he published *Molecular Biology of the Gene*, one of the most extensively used modern biology texts. He later wrote *The Double Helix* (1968), an informal and personal account of the DNA discovery and the roles of the people involved in it, which aroused some controversy.

In 1968 Watson assumed the leadership of the Laboratory of Quantitative Biology at Cold Spring Harbor, Long Island, N.Y., and made it a world centre for research in molecular biology. He concentrated its efforts on cancer research. In 1981 his *The DNA Story* (written with John Tooze) was published. From 1988 to 1992 at the National Institutes of Health, Watson helped direct the Human

Genome Project, a project to map and decipher all the genes in the human chromosomes, but he eventually resigned because of alleged conflicts of interests involving his investments in private biotechnology companies.

In early 2007 Watson's own genome was sequenced and made publicly available on the Internet. He was the second person in history to have a personal genome sequenced in its entirety. In October of the same year, he sparked controversy by making a public statement alluding to the idea that the intelligence of Africans might not be the same as that of other peoples and that intellectual differences among geographically separated peoples might arise over time as a result of genetic divergence. Watson's remarks were immediately denounced as racist. Though he denied this charge, he resigned from his position at Cold Spring Harbor and formally announced his retirement less than two weeks later.

RICHARD P. FEYNMAN

(b. May 11, 1918, New York, N.Y., U.S.—d. Feb. 15, 1988, Los Angeles, Calif.)

American theoretical physicist Richard Phillips Feynman was widely regarded as the most brilliant, influential, and iconoclastic figure in his field in the post-World War II era. Feynman remade quantum electrodynamics—the theory of the interaction between light and matter—and thus altered the way science understands the nature of waves and particles. He was co-awarded the Nobel Prize for Physics in 1965 for this work, which tied together in an experimentally perfect package all the varied phenomena at work in light, radio, electricity, and magnetism. The other cowinners of the Nobel Prize, Julian S. Schwinger of the United States and Tomonaga Shin'ichirō of Japan, had independently created equivalent theories, but it was Feynman's that proved the most original and far-reaching. The problem-solving tools that he invented—including pictorial representations of particle interactions known as Feynman diagrams—permeated many areas of theoretical physics in the second half of the 20th century.

Feynman studied physics as an undergraduate at the Massachusetts Institute of Technology and received his doctorate at Princeton University in 1942. At Princeton, with his adviser, John Archibald Wheeler, he developed an approach to quantum mechanics governed by the principle of least action. This approach replaced the wave-oriented electromagnetic picture developed by James Clerk Maxwell with one based entirely on particle interactions mapped in space and time. In effect, Feynman's method calculated the probabilities of all the possible paths a particle could take in going from one point to another.

During World War II Feynman was recruited to serve as a staff member of the U.S. atomic bomb project at Princeton University (1941–42) and then at the new secret laboratory at Los Alamos, New Mexico (1943–45). At Los Alamos he became the youngest group leader in the theoretical division of the Manhattan Project. With the head of that division, Hans Bethe, he devised the formula for predicting the energy yield of a nuclear explosive. Feynman also took charge of the project's primitive computing effort, using a hybrid of new calculating machines and human workers to try to process the vast amounts of numerical computation required by the project. He observed the first detonation of an atomic bomb on July 16, 1945, near Alamogordo, New Mexico, and, though his initial reaction was euphoric, he later felt anxiety about the force he and his colleagues had helped unleash on the world.

At war's end Feynman became an associate professor at Cornell University (1945–50) and returned to studying the fundamental issues of quantum electrodynamics. In 1950 he became professor of theoretical physics at the California Institute of Technology (Caltech), where he remained the rest of his career.

Five particular achievements of Feynman stand out as crucial to the development of modern physics. First, and most important, is his work in correcting the inaccuracies of earlier formulations of quantum electrodynamics, the theory that explains the interactions between electromagnetic radiation (photons) and charged subatomic particles such as electrons and positrons (antielectrons).

By 1948 Feynman completed this reconstruction of a large part of quantum mechanics and electrodynamics and resolved the meaningless results that the old quantum electrodynamic theory sometimes produced. Second, he introduced simple diagrams, now called Feynman diagrams, that are easily visualized graphic analogues of the complicated mathematical expressions needed to describe the behaviour of systems of interacting particles. This work greatly simplified some of the calculations used to observe and predict such interactions.

In the early 1950s Feynman provided a quantum-mechanical explanation for the Soviet physicist Lev D. Landau's theory of superfluidity—i.e., the strange, frictionless behaviour of liquid helium at temperatures near absolute zero. In 1958 he and the American physicist Murray Gell-Mann devised a theory that accounted for most of the phenomena associated with the weak force, which is the force at work in radioactive decay. Their theory, which turns on the asymmetrical "handedness" of particle spin, proved particularly fruitful in modern particle physics. And finally, in 1968, while working with experimenters at the Stanford Linear Accelerator on the scattering of high-energy electrons by protons, Feynman invented a theory of "partons," or hypothetical hard particles inside the nucleus of the atom, that helped lead to the modern understanding of quarks.

Feynman's lectures at Caltech evolved into the books *Quantum Electrodynamics* (1961) and *The Theory of Fundamental Processes* (1961). In 1961 he began reorganizing and teaching the introductory physics course at Caltech; the result, published as *The Feynman Lectures on Physics*, 3 vol. (1963–65), became a classic textbook. Feynman's views on quantum mechanics, scientific method, the relations between science and religion, and the role of beauty and uncertainty in scientific knowledge are expressed in two models of science writing, again distilled from lectures: *The Character of Physical Law* (1965) and *QED: The Strange Theory of Light and Matter* (1985).

ROSALIND FRANKLIN

(b. July 25, 1920, London, Eng.—d. April 16, 1958, London)

British scientist Rosalind Franklin contributed to the discovery of the molecular structure of deoxyribonucleic acid (DNA), a constituent of chromosomes that serves to encode genetic information.

Franklin attended St. Paul's Girls' School before studying physical chemistry at Newnham College, Cambridge. After graduating in 1941, she received a fellowship to conduct research in physical chemistry at Cambridge. But the advance of World War II changed her course of action: not only did she serve as a London air raid warden, but in 1942 she gave up her fellowship in order to work for the British Coal Utilisation Research Association, where she investigated the physical chemistry of carbon and coal for the war effort. Nevertheless, she was able to use this research for her doctoral thesis, and in 1945 she received a doctorate from Cambridge. From 1947 to 1950 she worked with Jacques Méring at the State Chemical Laboratory in Paris, studying X-ray diffraction technology. That work led to her research on the structural changes caused by the formation of graphite in heated carbons—work that proved valuable for the coking industry.

In 1951 Franklin joined the Biophysical Laboratory at King's College, London, as a research fellow. There she applied X-ray diffraction methods to the study of DNA. When she began her research at King's College, very little was known about the chemical makeup or structure of DNA. However, she soon discovered the density of DNA and, more importantly, established that the molecule existed in a helical conformation. Her work to make clearer X-ray patterns of DNA molecules laid the foundation for James Watson and Francis Crick to suggest in 1953 that the structure of DNA is a double-helix polymer, a spiral consisting of two DNA strands wound around each other.

From 1953 to 1958 Franklin worked in the Crystallography Laboratory at Birkbeck College, London. While there she completed her work on coals and on DNA and began a project on the molecular structure of the tobacco mosaic virus. She collaborated on studies showing that the ribonucleic acid (RNA) in that virus was embedded in its protein rather than in its central cavity and that this RNA was a single-strand helix, rather than the double helix found in the DNA of bacterial viruses and higher organisms. Franklin's involvement in cutting-edge DNA research was halted by her untimely death from cancer in 1958.

EDWARD O. WILSON

(b. June 10, 1929, Birmingham, Ala., U.S.)

American biologist Edward Osborne Wilson was recognized as the world's leading authority on ants. He was also the foremost proponent of sociobiology, the study of the genetic basis of the social behaviour of all animals, including humans.

Wilson received his early training at the University of Alabama (B.S., 1949; M.S., 1950). After receiving his doctorate in biology at Harvard University in 1955, he was a member of Harvard's biology and zoology faculties from 1956 to 1976. At Harvard he was later Frank B. Baird Professor of Science (1976–94), Mellon Professor of the Sciences (1990–93), and Pellegrino University Professor (1994–97). He was professor emeritus from 1997. In addition, Wilson served as curator in entomology at Harvard's Museum of Comparative Zoology (1973–97).

In 1955 Wilson completed an exhaustive taxonomic analysis of the ant genus *Lasius*. In collaboration with W.L. Brown, he developed the concept of "character displacement," a process in which populations of two closely related species, after first coming into contact with each other, undergo rapid evolutionary differentiation in order to minimize the chances of both competition and hybridization between them.

After his appointment to Harvard in 1956, Wilson made a series of important discoveries, including the determination that ants communicate primarily through the transmission of chemical substances known as pheromones. In the course of revising the classification of ants native to the South Pacific, he formulated the concept of the "taxon cycle," in which speciation and species dispersal are linked to the varying habitats that organisms encounter as their populations expand. In 1971 he

Sociobiologist Edward O. Wilson is pictured here with one of the ants he spent his career observing. Hugh Patrick Brown/Time & Life Pictures/ Getty Images

published *The Insect Societies*, his definitive work on ants and other social insects. The book provided a comprehensive picture of the ecology, population dynamics, and social behaviour of thousands of species.

In Wilson's second major work, *Sociobiology: The New Synthesis* (1975), a treatment of the biological basis of social behaviour, he proposed that the essentially biological principles on which animal societies are based also apply to humans. This thesis provoked condemnation from prominent researchers and scholars in a broad range of disciplines, who regarded it as an attempt to justify harmful or destructive behaviour and unjust social relations in human societies. In fact, however, Wilson maintained that as little as 10 percent of human behaviour is genetically induced, the rest being attributable to environment.

One of Wilson's most notable theories was that even a characteristic such as altruism may have evolved through natural selection. Traditionally, natural selection was thought to foster only those physical and behavioral traits that increase an individual's chances of reproducing. Thus, altruistic behaviour—as when an organism sacrifices itself in order to save other members of its immediate family— would seem incompatible with this process. In *Sociobiology* Wilson argued that the sacrifice involved in much altruistic behaviour results in saving closely related individuals—i.e., individuals who share many of the sacrificed organism's genes. Therefore, the preservation of the gene, rather than the preservation of the individual, was viewed as the focus of evolutionary strategy.

In later years, however, Wilson was inclined to think that highly social organisms are integrated to such an extent that they are better treated as one overall unit—a superorganism—rather than as individuals in their own right. This view was suggested by Charles Darwin himself in *On the Origin of Species* (1859). Wilson expounded on it in

Success, Dominance, and the Superorganism: The Case of the Social Insects (1997).

In *On Human Nature* (1978), for which he was awarded a Pulitzer Prize in 1979, Wilson discussed the application of sociobiology to human aggression, sexuality, and ethics. His book *The Ants* (1990) was a monumental summary of contemporary knowledge of those insects. In *The Diversity of Life* (1992), Wilson sought to explain how the world's living species became diverse and examined the massive species extinctions caused by human activities in the 20th century.

In his later career Wilson turned increasingly to religious and philosophical topics. In *Consilience: The Unity of Knowledge* (1998), he strove to demonstrate the interrelatedness and evolutionary origins of all human thought. In *Creation: An Appeal to Save Life on Earth* (2006), he developed further the evolutionarily informed humanism he had earlier explored in *On Human Nature*. In contrast to many other biologists, notably Stephen Jay Gould, Wilson believed that evolution is essentially progressive, leading from the simple to the complex and from the worse-adapted to the better. From this he inferred an ultimate moral imperative for humans: to cherish and promote the well-being of their species.

In 1990 Wilson and American biologist Paul Ehrlich shared the Crafoord Prize, awarded by the Royal Swedish Academy of Sciences to support areas of science not covered by the Nobel Prizes. His autobiography, *Naturalist*, appeared in 1994.

JANE GOODALL

(b. April 3, 1934, London, Eng.)

B ritish ethologist Jane Goodall is known for her exceptionally detailed and long-term research on the chimpanzees of Gombe Stream National Park in Tanzania.

Interested in animal behaviour from an early age, Goodall left school at age 18. She worked as a secretary and as a film production assistant until she gained passage to Africa. Once there, Goodall began assisting paleontologist and anthropologist Louis Leakey.

Her association with Leakey led eventually to her establishment in June 1960 of a camp in the Gombe Stream Game Reserve (now a national park) so that she could observe the behaviour of chimpanzees in the region. In 1964 she married a Dutch photographer who had been sent in 1962 to Tanzania to film her work (later they divorced). The University of Cambridge in 1965 awarded Goodall a Ph.D. in ethology; she was one of very few candidates to receive a Ph.D. without having first possessed an A.B. degree. Except for short periods of absence, Goodall and her family remained in Gombe until 1975, often directing the fieldwork of other doctoral candidates. In 1977 she cofounded the Jane Goodall Institute for Wildlife Research, Education, and Conservation in California; the centre later moved its headquarters to Washington, D.C.

Over the years Goodall was able to correct a number of misunderstandings about chimpanzees. She found, for example, that the animals are omnivorous, not vegetarian; that they are capable of making and using tools; and, in short, that they have a set of hitherto unrecognized complex and highly developed social behaviours. Her work served as a classic example of aggressive behavior in chimpanzees; she observed one of the animals intimidating rivals by banging two oilcans together. Goodall wrote a number of books and articles about various aspects of her work, notably *In the Shadow of Man* (1971). She summarized her years of observation in *The Chimpanzees of Gombe: Patterns of Behavior* (1986). Goodall continued to write and lecture about environmental and conservation issues into the early 21st century. The recipient of numerous honours, she was created Dame of the British Empire in 2003.

SIR HAROLD W. KROTO

(b. Oct. 7, 1939, Wisbech, Cambridgeshire, Eng.)

English chemist Sir Harold Walter Kroto, with Richard E. Smalley and Robert F. Curl, Jr., was awarded the 1996 Nobel Prize for Chemistry for their joint discovery of the carbon compounds called fullerenes.

Kroto received a Ph.D. from the University of Sheffield in 1964. He joined the faculty of the University of Sussex in 1967 and became a professor of chemistry there in 1985. In the course of his research, Kroto used microwave spectroscopy to discover long, chainlike carbon molecules in the atmospheres of stars and gas clouds. Wishing to study the vaporization of carbon in order to find out how these carbon chains formed, he went to Rice University (Houston, Texas), where Smalley had designed an instrument, the laser-supersonic cluster beam apparatus, that could vaporize almost any known material and then be used to study the resulting clusters of atoms or molecules.

In a series of experiments carried out in September 1985, the two men, along with Smalley's associate at Rice, Robert Curl, generated clusters of carbon atoms by vaporizing graphite in an atmosphere of helium. Some of the spectra they obtained from the vaporization corresponded to previously unknown forms of carbon containing even numbers of carbon atoms ranging from 40 to more than 100 atoms. Most of the new carbon molecules had a structure of C^{60}. The researchers recognized that this molecule's atoms are bonded together into a highly symmetrical, hollow structure that resembles a sphere or ball. C^{60} is a polygon with 60 vertices and 32 faces, 12 of which are pentagons and 20 of which are hexagons — the same geometry as that of a soccer ball.

In the 1985 paper describing their work, the discoverers chose the whimsical name buckminsterfullerene for C^{60}, after the American architect R. Buckminster Fuller, whose geodesic dome designs have a structure similar to that atom. The discovery of the unique structure of fullerenes, or buckyballs, as this class of carbon compounds came to be known, opened up an entirely new branch of chemistry.

RICHARD E. SMALLEY

(b. June 6, 1943, Akron, Ohio, U.S. — d. Oct. 28, 2005, Houston, Texas)

American chemist and physicist Richard Errett Smalley shared the 1996 Nobel Prize for Chemistry with Robert F. Curl, Jr., and Sir Harold W. Kroto for their joint discovery of carbon^{60} (C^{60}, or buckminsterfullerene, or buckyball) and the fullerenes.

Smalley received a Ph.D. from Princeton University in 1973. After postdoctoral work at the University of Chicago, he began his teaching career at Rice University (Houston, Texas) in 1976. He was named Gene and Norman Hackerman professor of chemistry there in 1982 and became a professor of physics in 1990.

It was at Rice University that Smalley and his colleagues discovered fullerenes, the third known form of pure carbon (diamond and graphite are the other two known forms). Smalley had designed a laser–supersonic cluster beam apparatus that could vaporize any material into a plasma of atoms and then be used to study the resulting clusters (aggregates of tens to many tens of atoms). On a visit to Smalley's lab, Kroto realized that the technique might be used to simulate the chemical conditions in the atmosphere of carbon stars and so provide compelling evidence for his conjecture that the chains originated in stars.

In a now-famous 11-day series of experiments conducted in September 1985 at Rice University by Kroto, Smalley, and Curl and their student coworkers James Heath, Yuan Liu, and Sean O'Brien, Smalley's apparatus was used to simulate the chemistry in the atmosphere of giant stars by turning the vaporization laser onto graphite. The study not only confirmed that carbon chains were produced but also showed, serendipitously, that a hitherto unknown carbon species containing 60 atoms formed spontaneously in relatively high abundance. The atoms of fullerenes are arranged in a closed shell. Carbon^{60}, the smallest stable fullerene molecule, consists of 60 carbon atoms that fit together to form a cage, with the bonds resembling the pattern of seams on a soccer ball. The molecule was given the name buckminsterfullerene because its shape is similar to the geodesic domes designed by the American architect and theorist R. Buckminster Fuller. A leading supporter of nanotechnology, Smalley played a key role in the establishment in 2000 of the National Nanotechnology Initiative, a federal research and development program.

ROBERT F. CURL, JR.

(b. Aug. 23, 1933, Alice, Texas, U.S.)

American chemist Robert Floyd Curl, Jr., with Richard E. Smalley and Sir Harold W. Kroto discovered the first fullerene, a spherical cluster of carbon atoms, in 1985. The discovery opened a new branch of chemistry, and all three men were awarded the 1996 Nobel Prize for Chemistry for their work.

Curl studied at Rice University (B.A., 1954) in Houston, Texas, and then completed his doctoral studies in chemistry at the University of California at Berkeley in 1957. He joined the faculty at Rice in 1958. In September 1985 Curl met with Kroto of the University of Sussex, Eng., and

Smalley, a colleague at Rice, and, in 11 days of research, they discovered fullerenes. They announced their findings to the public in the Nov. 14, 1985, issue of the journal *Nature*.

Although Kroto, Curl, and Smalley discovered this fundamental new form of carbon as a synthetic product in the course of attempting to simulate the chemistry in the atmosphere of giant stars, fullerenes were later found to occur naturally in tiny amounts on Earth and in meteorites. In addition, since the discovery of fullerenes, research on these compounds has accelerated. In the 1990s a method was announced for producing buckyballs in large quantities and practical applications appeared likely. In 1991 *Science* magazine named buckminsterfullerene their "molecule of the year."

Curl's later research focused on quartz tuning forks and the development of trace gas sensors. This research was aimed at creating sensors that could be used to generate arrays of quartz tuning forks. These arrays could then be used for the photoacoustic detection of gases. He also was developing improved technology to sequence DNA that employed high-powered lasers and fluorescent dyes.

STEPHEN JAY GOULD

(b. Sept. 10, 1941, New York, N.Y., U.S. — d. May 20, 2002, New York)

Stephen Jay Gould was an American paleontologist, evolutionary biologist, and science writer. Gould graduated from Antioch College in 1963 and received a Ph.D. in paleontology at Columbia University in 1967. He joined the faculty of Harvard University in 1967, becoming a full professor there in 1973.

Gould's technical research focused on the evolution and speciation of West Indian land snails. With Niles Eldredge, he developed in 1972 the theory of punctuated equilibrium, a revision of Darwinian theory proposing that the creation of new species through evolutionary change occurs not at slow, constant rates over millions of years but rather in rapid bursts over periods as short as thousands of years, which are then followed by long periods of stability during which organisms undergo little further change. Gould's theory was opposed by many, including American biologist Edward O. Wilson, who believed that evolution is essentially progressive, leading from the simple to the complex and from the worse-adapted to the better.

Gould also argued that population genetics is useful— indeed, all-important—for understanding relatively small-scale or short-term evolutionary changes but that it is incapable of yielding insight into large-scale or long-term ones, such as the Cambrian explosion. One must turn to paleontology in its own right to explain these changes, which might well involve extinctions brought about by extraterrestrial forces (e.g., comets) or new kinds of selection operating only at levels higher than the individual organism. Similar to Gould's theory on evolutionary change, much of his later work often drew criticism from other scientists.

Apart from his technical research, Gould became widely known as a writer, polemicist, and popularizer of evolutionary theory. In his books *Ontogeny and Phylogeny* (1977), *The Mismeasure of Man* (1981), *Time's Arrow, Time's Cycle* (1987), and *Wonderful Life* (1989), he traced the course and significance of various controversies in the history of evolutionary biology, intelligence testing, geology, and paleontology. From 1974 Gould regularly contributed essays to the periodical *Natural History*, and these were collected in several volumes, including *Ever Since Darwin* (1977), *The Panda's Thumb* (1980), and *Hen's Teeth and Horse's Toes* (1983). In *Rocks of Ages: Science and Religion in the Fullness of Life* (1999), Gould, who was then president of the American Association for the Advancement of Science, rejected the work of individuals who tried to integrate science and religion. According to Gould, science and religion were never at war but should remain separate. Gould's science writing is characterized by a graceful literary style and the ability to treat complex concepts with absolute clarity.

STEPHEN W. HAWKING

(b. Jan. 8, 1942, Oxford, Oxfordshire, Eng.)

English theoretical physicist Stephen William Hawking developed a theory of exploding black holes that drew upon both relativity theory and quantum mechanics. He also worked with space-time singularities.

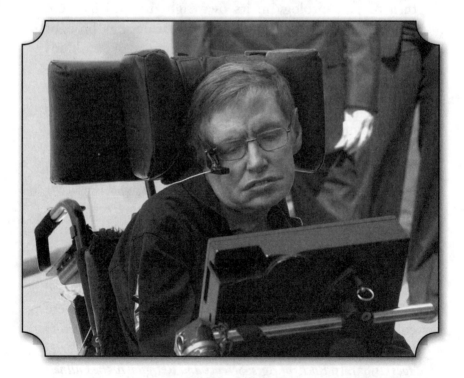

Stephen W. Hawking, 2007. Kim Shiflett/NASA

Hawking studied mathematics and physics at University College, Oxford (B.A., 1962), and Trinity Hall, Cambridge (Ph.D., 1966). He was elected a research fellow at Gonville and Caius College at Cambridge. In the early 1960s Hawking contracted amyotrophic lateral sclerosis, an incurable degenerative neuromuscular disease. He continued to work despite the disease's progressively disabling effects.

Hawking worked primarily in the field of general relativity and particularly on the physics of black holes. In 1971 he suggested the formation, following the big bang, of numerous objects containing as much as 1,000,000,000 tons of mass but occupying only the space of a proton. These objects, called mini black holes, are unique in that their immense mass and gravity require that they be ruled by the laws of relativity, while their minute size requires that the laws of quantum mechanics apply to them also. In 1974 Hawking proposed that, in accordance with the predictions of quantum theory, black holes emit subatomic particles until they exhaust their energy and finally explode. Hawking's work greatly spurred efforts to theoretically delineate the properties of black holes, objects about which it was previously thought that nothing could be known. His work was also important because it showed these properties' relationship to the laws of classical thermodynamics and quantum mechanics.

Hawking's contributions to physics earned him many exceptional honours. In 1974 the Royal Society elected him one of its youngest fellows. He became professor of gravitational physics at Cambridge in 1977, and in 1979 he was appointed to Cambridge's Lucasian professorship of mathematics, a post once held by Isaac Newton. Hawking was made a Commander of the British Empire (CBE) in 1982 and a Companion of Honour in 1989. He received the Copley Medal from the Royal Society in 2006.

Stephen W. Hawking (centre) *experiencing zero gravity aboard a modified Boeing 727, April 2007. NASA*

His publications include *The Large Scale Structure of Space-Time* (1973; coauthored with G.F.R. Ellis), *Superspace and Supergravity* (1981), *The Very Early Universe* (1983), and the best-sellers *A Brief History of Time: From the Big Bang to Black Holes* (1988), *The Universe in a Nutshell* (2001), and *A Briefer History of Time* (2005).

J. CRAIG VENTER

(b. Oct. 14, 1946, Salt Lake City, Utah, U.S.)

American geneticist, biochemist, and businessman John Craig Venter pioneered new techniques in genetics and genomics research and headed the private-sector enterprise, Celera Genomics, in the Human Genome Project (HGP).

Soon after Venter was born, his family moved to the San Francisco area, where swimming and surfing occupied his free time. After high school Venter joined the U.S. Naval Medical Corps and served in the Vietnam War. On returning to the U.S., he earned a B.A. in biochemistry (1972) and then a doctorate in physiology and pharmacology (1975) at the University of California, San Diego. In 1976 he joined the faculty of the State University of New York at Buffalo, where he was involved in neurochemistry research. In 1984 Venter moved to the National Institutes of Health (NIH), in Bethesda, Md., and began studying genes involved in signal transmission between neurons.

While at the NIH, Venter became frustrated with traditional methods of gene identification, which were slow and time-consuming. He developed an alternative technique using expressed sequence tags (ESTs), small segments of deoxyribonucleic acid (DNA) found in expressed genes that are used as "tags" to identify unknown genes in other organisms, cells, or tissues. Venter used ESTs to rapidly identify thousands of human genes. Although first received with skepticism, the approach later gained increased acceptance; in 1993 it was used to identify the gene responsible for a type of colon cancer. Venter's attempts to patent the gene fragments that he identified, however, created a furor among those in the scientific community who believed that such information belonged in the public domain.

Venter left the NIH in 1992 and, with the backing of the for-profit company Human Genome Sciences, in Gaithersburg, Md., established a research arm, The Institute for Genomic Research (TIGR). At the institute a team headed by American microbiologist Claire Fraser,

Venter's first wife, sequenced the genome of the microorganism *Mycoplasma genitalium*.

In 1995, in collaboration with American molecular geneticist Hamilton Smith of Johns Hopkins University, in Baltimore, Md., Venter determined the genomic sequence of *Haemophilus influenzae*, a bacterium that causes earaches and meningitis in humans. The achievement marked the first time that the complete sequence of a free-living organism had been deciphered, and it was accomplished in less than a year.

In 1998 Venter founded Celera Genomics and began sequencing the human genome. Celera relied on whole genome "shotgun" sequencing, a rapid sequencing technique that Venter had developed while at TIGR. The shotgun technique is used to decode small sections of DNA (about 2,000–10,000 base pairs [bp] in length) of an organism's genome. These sections are later assembled into a full-length genomic sequence. This is in contrast to older genome sequencing techniques, in which a physical map of an organism's genome is generated by ordering of segments of chromosomes before sequencing begins; sequencing then entails the analysis of long, 150,000 bp sections of DNA. Celera began decoding the human genome at a faster rate than the government-run HGP.

Venter's work was viewed at first with skepticism by the NIH-funded HGP group, led by geneticist Francis Collins; nevertheless, at a ceremony held in Washington, D.C., in 2000, Venter, Collins, and U.S. Pres. Bill Clinton gathered to announce the completion of a rough draft sequence of the human genome. The announcement emphasized that the sequence had been generated through a concerted effort between Venter's private company and Collins's public research consortium. The HGP was completed in 2003.

In addition to the human genome, Venter contributed to the sequencing of the genomes of the rat, mouse, and fruit fly. In 2006 he founded the J. Craig Venter Research Institute (JCVI), a not-for-profit genomics research support organization. In 2007, researchers funded in part by the JCVI successfully sequenced the genome of the mosquito *Aedes aegypti*, which transmits the infectious agent of yellow fever to humans.

FRANCIS COLLINS
(b. April 14, 1950, Staunton, Va., U.S.)

American geneticist Francis Collins discovered genes causing genetic diseases and led the U.S. National Institutes of Health (NIH) public research consortium in the Human Genome Project (HGP).

Homeschooled by his mother for much of his childhood, Collins took an early interest in science. He received a B.S. from the University of Virginia (1970), went on to Yale University to earn an M.S. and a Ph.D. (1974), and earned an M.D. (1977) at the University of North Carolina at Chapel Hill. In 1984 Collins joined the staff of the University of Michigan at Ann Arbor as an assistant professor. His work at Michigan would earn him a reputation as one of the world's foremost genetics researchers. In 1989 he announced the discovery of the gene that causes cystic fibrosis. The following year a Collins-led team found the gene that causes neurofibromatosis, a genetic disorder that generates the growth of tumours. He also served as a leading researcher in a collaboration of six laboratories that in 1993 uncovered the gene that causes Huntington chorea, a neurological disease.

In 1993 Collins, by then a full professor, left Michigan to take the post as head of the National Human Genome Research Institute (NHGRI) of the NIH, which had begun work on the HGP three years earlier with a stated goal of completing the sequencing project in 15 years at a cost of $3 billion by coordinating the work of a number of leading academic research centres around the country, in collaboration with the U.S. Department of Energy and the Wellcome Trust of London. Driven by a sincere interest in successful research that could help humanity, Collins was an obvious choice for the job, and he willingly took a sizable pay cut to participate in a historic project.

The necessity of a government effort was questioned when a rival operation, Celera Genomics, emerged in 1998 and appeared to be working even faster than the HGP at deciphering the human deoxyribonucleic acid (DNA) sequence. Headed by American geneticist and businessman J. Craig Venter, a former NIH scientist, Celera had devised its own, quicker method—though some scientists, Collins among them, questioned the accuracy of the work. However, in the end the public and private endeavours came together. On June 26, 2000, Collins, Venter, and U.S. Pres. Bill Clinton gathered in Washington, D.C., to announce that the rough draft sequence of the DNA in the human genetic map had been completed through the combined effort of Collins's public research consortium and Venter's private company.

The breakthrough was hailed as the first step toward helping doctors diagnose, treat, and even prevent thousands of illnesses caused by genetic disorders. In April 2003, following further analysis of the sequence, the HGP came to a close. The announcement of the completion of the HGP coincided with the 50th anniversary of American geneticist and biophysicist James D. Watson and British biophysicist Francis Crick's publication on the structure of DNA.

A practicing Christian, Collins freely expressed the awe he experienced as a leader in the uncloaking of one of the mysteries of life. As concerns arose about the moral and ethical implications of the research he had conducted, Collins actively cautioned against misuse of genetic information. At congressional hearings in July 2000, Collins urged the passage of federal law to set guidelines on how individuals' genetic information could be handled. "The potential for mischief is quite great," he said. On Aug. 1, 2008, Collins resigned from his position as director of the NHGRI in order to pursue broader, more flexible research opportunities.

STEVEN PINKER

(b. Sept. 18, 1954, Montreal, Can.)

Canadian-born American experimental psychologist Steven Pinker was known for his evolutionary interpretation of language acquisition in humans. Pinker studied cognitive science at McGill University in Montreal, where he received his B.A. in 1976. He earned a Ph.D. in experimental psychology at Harvard University in 1979. After stints as an assistant professor at Harvard (1980–81) and Stanford University (1981–82), he joined the Department of Brain and Cognitive Sciences at the Massachusetts Institute of Technology (MIT). In 1989 he was appointed full professor at MIT and became director of the university's Center for Cognitive Neuroscience.

His early studies on the linguistic behaviour of children led him to endorse noted linguist Noam Chomsky's assertion that humans possess an innate facility for understanding language. Eventually Pinker concluded that this facility arose as an evolutionary adaptation. He expressed this conclusion in his first popular book, *The Language Instinct*, which became a runaway best-seller and was rated among the top 10 books of 1994 by the *New York Times*.

The book's best-selling sequel, *How the Mind Works*, earned a nomination for the Pulitzer Prize for general nonfiction. In *How the Mind Works* (1997), Pinker discussed the development of the human brain in terms of natural selection, applying a Darwinian perspective to a wide range of mental faculties. He expounded a scientific method that he termed "reverse engineering." The method, which involved analyzing human behaviour in an effort to understand how the brain developed through the process of evolution, gave him a way to explain various cognitive phenomena, such as logical thought and three-dimensional vision.

In *Words and Rules: The Ingredients of Language* (1999), Pinker focused on the human faculty for language, offering an analysis of the cognitive mechanisms that make language possible. Exhibiting a lively sense of humour and a talent for explaining difficult scientific concepts clearly, he argued that the phenomenon of language depended essentially on two distinct "ingredients," or mental processes—the memorization of words and the manipulation of them with rules of grammar. Among Pinker's later books were *The Blank Slate: The Modern Denial of Human Nature* (2002) and *The Stuff of Thought: Language as a Window into Human Nature* (2007).

Pinker's work, while enthusiastically received in some circles, stirred controversy in others. Predictably, there were religious and philosophical objections to Pinker's strictly biological approach to the mind, but scientific questions were raised as well. Many scientists, including paleobiologist Stephen Jay Gould, felt that the data on natural selection were as yet insufficient to support all of Pinker's claims and that other possible influences on the brain's development existed. Although he conceded that there was much research left to be done, Pinker—along with a considerable number of other experts—remained convinced that he was on the right track.

GLOSSARY

abreaction The discharging of unconscious emotional material through verbalization.

anatomical How the body of a human or animal is constructed.

binomial nomenclature The uniform system for naming natural genera and species.

climatology The study of climates and meteorological phenomena.

diamagnetism Being repelled by a magnet.

dissection A detailed analysis through cutting and exploration of human or animal anatomy.

eccentric Deviating from a standard elliptical orbit.

epicycle A small circle, the centre of which moves on the circumference of a larger circle at whose centre is Earth.

equant A circle around whose circumference a planet moves uniformly.

equinox Two times a year when the Sun crosses the celestial equator, creating a day during which daylight and nighttime are of roughly equal length.

eugenics The theory that the human race can be improved by selectively breeding specific individuals with one another.

ferromagnetism The result of substances such as iron and nickel that are extremely susceptible to electro-magnetic forces.

geocentric Earth-centred.

harbinger An event that foreshadows a different, future event.

heliocentric Sun-centred.

homeopathy A system of therapy based on the concept that illness-bearing substances have a curative effect when given in very dilute quantities to sick people with a disease caused by the same substances.

humours The four main bodily fluids—blood, yellow bile, black bile, and phlegm—linked to ancient diseases and cures.

linkage The phenomenon that certain features are consistently inherited together.

naturalist Someone who studies and knows a great deal about natural history, especially with regard to zoology or botany.

paramagnetism When a substance in which an induced magnetic field is parallel and proportional to the intensity of the magnetizing field.

piezoelectricity The generation of electricity or of electric polarity in dielectric crystals subjected to mechanical stress.

quantitative Relating to or based on quantity.

stoichiometry The complete depiction of the principles of chemical combining proportions.

syllogism A deductive argument that has a major premise, a secondary or minor premise, and a conclusion; going from general to specific reasoning to reach a conclusion.

taxonomy The classification of organisms in an ordered way that highlights natural relationships.

thermodynamics The study of the relationships and conversions between heat and other forms of energy.

ungulates Creatures that have hooves.

FOR FURTHER READING

Ackerman, Jane. *Louis Pasteur and the Founding of Microbiology*. Greensboro, NC: Morgan Reynolds Publishing, 2004.

Bird, Kai, and Sherwin, Martin J. *American Prometheus: The Triumph and Tragedy of J. Robert Oppenheimer*. Conshohocken, PA: Atlantic Books, 2008.

Bowman-Kruhm, Mary. *The Leakeys: A Biography*. Westport, CT: Greenwood Press, 2005.

Brown, Kevin. *Penicillin Man: Alexander Fleming and the Antibiotic Revolution*. Salem, MA: The History Press, 2005.

Cousteau, Jacques. *The Human, the Orchid, and the Octopus: Exploring and Conserving Our Natural World*. New York, NY: Bloomsbury USA, 2008.

Darwin, Charles. *The Origin of the Species: 150th Anniversary Edition*. New York, NY: Penguin Group, 2003.

da Vinci, Leonardo, edited by H. Anna Suh. *Leonardo's Notebook*. New York, NY: Black Dog and Levanthal Publishers, Inc., 2005.

Finocchiaro, Maurice A., ed. *The Essential Galileo*. Indianapolis, IN: Hackett Publishing Company, Inc., 2008.

Frankenberry, Nancy H. *The Faith of Scientists: In Their Own Words*. Princeton, NJ: Princeton University Press, 2008.

Goldsmith, Barbara. *Obsessive Genius: The Inner World of Marie Curie*. New York, NY: W.W. Norton & Company, Inc., 2005.

Greene, Meg. *Jane Goodall: A Biography*. Westport, CT: Greenwood Press, 2005.

Hawking, Stephen. *A Briefer History of Time*. New York, NY: Bantam, 2008.

Jardine, Lisa. *The Curious Life of Robert Hooke: The Man Who Measured London*. New York, NY: Harper Perennial, 2005.

Kluger, Jeffrey. *Splendid Solution: Jonas Salk and the Conquest of Polio*. New York, NY: Berkley Books, 2006.

MacGillivray, Alex. *Rachel Carson's Silent Spring*. Hauppauge, NY: Barron's Educational Series, 2004.

Neffe, Jurgen. *Einstein: A Biography*. New York, NY: Farrar, Strauss and Giroux, 2007.

Rose, Steven, ed. *The Richness of Life: The Essential Stephen Jay Gould*. New York, NY: W.W. Norton & Company, Inc., 2006.

Thurschwell, Pamela. *Sigmund Freud*. New York, NY: Routledge, 2009.

Van Gorp, Lynn. *Gregor Mandel: Genetics Pioneer*. Mankato, MN: Compass Point, 2009.

Whitaker, Andrew. *Einstein, Bohr, and the Quantum Dilemma: From Quantum Theory to Quantum Information*. New York, NY: University Press, 2006.

Index